TOWARD A
UNIFIED THEORY
OF MANAGEMENT

McGraw-Hill Series in Management

KEITH DAVIS, CONSULTING EDITOR

ALLEN: MANAGEMENT AND ORGANIZATION

ALLEN: THE MANAGEMENT PROFESSION

BOWMAN: MANAGEMENT: ORGANIZATION AND PLANNING

DAVIS: HUMAN RELATIONS AT WORK

DAVIS AND SCOTT: READINGS IN HUMAN RELATIONS

FLIPPO: PRINCIPLES OF PERSONNEL MANAGEMENT

GRIMSHAW AND HENNESSEY: ORGANIZATIONAL BEHAVIOR

HARBISON AND MYERS: MANAGEMENT IN THE INDUSTRIAL WORLD

JOHNSON, KAST, AND ROSENZWEIG: THE THEORY AND MANAGEMENT OF SYSTEMS

KEITH AND GUBELLINI: BUSINESS MANAGEMENT

KOONTZ: TOWARD A UNIFIED THEORY OF MANAGEMENT

KOONTZ AND O'DONNELL: PRINCIPLES OF MANAGEMENT

KOONTZ AND O'DONNELL: READINGS IN MANAGEMENT

MAIER: PROBLEM-SOLVING DISCUSSIONS AND CONFERENCES: LEADERSHIP METHODS AND SKILLS

MAYER: PRODUCTION MANAGEMENT

MC DONOUGH: INFORMATION ECONOMICS AND MANAGEMENT SYSTEMS

MC NICHOLS: POLICY MAKING AND EXECUTIVE ACTION

MINER: THE MANAGEMENT OF INEFFECTIVE PERFORMANCE

PIGORS AND PIGORS: CASE METHOD IN HUMAN RELATIONS

SALTONSTALL: HUMAN RELATIONS IN ADMINISTRATION

SARTAIN AND BAKER: THE SUPERVISOR AND HIS JOB

SCHREIBER, JOHNSON, MEIER, FISCHER, AND WEWELL: CASES IN MANUFACTURING MANAGEMENT

STEINER: MANAGERIAL LONG-RANGE PLANNING

SUTERMEISTER: PEOPLE AND PRODUCTIVITY

TANNENBAUM, WESCHLER, AND MASSARIK: LEADERSHIP AND ORGANIZATION

VANCE: INDUSTRIAL ADMINISTRATION

VANCE: MANAGEMENT DECISION SIMULATION

A SYMPOSIUM HELD AT THE
GRADUATE SCHOOL OF BUSINESS ADMINISTRATION
UNIVERSITY OF CALIFORNIA, LOS ANGELES
NOVEMBER 8 AND 9, 1962

TOWARD A UNIFIED THEORY OF MANAGEMENT

EDITED BY **HAROLD KOONTZ**

McGraw-Hill Book Company

NEW YORK   SAN FRANCISCO   TORONTO   LONDON

II

Toward a Unified Theory of Management

PARTICIPANTS IN THE SYMPOSIUM

Prof. H. H. Albers
STATE UNIVERSITY OF IOWA

Prof. G. L. Bach
CARNEGIE INSTITUTE OF TECH-
NOLOGY

Prof. F. E. Balderston
UNIVERSITY OF CALIFORNIA,
LOS ANGELES

Dr. William Ballhaus
NORTHROP AIRCRAFT COMPANY

Prof. Warren G. Bennis
MASSACHUSETTS INSTITUTE OF
TECHNOLOGY

Prof. Robert Blake
UNIVERSITY OF TEXAS

Prof. George Brown
UNIVERSITY OF CALIFORNIA,
LOS ANGELES

Mr. Wilfred Brown
GLACIER METAL COMPANY, LTD.

Mr. Warren Cannon
MC KINSEY FOUNDATION FOR
MANAGEMENT RESEARCH, INC.

Prof. Joseph Carrabino
UNIVERSITY OF CALIFORNIA,
LOS ANGELES

Prof. Fred E. Case
UNIVERSITY OF CALIFORNIA,
LOS ANGELES

Gen. John W. Cave
UNIVERSITY OF CALIFORNIA,
LOS ANGELES

Dean Richard M. Cyert
CARNEGIE INSTITUTE OF TECH-
NOLOGY

Prof. Ernest Dale
CORNELL UNIVERSITY

Prof. Keith Davis
ARIZONA STATE UNIVERSITY

Prof. Ralph C. Davis
OHIO STATE UNIVERSITY

Prof. Robert Dubin
UNIVERSITY OF OREGON

Mr. Donald Elliot
MEAD JOHNSON & COMPANY

Prof. George J. Feeney
NEW YORK UNIVERSITY

Prof. William M. Fox
UNIVERSITY OF FLORIDA

Dr. T. Keith Glennan
CASE INSTITUTE OF TECHNOLOGY

Prof. Billy E. Goetz
MASSACHUSETTS INSTITUTE OF
TECHNOLOGY

Prof. Mason Haire
UNIVERSITY OF CALIFORNIA,
BERKELEY

Prof. James Jackson
UNIVERSITY OF CALIFORNIA,
LOS ANGELES

Dean Neil H. Jacoby
UNIVERSITY OF CALIFORNIA,
LOS ANGELES

Mr. Andrew F. Kay
NON-LINEAR SYSTEMS, INC.

Mr. E. D. Kemble
GENERAL ELECTRIC COMPANY

Prof. Harold Koontz
UNIVERSITY OF CALIFORNIA,
LOS ANGELES

Prof. Preston P. Le Breton
UNIVERSITY OF WASHINGTON

Prof. Alan Manne
STANFORD UNIVERSITY

Prof. James C. March
CARNEGIE INSTITUTE OF TECH-
NOLOGY

Mr. Harry M. Markowitz
THE RAND CORPORATION

Prof. Jacob Marschak
UNIVERSITY OF CALIFORNIA,
LOS ANGELES

Prof. Fred Massarik
UNIVERSITY OF CALIFORNIA,
LOS ANGELES

Prof. Dalton E. McFarland
MICHIGAN STATE UNIVERSITY

Prof. C. B. McGuire
UNIVERSITY OF CALIFORNIA,
BERKELEY

Prof. John F. Mee
INDIANA UNIVERSITY

Prof. David W. Miller
COLUMBIA UNIVERSITY

Mr. John R. Moore
AUTONETICS DIVISION, NORTH
AMERICAN AVIATION, INC.

Mr. Richard F. Neuschel
MC KINSEY & COMPANY, INC.

Prof. Cyril O'Donnell
UNIVERSITY OF CALIFORNIA,
LOS ANGELES

Mr. Gordon D. Osborn
U.S. BUREAU OF THE BUDGET

Mr. George L. Parkhurst
STANDARD OIL COMPANY OF
CALIFORNIA

Prof. Harry Roberts
UNIVERSITY OF CHICAGO

Acting Dean George W. Robbins
UNIVERSITY OF CALIFORNIA,
LOS ANGELES

Prof. F. J. Roethlisberger
HARVARD UNIVERSITY

Prof. Robert Schlaifer
HARVARD UNIVERSITY

Dr. Warren Schmidt
UNIVERSITY OF CALIFORNIA,
LOS ANGELES

Prof. Herbert A. Shepard
CASE INSTITUTE OF TECHNOLOGY

Dr. Martin Shubik
THOMAS J. WATSON RESEARCH
CENTER, IBM CORPORATION

Prof. Ronald S. Shuman
UNIVERSITY OF OKLAHOMA

Prof. Herbert A. Simon
CARNEGIE INSTITUTE OF TECH-
NOLOGY

Mr. Bart W. Sorge
UNITED GEOPHYSICAL
CORPORATION

Prof. R. Clay Sprowls
UNIVERSITY OF CALIFORNIA,
LOS ANGELES

Prof. George A. Steiner
UNIVERSITY OF CALIFORNIA,
LOS ANGELES

Mr. Henry K. Swenerton
GLADDING, MC BEAN & COMPANY

Prof. Robert Tannenbaum
UNIVERSITY OF CALIFORNIA,
LOS ANGELES

Prof. Harvey M. Wagner
STANFORD UNIVERSITY

Dr. Allen Wallis
UNIVERSITY OF ROCHESTER

Prof. C. Edward Weber
UNIVERSITY OF PITTSBURGH

Prof. William B. Wolf
UNIVERSITY OF HAWAII

RECORDERS

Prof. Leland Burns
Prof. James Clark
Prof. David Huff
Prof. Clarence Huizenga
Prof. Harold Kassarjian
Mr. Kenneth MacCrimmon
Prof. Anthony Raia
Prof. Barry Richman

UNIVERSITY OF CALIFORNIA, LOS ANGELES

MORNING: WELCOME

Acting Dean George W. Robbins
Graduate School of Business Administration
University of California, Los Angeles

Dr. Franklin D. Murphy, Chancellor
University of California, Los Angeles

APPROACHING A THEORY OF MANAGEMENT

Chairman: Prof. Harold Koontz
University of California, Los Angeles

THE FUNCTIONAL APPROACH TO MANAGEMENT

Prof. Ernest Dale, Cornell University

CONTRIBUTIONS OF THE BEHAVIORAL SCIENCES TO A
GENERAL THEORY OF MANAGEMENT

Prof. Fritz J. Roethlisberger, Harvard University

THE DECISION THEORY APPROACH

Prof. Robert Schlaifer, Harvard University

APPROACHING THE THEORY OF MANAGEMENT

Prof. Herbert A. Simon

AFTERNOON: SYNDICATE DISCUSSIONS IN TERMINOLOGIES,
METHODOLOGIES, AND CONTRIBUTIONS

EVENING: Chairman: Prof. George A. Steiner
University of California, Los Angeles

MANAGERIAL PLANNING AT THE UNIVERSITY OF CALI-
FORNIA

Acting Dean George W. Robbins
Graduate School of Business Administration
University of California, Los Angeles

MORNING: TERMS, METHODS, AND CONTRIBUTIONS:
CAN THEY BE SYNTHESIZED?

A Summary of Syndicate Discussions
Prof. Robert Tannenbaum
University of California, Los Angeles

THE PRACTICING MANAGER AND MANAGE-
MENT THEORY AND RESEARCH

Chairman: Prof. Cyril O'Donnell
University of California, Los Angeles

MANAGEMENT THEORY FROM MANAGEMENT PRACTICE:
THE CONCEPT OF CONTRACTION

Mr. Wilfred Brown, Chairman

Glacier Metal Company, Ltd.
Alperton Wembley, Middlesex, England

WHAT CAN MANAGEMENT THEORY DO FOR THE PRAC-
TICING MANAGER?

Dr. William F. Ballhaus
Executive Vice President
The Northrop Corporation
Los Angeles, California

WHAT THE PRACTICING MANAGER EXPECTS FROM MAN-
AGEMENT THEORY AND RESEARCH

Mr. Edward D. Kemble
Manager of Management Research
The General Electric Company
Ossining, New York

MANAGEMENT'S NEED FOR THEORY AND RESEARCH

Mr. Richard Neuschel, Director
McKinsey & Company, Inc.
New York, New York

THE ROLE OF THE UNIVERSITY IN MANAGE-MENT THEORY AND RESEARCH

Chairman: Prof. Jacob Marschak
University of California, Los Angeles

Prof. G. L. Bach (Former Dean)
Carnegie Institute of Technology

Dr. Allen Wallis, President
University of Rochester

Dean Neil H. Jacoby
University of California, Los Angeles

CELEBRATION DINNER

Chairman: Prof. J. Fred Weston
University of California, Los Angeles

Address: "MANAGEMENT WITHOUT THE BENEFIT OF
THEORY"
Dr. Donald McLaughlin, Chairman of the
Regents
University of California
President, Homestate Mining Company
San Francisco, California

PREFACE

This book is a summary of papers presented in discussions held by an invited group of management theorists, business school administrators, and management practitioners who met at the Graduate School of Business Administration of the University of California, Los Angeles, in November, 1962. Built around the theme of "Management Theory and Research: Their Role in Improved Management," the symposium concentrated on the varieties of approaches to management theory and research, the problems of synthesis, the needs and contributions of practitioners, and the role of the business schools in this important area.

The occasion of the seminar was a celebration of the opening of the new Graduate School of Business building at the University of California, Los Angeles. However, the seminar was largely sparked by a paper written by the editor on "Making Sense of Management Theory," which appeared in the *Harvard Business Review* (July-August, 1962) and prior thereto in a slightly different form as "The Management Theory Jungle" in the *Journal of the Academy of Management* (December, 1961). Although so sparked, its format, program, and invited participants were determined by a committee of the Graduate School of Business Administration of the University of California, Los Angeles.

The objective of the seminar was to bring together eminent scholars with diverse research and analytical approaches to management, as well as perceptive and experienced practitioners of the managerial art from business, education, and government. The more specific long-range goal was to make beginnings in clarifying some of the language of management, in integrating the study of management and its underlying disciplines, and in carving out a general theory of management—a conceptual scheme of ideas or statements—that explains or accounts for phenomena of management. Although this long-term goal could not be accomplished in so short a symposium, it was hoped that some understanding of these matters could be developed.

Prepared papers were presented by seven scholars of management, including three current or former business school deans, and by four eminent practitioners of management. In addition, discussions were held by the sixty-one participants in the seminar. Some of these were in eight syndicate groups and some in general discussion by the entire groups of symposium participants.

The editor has included in this book the eleven papers presented, plus his paper which largely gave the symposium its theme. He has also included Prof. Robert Tannenbaum's summary of the group discussions and excerpts of the general discussions, freely edited around certain major topics to which the participants addressed themselves. In addition, the editor has written a summary chapter interpreting the findings of the symposium.

Although the symposium might be referred to, as one of its participants did, as a "grand conversation," it is believed that the thoughts expressed and the contributions made by the participants are such as to justify their publication so that a wider audience may gain from these insights. With greater understanding of the nature and role of management theory and research and its importance to the future of effective management teaching and practice, it has seemed that the need for dissemination of the results of this seminar is too great not to make them available in published form.

The Graduate School of Business of the University of California, Los Angeles, the participants, and the editor are indebted to the McKinsey Foundation for Management Research, Inc., and the Western Management Sciences Institute for generous financial support in making this seminar possible. The editor knows that all these parties would join him in acknowledging a debt to Mr. Donald Kirchner of the UCLA Graduate School for handling the physical arrangements of the conference and to Miss Natalie Newman for her diligent work in assisting Mr. Kirchner and in preparing this manuscript for publication.

HAROLD KOONTZ

CONTENTS

Preface   v

Chapter I: MAKING SENSE OF MANAGEMENT THEORY
              Harold Koontz   2

Chapter II: APPROACHING A THEORY OF MANAGE-
              MENT   18

              A. The Functional Approach to Management
                  Ernest Dale   21
              B. Contributions of the Behavioral Sciences
                  to a General Theory of Management
                  Fritz J. Roethlisberger   41
              C. Decision Theory and Management Theory
                  Robert Schlaifer   68
              D. Approaching the Theory of Management
                  Herbert A. Simon   77

Chapter III: TERMS, METHODS, AND CONTRIBUTIONS:
              CAN THEY BE SYNTHESIZED?   86

              A. Observations on Large Group and Syndi-
                  cate Discussions   *Robert Tannenbaum*   88
              B. The Problems of Synthesis: A Discussion   97
              C. The Classical Approach and Theory: A
                  Discussion   108
              D. Decision Theory as a Basis of Management
                  Theory and Research: A Discussion   112

Chapter IV: THE PRACTICING MANAGER AND MAN-
              AGEMENT THEORY AND RESEARCH   120

              A. Management Theory from Management
                  Practice: The Concept of Contraction
                  Wilfred Brown   123
              B. What Can Management Theory Do for the
                  Practicing Manager?   *William F. Ballhaus*   141

C. What the Practicing Manager Expects from Management Theory and Research *E. D. Kemble* 150

D. Management's Need for Theory and Research *Richard F. Neuschel* 176

Chapter V: **THE ROLE OF THE UNIVERSITY IN MANAGEMENT THEORY AND RESEARCH** 187

A. Universities, Business Schools, and Business *G. L. Bach* 189

B. The University and Development of Management Knowledge *W. Allen Wallis* 204

C. The Role of the University in Management Research *Neil H. Jacoby* 207

D. Research and Business Schools: A Discussion 217

E. What Should the University Business Schools Do? A Discussion 226

Chapter VI: **MANAGEMENT THEORY AND RESEARCH: SOME CONCLUSIONS** *Harold Koontz* 235

Index 267

1 MAKING SENSE OF MANAGEMENT THEORY [1]

Harold Koontz

Every thoughtful business executive who wants to make his practice of management more effective should be concerned with the development of an accurate and useful theory of management.

[1] Reprinted by permission from *Harvard Business Review*, vol. 40, no. 4, pp. 24–48, July–August, 1962. Although not given as a part of the symposium, this paper was an important factor in keynoting the seminar. This paper is a special adaptation of an original paper, "The Management Theory Jungle," *Journal of the Academy of Management*, vol. 4, no. 3, pp. 174–188, December, 1961. As a result of Professor Koontz's provocative analysis of the confusion existing in the state of management theory, the Graduate School of Business, University of California, Los Angeles, decided to make the theme of the symposium "Management Theory and Research: Their Role in Improved Management." This paper was submitted to all participants and was the subject of much discussion during the conference.

Any art—and managing is surely one of the most important arts —is improved by the discovery, understanding, and proper application of theory by those who know how to use it. The popular notion that theory and practice are opposites overlooks the fact that good theory underlies and improves practice.

While problems of managing have existed since the dawn of organized life, the systematic examination of management problems is, with few exceptions, the product of the present century and especially of the past two decades. Moreover, until recent years, almost all of those who have attempted to analyze the management process and look for some scientific underpinnings to help the practice of management were alert and perceptive practitioners of the art who could base their speculations on many years of experience. Thus, the earliest meaningful writing came from such experienced business management practitioners as Henri Fayol, James D. Mooney, Alvin Brown, Oliver Sheldon, Chester Barnard, and Lyndall F. Urwick. Although not based on questionnaires, controlled interviews, or mathematics, the observations of such men can hardly be regarded as "armchair."

The noteworthy absence of academic writing and research in the formative years of modern management theory is now more than atoned for by a deluge of research and writing pouring from academic halls. What is interesting (but perhaps nothing more than a sign of the unsophisticated adolescence of management theory) is how the current flood has brought with it waves of differences and confusion. This welling of interest from every corner should not upset anyone concerned with seeing the frontiers of knowledge pushed back and the intellectual base of practice broadened. But what *is* upsetting to practicing managers, and, in fact, to all who see great potential social good emanating from improved management, is that the varied approaches to management theory have led to a kind of confused and destructive jungle warfare. Particularly in academic writings, the primary interests of many would-be cult leaders seem to be to carve out a distinct (and hence, original) approach to management. To defend this originality, and thereby gain a place in posterity (or at least to gain a publication which will justify academic status or promotion), these writers seem to have become overly concerned with downrating, and sometimes misrepresenting, what anyone else has said, or thought, or done.

Therefore, my purpose here will be to avoid allying myself with this or that theoretical fad, and to shed some light on the issues and problems involved in the management theory area today. So that some of the more worthwhile literature on this subject may be made useful to those who manage, I will—at the risk of serious oversimplification—classify the various "schools" of management theory into six main groups:

The Management Process School. This approach to management theory perceives management as a process of getting things done by people who operate in organized groups. By analyzing the process, establishing a conceptual framework for it, and identifying the principles underlying the process, this approach builds a theory of management. It regards management as a process that is essentially the same whether in business, government, or any other enterprise, and which involves the same *process*, whether at the level of president or foreman in a given enterprise. It does, however, recognize that the environment of management differs widely between enterprises and levels. According to this school, management theory is seen as a way of summarizing and organizing experience so that practice can be improved.

Often referred to (especially by its critics) as the "traditional" or "universalist" school, this school was actually fathered by Henri Fayol. However, many of his offspring did not know of their parent, since Fayol's work was eclipsed by the brighter light of his contemporary, Frederick W. Taylor, and since the first widely available English translation of Fayol was not made until 1949.[2] Other than Fayol, most of the early contributors to this school dealt only with the organization portion of the manage-

[2] *General and Industrial Management* (New York, Pitman Publishing Corporation, 1949); also Frederick W. Taylor, *Scientific Management* (New York, Harper & Brothers, 1911). Also see Lyndall F. Urwick, *Elements of Administration* (New York, Harper & Brothers, 1944); Harold Koontz and Cyril O'Donnell, *Principles of Management* (New York, McGraw-Hill Book Company, Inc., 1959); William H. Newman and Charles E. Summer, Jr., *The Process of Management* (Englewood Cliffs, New Jersey, Prentice-Hall, Inc., 1961).

ment process, largely because of their greater experience with this facet of management and the simple fact that planning and control, as well as the function of staffing, were given little attention by managers before 1940.

This school bases its approach to management theory on several fundamental beliefs. Specifically:

1. Managing is a process which can best be dissected intellectually by analyzing the manager's functions.

2. Long experience with management in a variety of enterprise situations can be grounds for the distillation of certain fundamental truths or generalizations—usually referred to as principles—that have a clarifying and predictive value in the understanding and improvement of managing.

3. These fundamental beliefs can become focal points for useful research both to ascertain their validity and to improve their meaning and applicability in practice.

4. Such beliefs can furnish elements, at least until disproved, of a useful theory of management.

5. Managing is an art, but, like medicine or engineering, one which can be improved by reliance on sound underlying principles.

6. Principles in management, like principles in the biological and physical sciences, are true even if exceptions or compromises of the "rules" prove effective in a given situation.

7. While there are, of course, many factors which affect the manager's environment, management theory need not encompass *all* knowledge in order for it to serve as a scientific or theoretical foundation for management practice.

The basic approach this school takes, then, is to look first at the functions of managers—planning, organizing, staffing, directing, and controlling—and to distill from these functions certain fundamental principles that hold true in the understandably complicated practice of management.

Also, purely to make the area of management theory intellectually manageable, those who subscribe to this school do not usually attempt to include in the theory the entire areas of sociology, economics, biology, psychology, physics, chemistry, and so on. This is done not because these other areas of knowledge are unimportant and have no bearing on management, but merely because no real progress has ever been made in science or art without significant partitioning of knowledge. Yet anyone would be foolish not to realize that a function which deals with people in their various activities of producing and marketing anything from money to religion and education is completely independent of the physical, biological, and cultural universe in which we live.

The Empirical School. This second approach to management is taken by those scholars who identify management as a study of experience, sometimes with intent to draw generalizations but often merely as a means of transferring this experience to practitioners and students. Typical of this school are those who see management or "policy" as the study and analysis of cases, as does Ernest Dale in his "comparative approach."[3]

The empirical school seems to be founded on the premise that if we analyze the experience of successful managers, or the mistakes made in management, we will somehow learn the application of the most effective kinds of management techniques.

No one can deny the importance of studying managers' experience, or of analyzing the "how it was done" of management. But management, unlike law, is not a science based on precedent, and situations in the future which are exactly comparable to the past are exceedingly unlikely to occur. Indeed, there is a positive danger in relying too much on past experience or on the undistilled history of managerial problem solving, since a technique or approach found "right" in the past will seldom fit a situation of the future.

But this is denied by advocates of the empirical approach. As a case in point, Ernest Dale, after claiming to find "so little practical value" in the principles enunciated by the universalists, curiously drew certain "generalizations" or "criteria" from his valuable study of *The Great Organizers*.

By emphasizing the study of past experience, the empirical theorists may generate sufficient research and new ideas to hasten the day when principles of management can be verified. It is also possible that the proponents of this school may come up with a more useful framework of principles than has been supplied by the management process school. But once this group starts to draw generalizations from its research (and it must do so, unless its members are satisfied to exchange meaningless and structure-

---

[3] *The Great Organizers* (New York, McGraw-Hill Book Company, Inc., 1960), pp. 11–28.

less experiences), this approach will end up much the same as the management process school.

The Human Behavior School. This approach to the analysis of management is based on the central thesis that, since managing involves getting things done with and through people, the study of management must be centered on interpersonal relations. Variously called the "human relations," "leadership," or "behavioral sciences" approach, this school brings to bear "existing and newly developed theories, methods, and techniques of the relevant social sciences upon the study of inter- and intrapersonal phenomena, ranging fully from the personality dynamics of individuals at one extreme to the relations of cultures at the other."[4] In other words, this school concentrates on the "people" part of management and rests on the principle that since people work together in groups to accomplish objectives, "people should understand people," and has as its primary focus the motivation of the individual as a sociopsychological being.

Adherents of this school, as a result, have a heavy orientation toward psychology and social psychology; nevertheless, the emphasis of various groups within this school varies widely. There are those who emphasize human relations as an art that the manager should advantageously understand and practice. Some focus attention on the manager as a leader and sometimes equate managership with leadership, thus, in effect, tending to treat all group activities as "managed" situations. Still others see the study of group dynamics and interpersonal relationships as simply a study of sociopsychological relationships and seem, therefore, merely to be attaching the term management to the field of social psychology.

It can hardly be denied that management must deal with human behavior; nor can it be disputed that the study of human interactions, whether in the environment of management or in unmanaged situations, is important and useful. And it would be a serious mistake to regard good leadership as unimportant

[4] See Robert Tannenbaum, Irving R. Weschler, and Fred Massarik, *Leadership and Organization* (New York, McGraw-Hill Book Company, Inc., 1961), p. 9; see also Robert Dubin, *Human Relations in Administration: The Sociology of Organization* (Englewood Cliffs, New Jersey, Prentice-Hall, Inc., 1961).

to good managership. But whether the field of human behavior is equivalent to the field of management is quite another thing. Perhaps it is like calling cardiology the study of the human body.

The Social System School. Closely related to the human behavior school (and often confused with it) is the school which includes those researchers who look upon management as a social system, that is, as a system of cultural interrelationships. Sometimes, as in the case of James G. March and Herbert A. Simon,[5] the system is limited to formal organizations, and the term organization is used as a synonym for enterprise, and not as the equivalent of the authority-activity concept used most often in practice. In other cases, the system is not limited to formal organizations, but rather encompasses any kind of a system of human relationships.

Heavily sociological in nature, this approach to management does essentially what any study of sociology does: identifies the nature of the cultural relationships of various social groups and attempts to show these as a related, and usually integrated, system.

The spiritual father of this ardent and vocal school of management theorists is the late Chester Barnard.[6] In searching for an answer to fundamental explanations underlying the managing process, this thoughtful business executive developed a theory of cooperation grounded in the needs of the individual to overcome, through cooperation, the biological, physical, and social limitations of himself and his environment. Barnard then carved from the total of cooperative systems so engendered one set of interrelationships which he defined as "formal organization." His formal organization concept—quite unlike that usually held by management practitioners—consists of any cooperative system in which there are persons able to communicate with each other and willing to contribute action toward a conscious common purpose.

The Barnard concept of cooperative systems pervades the work of many contributors to the social system school of management. For example, Herbert A. Simon at one time defined the subject of organization theory and the nature of human organiza-

---

[5] *Organizations* (New York, John Wiley & Sons, Inc., 1958).

[6] *The Functions of the Executive* (Cambridge, Harvard University Press, 1938).

tions as "systems of interdependent activity, encompassing at least several primary groups and usually characterized, at the level of consciousness of participants, by a high degree of rational direction of behavior toward ends that are objects of common knowledge."[7] Simon and others subsequently have apparently expanded this concept of social systems to include any cooperative and purposeful group interrelationship or behavior.

Basic sociology, the analysis of concepts of social behavior, and the study of group behavior in the framework of social systems do have great value in the field of management. But one may well ask whether this *is* management. Is the field of management the same as the field of sociology? Or is sociology an important underpinning like language, psychology, physiology, mathematics, and other fields of knowledge? Must management be defined in terms of the universe of knowledge?

The Decision Theory School. Another approach undertaken by a growing number of scholars might be referred to as the decision theory school. This group concentrates on rational approaches to decision making—the selection of a course of action or of an idea from various possible alternatives.[8] In its approach, this school may deal with the decision itself, or with the persons or organizational group who make the decision, or with an analysis of the decision process. Some limit themselves primarily to the economic rationale of the decision, while others regard anything that happens in an enterprise as the subject of their analysis. Still others expand decision theory so it covers the psychological and sociological aspects of decisions and decision makers.

Thus, by expanding the horizons of decision theory well beyond the process of evaluating alternatives, many use the subject as a springboard from which to bound into an examination of the entire sphere of human activity (including the nature of the organization structure, the psychological and social reactions of individuals and groups, the development of basic information for

[7] "Comments on the Theory of Organizations," *American Political Science Review*, December, 1952, p. 1130.

[8] See R. Duncan Luce and Howard Raiffa, *Games and Decisions* (New York, John Wiley & Sons, Inc., 1957); David W. Miller and Martin K. Starr, *Executive Decisions and Operations Research* (Englewood Cliffs, New Jersey, Prentice-Hall, Inc., 1960).

decisions, and the analysis of value considerations with respect to goals, communications networks, and incentives). As one would expect, when the decision theorists study the small but central area of decision *making*, they are led by this keyhole look at management to consider the entire field of enterprise operation and its environment. The result is that decision theory tends to become a broad view of the enterprise as a social system, rather than merely a neat and narrow concentration on decision.

The Mathematical School. Although mathematical methods can be (and have been) used by any school of management theory, I have chosen to group under this heading those theorists who see management as a system of mathematical models and processes. Perhaps the most widely known group comprises the operations researchers or operations analysts, who have sometimes anointed themselves with the rather pretentious name of "management scientists." The abiding belief of this group is that if management, or organization, or planning, or decision making is a logical process, it can be expressed in terms of mathematical symbols and relationships.[9]

There can be no doubt of the great usefulness of mathematical approaches to any field of inquiry. This type of approach forces upon the analyst the definition of a problem or problem area; conveniently allows the insertion of symbols for unknown data; and, due to its logical methodology—developed by years of scientific application and abstraction—furnishes a powerful tool for solving or simplifying complex phenomena. But it is even harder to see mathematics as a truly separate school of management theory than it is to see it as a separate school in physics, chemistry, engineering, or medicine. I only deal with it here because a kind of cult appears to have developed around mathematical analysts who have subsumed to themselves this area of management.

In pointing out that mathematics is a tool, rather than a school, I have no intention of underestimating the impact of

---

[9] See Miller and Starr, *op. cit.;* Joseph F. McCloskey and Florence N. Trefethen, *Operations Research for Management* (Baltimore, Johns Hopkins Press, 1954); C. West Churchman, Russell L. Ackoff, and E. Leonard Arnoff, *Introduction to Operations Research* (New York, John Wiley & Sons, Inc., 1957).

mathematics on the science and practice of management. By bringing to this immensely important and complex field the tools and techniques of the physical sciences, the mathematicians have already made an immense contribution to orderly thinking. They have forced on people in management the means as well as the desirability of seeing many problems more clearly; they have pressed on scholars and practitioners the need for establishing goals and measures of effectiveness; they have been extremely helpful in getting people to view the management area as a logical system of relationships; and they have caused people in management to review and occasionally reorganize information sources and systems so that mathematics can be given sensible quantitative meaning. But even with this meaningful contribution, and the greater sharpness and sophistication of planning which has resulted, I cannot see that mathematics is management theory any more than it is astronomy.

MAJOR ENTANGLEMENTS

When these various schools or approaches to management theory have been outlined, it becomes clear that these intellectual cults do not draw greatly differing inferences from the physical and cultural environment surrounding businessmen. Why, then, have there been so many disputes among them? And why such a struggle (particularly among our academic brethren) to gain a place in the sun by denying the approaches of others? Like the widely differing and often contentious denominations of Christianity, all have essentially the same goals and deal with essentially the same world.

While there are many sources of the mental entanglement in the management theory jungle, the major ones seem to me to be:

The Semantics Jungle. As is so often true when intelligent men argue about basic problems, much of the trouble lies in the meaning of key words. The semantics problem is particularly severe in the field of management. There are even difficulties related to the meaning of the word "management." Most people would agree that it means getting things done through and with people, but do they mean only in formal organizations or in all group activities? Do they mean by governing, leading, or teaching?

Perhaps the greatest single semantic confusion lies in the word "organization." Most members of the management process school use it to define the activity-authority structure of an enterprise. Certainly most managers think that they are "organizing" when they establish a framework of activity grouping and authority relationships. In this case, organization represents the formal framework within an enterprise that furnishes the environment in which people perform. Yet a large number of organization theorists conceive of organization as the sum total of human relationships in any group activity; they thus seem to make it equivalent to *social* structure. And some use organization to mean *enterprise*.

Other semantic entanglements might be mentioned. Decision making is regarded by some as a process of choosing from among alternatives; by others as the total managerial task and environment. Leadership, often made synonymous with managership by some, is analytically separated by others. Communications may mean anything from a written or oral report to a vast network of formal and informal relationships. Human relations can imply a psychiatric manipulation of people, *or* it can refer to the study and art of understanding people and their interpersonal relationships.

Different Views of Management. As was indicated in the discussion of semantics, management has far from a standard meaning, although most agree that it involves getting things done through and with people. But does it mean dealing with *all* human relationships? Is a street peddler a manager? Is a parent a manager? Is a leader of a disorganized mob a manager? Does the field of management equal the fields of sociology and social psychology combined? Is it the equivalent of the entire system of social relations?

While I recognize that sharp lines cannot be drawn in management any more than they can in medicine or engineering, surely there can be a sharper distinction drawn than at present. With the plethora of management writing and with experts calling almost everything under the sun management, can one expect management theory to be regarded as very useful or scientific by the manager on the firing line?

The A Priori Assumption. Confusion in management theory has also been heightened by the tendency of many newcomers in the field to cast aside significant observations and analyses of the past on the grounds that they are a priori in nature. This accusation is often made by those who wish to cast aside the work of Fayol, Mooney, Brown, Urwick, and others who are branded as "universalists." To make the assumption that the distilled experiences of men such as these represent a priori reasoning is to forget that experience in and with managing *is* empirical. While the conclusions arrived at by perceptive and experienced practitioners of the art of management are not infallible, they do represent an experience which is certainly real and not armchair. No one could deny, I feel sure, that the ultimate test of accuracy of management theory must be practice; management theory and science must be developed from the real life of managing.

Misunderstanding of Principles. Those people who feel that they gain caste by advancing a particular notion or approach often delight in throwing away anything which smacks of management principles. Some refer to principles as platitudes, forgetting that a platitude is still a truism and a truth does not become worthless because it is familiar. (As Robert Frost has written, "Most of the changes we think we see in life are merely truths going in or out of favor.") Others cast away the principles of Fayol and other practitioners and draw *apparently* different generalizations from their study of management. But new generalizations which are discovered often turn out to be the same fundamental truths that certain criticized "universalists" have discovered, only expressed in different language.

One of the favorite tricks of the managerial theory group is to disprove a whole framework of principles by reference to one principle which the observer sees disregarded in practice. Thus, many critics of the universalists point to the well-known cases of dual subordination in organized enterprise, coming to the erroneous conclusion that there is no substance to the principle of unity of command. But this does not prove that there is no *cost* to a business by designing around, or disregarding, the principle of unity of command; nor does it prove that there were not other advantages which offset the costs, as there often are in cases of establishing functional supervision in organization.

Perhaps the most hackneyed stand-by for those who would disprove the validity of *all* principles by referring to a single one is the misunderstanding surrounding the principle of span of management (or span of control). The usual source of authority quoted by those who criticize is Sir Ian Hamilton, who never intended stating a universal principle (but rather was attempting to make a personal observation in a book of reflections on his army experience) when he said that he found it wise to limit his span to three to six subordinates.

No modern universalist relies on this single observation, and, indeed, few can or will state an absolute or universal numerical ceiling. Even Lyndall F. Urwick's often-cited limit of six subordinates (a limit which is by no means accepted as universal even by the universalists) is hedged and modified by requirements of "direct supervision" and "interlocking operations" of subordinates; in fact, these conditions tend to make the numerical limit meaningless.

What concerns those who feel that a recognition of fundamental truths, or generalizations, may help in the diagnosis and study of management, and who *know* from managerial experience that such truths or principles do serve an extremely valuable purpose, is the tendency for some analysts to prove the wrong things through either misstatements or misapplication of principles.

A classic case of such misunderstanding and misapplication is in Chris Argyris' otherwise interesting and valuable book, *Personality and Organization*. Argyris concludes that "formal organization principles make demands of relatively healthy individuals that are incongruent with their needs," and that "frustration, conflict, failure, and short-time perspective are predicted as results of this basic incongruency."[10] I wonder whether this startling conclusion—the exact opposite of what "good" formal organization based on "sound" organization principles ought to cause—is not explained by the fact that, of four "principles" Argyris quotes, one is not an organization principle at all but the

10 New York, Harper & Brothers, 1957, p. 74.

economic principle of specialization, three other principles are interpreted incorrectly, and other applicable organization and management principles are not even considered.

Mutual Reluctance to Understand. What has been said above leads one to the conclusion that much of the management theory jungle thrives on the unwillingness or inability of the management theorists to understand each other. Doubting that it is inability (because one must assume that a person interested in management theory is able to comprehend, at least in concept and framework, the approaches of the various schools), I can only come to the conclusion that the roadblock to understanding is unwillingness.

Perhaps this unwillingness is an outgrowth of the professional "walls" developed by learned disciplines. Perhaps the unwillingness stems from a fear that some new discovery will undermine professional and academic status built upon the acceptability of one approach or another. Or perhaps it is fear of professional or intellectual obsolescence. Whatever the cause, it seems that these walls will not be torn down until it is realized that they exist, until all cultists are willing to look at the approach and content of other schools, and until, through the exchange and understanding of ideas, some order may be brought from the present chaos.

DISENTANGLING THE JUNGLE

It is important that steps be taken to disentangle the management theory jungle. In a field where the many blunders of an unscientifically based managerial art can be so costly to society, delays cannot be tolerated. Practicing business executives should not only participate in the disentanglement process but insist that the academics also do their share. Let me end this discussion by offering a program of action.

First, we need to define management as a field of specific knowledge. This definition need not follow sharp, detailed, and inflexible lines, but neither should the definition be without fairly specific content. Because management is based in reality, life, and practice, I would suggest that it be defined in the light of the able and discerning practitioner's frame of reference. A science unrelated to the art it intends to serve is not likely to be very productive.

Although the study of managements made by many persons, including myself, in various enterprises, in various countries, and at various levels may be neither representative nor adequate, I have come to the conclusion that managing is the art of getting things done through and with people in *formally organized groups*. It is the art of creating an environment in which people can perform as individuals and yet cooperate toward attainment of group goals. It is the art of removing blocks to such performance, a way of optimizing efficiency in reaching goals. If this kind of definition of the field is unsatisfactory, I look forward, at least, to an agreement that the area should be defined so as to reflect the field of the practitioner and that those actually in management should arrive at such a definition.

In defining the field, too, it seems imperative to me that we draw some limits for purposes of analysis and research and that we distinguish between tools and content. We should not attempt to cover the entire cultural, biological, and physical universe when we deal with management. Moreover, we must recognize that mathematics, operations research, accounting, economic theory, sociometry, and psychology, to mention a few, are significant *tools* of management, but not, in themselves, a part of the *content* of the field.

Next, we need to integrate the study of management with other disciplines. If recognition of the proper content of the management field were achieved, I believe that the present cross fire of misunderstanding might tend to disappear. Management would be regarded as a specific discipline, and other disciplines would be looked upon as important bases of the field. Under these circumstances, the allied and underlying disciplines would be welcomed by the business and public administration schools, as well as by practitioners, as loyal and helpful associates. Integration of management and other disciplines would therefore not be difficult.

We then must clarify much of the language of management. I would expect that much of the need for clarification of the language of management would be satisfied by clear definition of the field as a body of knowledge. Yet there would still remain certain semantic problems which would require special clarification. While there are not too many places where semantics are important, there are such terms as "organization," "responsibility," "staff," and "policy" which cause confusion in thinking through confusion in meaning. Here again, I would suggest the adoption of the language of intelligent practitioners, unless the words are used by them so inexactly as to require special clarification. At least, we should not complicate an already complex field by developing a scientific or academic jargon which would build a language barrier between the theorist and the practitioner.

Finally, we should show a willingness to distill and test fundamentals. Certainly, the test of the maturity and usefulness of a science is the sharpness and validity of the principles underlying it. No science now regarded as mature started out with a complete statement of incontrovertibly valid principles. Even the oldest sciences, such as physics, keep revising their underlying laws and discovering new principles. Yet such sciences have proceeded for centuries on the basis of generalizations, some laws, some principles, and some hypotheses.

One understandable source of the inferiority of the social sciences is the recognition that they are so-called inexact sciences. On the other hand, even the so-called exact sciences are subject to a great deal of inexactness, have principles which are not completely proved, and use art in the design of practical systems and operations. The oft-encountered defeatist attitude of the social sciences, of which management is one, overlooks the fact that management may be explained, practice may be improved, and the goals of research may be made more meaningful, if we encourage attempts at perceptive distillation of experience by stating principles (or generalizations) and placing them in a logical framework. The practicing manager—the business or government executive—can either do this himself or open his experience to the scrutiny and analysis of the management researcher. It is hoped he will increasingly do so.

CONCLUSION

If we are to clarify management theory, as I hope we eventually will (with the help of experienced managers), we will need special criteria to make our studies more understandable and useful to the businessman. Here are the yardsticks by which such a theory might be judged:

1. A theory should deal with an area of knowledge and inquiry that is "manageable"; no great advances in scientific knowledge were made as long as man contemplated the whole universe.

2. A theory should be *useful* in improving management practice, and the tasks and needs of the executive himself must be the central focus.

3. No theory should be hampered by semantic obstacles; useless jargon not understandable to the practicing manager should be eliminated.

4. An effective theory should give direction and efficiency to management research and teaching.

5. Finally, a worthwhile theory must recognize that it is but a part of a larger universe of knowledge and theory and need not actually encompass that universe.

·· APPROACHING
11 A THEORY
OF MANAGEMENT

There are many persons, including the editor, who believe that management research, teaching, and practice will not make the progress desired and justified by the needs of broad social goals until there is developed at least a rudimentary theory of management. What seems to be needed is a systematic conceptual framework upon which the major ideas and findings of management practice can be arranged, one which will show where research efforts should be aimed to prove or disprove hypotheses and to fill perceived gaps in knowledge, and one which will help teaching by acting as a means for distilling management knowledge.

In the editor's opinion, the field of management is both one of the oldest and most socially important areas of practice, but also one of the newest in the development and application of scientific knowledge. It is recognized that management, like other

A THE FUNCTIONAL[1]
APPROACH
TO MANAGEMENT

Ernest Dale[2]

The historian, E. H. Carr, cites the following case: Webb is driving home from a party at which he had more alcohol than he could normally take, in a car whose brakes turn out to be seriously defective. At a blind corner where visibility is extremely poor, he hits and kills Jones, who was crossing the road to buy cigarettes at the corner shop.

There is, of course, a police investigation of the causes of the accident. Was it due to the defective brakes of the car, which had been checked only the week before? In that case the garage owner might be hauled into court. Was it due to Webb's drunken condition? Then a criminal action might be in order. Or should the road authorities be cited for negligence because the blind corner had previously been brought to their attention?

[1] "Functional action: that which is performed as a means to the attainment of an extrinsic end; often purposive." E. E. Eubank, *The Concepts of Sociology*, 1932.

[2] The author wishes to express his grateful thanks for ideas drawn from his former teachers and lecturers at Cambridge; to Sir Dennis Robertson, Ludwig Wittgenstein, and especially to the basic standards of E. H. Carr and his recent BBC lectures; to Col. Ilia A. Tolstoy, and to Prof. Harold Koontz for having been so generous as to provide the idea for the paper and a forum to present it; and to Alice Smith for editorial services.

social sciences, must wait for years of investigation
before a truly mature science and theory can be de
there are many persons who believe that even ine
and unproved theories help to show the way t
practice and to more effective analysis and research.

Despite the clear need for the development of n
theory and science, if the material and human resou
societies are to be utilized more effectively and efficien
the attainment of goals, there has appeared to be a
confusion and conflict. This has led, perhaps, also to
talents, arising from too many interschool rivalries and
standings, particularly among those who are undertakin
and investigation in management. The nature of this
ment and confusion, as perceived by the editor, were
in the previous chapter.

In order to place some of the differences in perspect
outstanding management scholars were asked to prese
views from the vantage point of research and analysis th
done. The following papers do appear to highlight some
differences and approaches. But they also show how an int
approach to management can make use of various und
disciplines and a variety of investigations. Perhaps these
indicate that management, like other scientifically based ar
depend, at least in part, on an eclecticism which is comn
other fields of knowledge. However, even though manag
may develop largely as an eclectic science, it, like other fie
knowledge, does almost certainly include a basic discipline v
is not found in other contributing scientific areas.

At this point two gentlemen (possibly they are social scientists) break into the investigation and explain in a very articulate and persuasive fashion that if Jones had not run out of cigarettes, he would not have crossed the road and would not have been killed. Jones himself, therefore, was primarily responsible for his own death. If he had not been a heavy smoker, he would still be alive.

The police, who have the solid basis of law to go on, naturally ask the two gentlemen to leave the room and not come back so that a serious inquiry can proceed. Jones *was* killed because he smoked cigarettes, but this does not alter the fact that he was acting in a perfectly legal way in crossing the road, provided he exercised due care in doing so. Nor, of course, was it illegal for him to smoke cigarettes.

In management, however, there is less basis to build on, and it is, therefore, important to develop a functional approach that is comprehensive enough to enable management to use the various approaches suggested—all of which may contain some truth—to the extent that they are applicable. This functional approach can perhaps be used in evaluating the various theories presented at this conference, and possibly some additional ones. It is a comparative approach of determining the applicability and mix of different theories to the solution of specific problems within the enterprise. Its operation might be defined as: describing and analyzing *what happened* (the basis on which the facts were selected), *why* it happened (the explanation), and *what is likely to happen* (the prediction). This approach to management, which as such has some interesting aspects, has sanction from the comparative field of history.

The Selection of the Facts

For much of the managerial process we have to rely on the record of the facts of the past. It provides the only real test of managerial experience. Hence the large number of cases, histories, and episodes used as illustrations and support for theories in managerial literature. These illustrations are based on the experience of the authors or on field studies.

However, it is just not possible to describe the past by telling "simply how it really was" or to use merely "the factual approach" that Alfred P. Sloan called for. A fact is defined as "a datum of experience as distinct from conclusions." What do we require of the facts? First of all, whatever facts are used must be accurate. A. E. Housman once stated that "accuracy is a duty, not a virtue,"[3] but writings on management are not always up to this standard.

It is physically impossible to capture all the facts of a case. It is rarely possible to tape-record all conversations bearing on it; and if it were, knowledge that their words were being recorded would influence the participants. Further, even tape recording cannot capture the *arrières-pensées*—that could be done only by prolonged psychoanalysis. And even then, two men's interpretations of a negotiation would be quite different though both were quite honest in presenting their views of what happened. It is no wonder that Mr. Durant's account of his negotiations with the du Ponts regarding the relinquishment of his interests in General Motors in 1920 differs substantially—and quite honestly—from that of the du Ponts.

Facts do not speak for themselves. It is the management writer and analyst who decides which facts to use. Talcott Parsons explained this by calling science "a selective system of cognitive orientations to reality."[4] Many of the facts of the management writer are selected for him by people who believe them, or perhaps want others to believe them. The small number of interesting and revealing company histories bears testimony to the widespread process of self-serving preselection.

Telling the truth but not the whole truth is common; sometimes the informant is incapable of perceiving the whole truth. I recall a speaker at a management conference who cited the following as "proof" of the excellence of his company's personnel policies: "During the 1930s, after the wage and hour law went through, our employees used to sneak back and put in extra time after punching out—time for which they were not paid—

---

[3] M. Manilii, *Astronomicon: Liber Primus*, 2d ed., 1937, p. 87.

[4] Talcott Parsons and E. Shils, *Toward a General Theory of Action*, 3d ed., 1954, p. 167.

because they wanted to help the company out." His hearers were rightly skeptical, not of the fact that the employees actually did "sneak" back but of the reason given for their apparent devotion. How much, they wondered, had the employees been made to feel, "Gad, I'd better," particularly in view of the employment situation at the time. The speaker, however, remained honestly convinced that his view was the correct one.

Nor is this an isolated case. One should, therefore, judge any account of managerial performance only if one knows the basis or criteria used in selecting the facts.

Perhaps there are two principal bases on which managerial facts are selected today; one is the assumption that managers attempt to maximize their profits; a second, that managers try to "satisfice" or find solutions to problems that are "good enough."

If the facts are selected on the first basis, then an account of a managerial case or process will be largely concerned with management's economic efforts—cutting costs, improving the utilization of capital, expanding markets, and products. And perhaps this account is more representative of the corporations which lead in rate of return on investment and profit increases over a period.

The second approach might possibly cover any action from profit maximization to long-term contracts requiring payment of high sums to managers who are losing increasing sums of money for their corporations each year. Both types of managers might "satisfice" their stockholders—the latter by promising them pie in the sky later on. This would be "good enough" at least for a period of time, or until it became clear that the promises were never going to materialize.

Hence one way of judging the value of any managerial account is to know the author's values and judge his performance on how he selects his facts. "Tell me your managerial assumptions (or prejudices), and I'll tell you your conclusions." If the writer (or manager) fails to state his underlying values, then one should study the man—the record of his thinking, speaking, writing, and acting—so as to understand why he writes the way he does and what conclusions he is likely to arrive at. Such an analysis of management writings *ad hominem* was perhaps most brilliantly made by R. K. Bendix and Lloyd N. Fisher.[5]

Plausibility of the Explanation

Once we have an account of the management action and understand the basis of selecting the facts, we then have to judge the soundness of the explanations—why a manager acts in a certain way; why one company appears to be more successful than another. Here we have to rely on the *plausibility* of the explanation. It should picture reality. This is the central idea of the *Tractatus* by the most famous philosopher of our time, Ludwig Wittgenstein. A new view of the essential nature of propositions occurred to him, namely, that a proposition is a picture, when he saw a newspaper that described the occurrence and location of an automobile accident by means of a diagram or map.[6]

But among the many managerial interpreters, whose picture is the most real? Perhaps we might reply:

1. An explanation that is verbally intelligible and understandable may be said to be better than one that is not. As Wittgenstein put it: "The riddle does not exist," and "Everything that can be said can be said clearly."[7] Probably many writers on management science fail on the score of intelligibility and clarity.

2. It is an explanation that strikes a reader as truer or more realistic than others, either because it coincides with his own experience or gives him new insights which account for phenomena that his previous theories have not explained.

For example, when we judge between two explanations of why corporations buy one vendor's computers rather than those of another, it seems to be more plausible, on the basis of our knowledge of our own and others' buying motivations, to say that one vendor's products are chosen because they enable the

[5] "The Perspectives of Elton Mayo," *Review of Economics and Statistics,* vol. 34, pp. 312–321.

[6] Norman Malcolm, *Ludwig Wittgenstein, A Memoir,* Oxford University Press, Fair Lawn, N.J., 1962, pp. 68–69.

[7] *Ibid.,* p. 22.

users to save more time and money, rather than to conclude that they are popular because they are "more human" ("You like to shake hands with them") or look more like sex symbols. There may be a grain of truth in the second explanation, but it seems very small in comparison with the weight of the evidence. Many of the "explanations" of the conduct of managers or employees in the literature appear to belong largely in this category of *Alice in Wonderland* studies.

Elton Mayo's work is an example of a new theory which accounted for developments that previous "economic man" theories —as exemplified by the views of Frederick W. Taylor—did not encompass. Some of Mayo's own conclusions may be challenged, but he did stimulate the search for fresh ideas and theories more in accord with the facts. Simon and March's *Organizations*[8] may similarly stimulate widespread testing of their propositions.

But should one not be suspicious of any theory, e.g., Taylor's or Mayo's, which attempts to explain "everything"? Thus Freud and Adler developed theories, entirely different from each other, which were supposed to be so all-embracing that there is no conceivable human behavior that could contradict them.[9]

As soon as one begins to explain too much by too little one is in danger of selecting facts to suit conclusions, and of departing from reality in all but a few instances. Thus characterization of the management of a country mainly by the typology of "authoritarian," "paternalistic," "constitutional," and "democratic"[10] may be relevant in a country like the United States when applied to union-management relations (though not to the managerial *raison d'être*) but could hardly explain the nature of management in countries where unions are marginal in most managerial decisions and achievements.

Finally there are explanations which are not explanations: tautologies like, "the greater the uniformity of the group, the

8 John Wiley & Sons, Inc., New York, 1958.

9 Karl Popper, "Philosophy of Science" in C. A. Mace (ed.), *British Philosophy in the Mid-century*, George Allen & Unwin, London, 1957, p. 161.

10 Frederick Harbison and Charles A. Myers, *Management in the Industrial World*, McGraw–Hill Book Company, Inc., New York, 1959, pp. 50–64.

fewer dissenters present,"[11] or "Industrialization refers to the actual course of transition from the traditional society toward industrialism. Industrialism is an abstraction, a limit approached through historical industrialization. Industrialism is the concept of the fully industrialized society, that which the industrialization process inherently tends to create."[12] As Neil W. Chamberlain observed in reviewing the book containing this quotation in *The American Economic Review* (June, 1961), "Gertrude Stein could have done no better."

Predictability

A final test of the validity of a theory is the extent to which it makes possible the prediction of the results of a given action. It is the least likely to possess this quality when it claims universal predictability.

For example, take the claim that a knowledge of the principles of management enables its possessor to manage anything with at least fair success.[13] This would appear to be false, first, on the a priori ground that no one individual could be a good administrator of religious, academic, military, and business institutions, of a communist and a democratic enterprise, because the philosophies that underlie each type of activity vary so widely that no one man could hold them all. Jackson Martindell, President of the American Institute of Management, declared at a lecture at Cornell University that his findings show that the three best-managed organizations are the Standard Oil Company of New Jersey, the Roman Catholic Church, and the Communist Party. Applying the doctrine of complete universality of management, can anyone imagine the consequences of an executive

[11] Harold Guetzkow (ed.), *Groups, Leadership, and Men,* Carnegie Press, Carnegie Institute of Technology, Pittsburgh, Pa., 1951.

[12] *Industrialism and Industrial Man,* Clark Kerr, John T. Dunlop, Frederick H. Harbison, and Charles A. Myers, Harvard University Press, Cambridge, Mass., 1960, p. 33. This book covers a five-year period of work of seventy-eight persons of all nationalities, sponsoring forty projects in thirty-five countries and producing twelve books with no systematic testing of the "key" categories (and apparent absence of concepts or theories).

[13] " 'He who can manage,' says Lawrence A. Appley, the President of A.M.A., 'can manage anything.' " Osborn Elliot, *Men at the Top,* Harper & Row, Publishers, Incorporated, New York, 1959, p. 81.

"merry-go-round" of the three "chief executives" of these organizations? To help managers out of this dilemma could social scientists do more to refine the concepts and applications of the "universality and transferability of management"?

Second, the idea of the universal manager is largely contradicted by experience. To cite just one example, the frustration and powerlessness many businessmen experience when they enter government is well known. Also, many of the cases that appear to prove the existence of the universal manager turn out on closer examination to be nothing of the kind. A man is made president of a company in an industry in which he has had no experience, but it develops that he is really managing only a segment of it in which he *has* had experience—raising funds, for example. Production and marketing continue to be governed by those with long industry experience. Or to take another case: It seems to be naïve to imagine that military men who switch to industry are chosen for their posts for their managerial ability in view of the importance of military contracts to many companies.

All this is not to deny the validity of the usefulness of a knowledge of, say, organization, or the other management techniques. If nothing else, familiarity with what has been thought and done in these areas will save a man a great deal of mental, and possibly actual, trial and error.

Thus, considering the multiplicity of the factors, the lack of some of the necessary data, and the changeability and uncertainty of others in the field of management, short-run predictions of limited application are all that we can hope for. The theories should be regarded more or less as what Alfred Marshall called "engines of thinking," which may enable those who know them to draw more nearly correct conclusions about the future.

One such generalization which may have some predictive value is that an enterprise or a particular province, state, or country which plays a leading role in the advancement of the particular economic unit in one period is unlikely to play a similar role in the next period. The philosophies, systems, and methods of the previous period may not be sufficiently adapted to the changing circumstances of the new time:

As the prophet dies and the generation which had known him and was directly influenced by him passes away, the miracles are forgotten and impact of the extraordinary feats starts to decline . . . once the inner impulse vanishes . . . dynamic reality ceases to exist . . . the regime is bound to degenerate into natural rule serving the lower impulses of whoever happens to be the stronger.[14]

Such a group may have "a dominant orientation toward a lost golden age, while life is lived sluggishly along on the present."[15] The relative decline of management in England, of New England in our own country, and of the seventy of the 100 largest corporations in 1910 which no longer make the list today are examples. So is the current decline of some management groups today.[16] Many groups pay what Veblen once called "the penalty of being first."

Perhaps one way of partially continuing supremacy would be to investigate the possibility of prediction through comparative analysis, endeavoring to examine similar results of various types of action in *comparable* situations and using these new insights for prediction and a guide to action.

DEVELOPING A FUNCTIONAL APPROACH

Thus selection, explanation, and predictability might be the criteria used in examining and applying the various management theories—old or new—for the solution of management problems. This is not to say that every theory is as good as every other theory—but some are useful in some situations, to a greater or a lesser degree, and some in others—and application of the three criteria to the particular situation may afford a guide to decision.

The use of these criteria can be illustrated by their application to the principal theories so excellently collected and analyzed by Prof. Harold Koontz:

1. The operational approach
2. The human relations approach
3. The management science approach

[14] "Ibn Khaldun" quoted in Ernest Dale, *The Great Organizers*, McGraw-Hill Book Company, Inc., New York, 1960, p. 18.

[15] R. S. Lynd, *Knowledge for What?* Princeton University Press, Princeton, N.J., 1939, p. 88.

[16] Ernest Dale, "Executives Who Can't Manage," *The Atlantic Monthly*, July, 1962.

The following analysis is limited, principally because of lack of space, and should be considered illustrative only:

The Operational Approach

In the operational approach, past operations are studied to determine facts; theories are developed to explain the facts; and lastly the facts and theories are used to make predictions about future operations.[17]

From his observations of business, for example, Fayol drew many of what have been called the "classical" principles of organization. Some of these, such as the "scalar principle"—or pyramid of authority—are merely descriptive of what he actually found in observing organizations in general. Others, such as the idea of making responsibility and authority equal and the "unity of command," were undoubtedly arrived at by observing difficulties that appeared to arise and embodied an attempt to correct them. The same is true of Fayol's successors, such as Mooney and Reiley, Urwick, and Gulick.

In recent years, there has been considerable disagreement with the principles arrived at by these thinkers from their observations of actual operations. It is not necessary to repeat the attacks in detail; suffice it to say that the approach has been considered too mechanistic, and the predictions derived from it tautologous or just plain wrong.

But what we have called the operational principles still survive and are used by practitioners in the corporations and in nonprofit, governmental, and military institutions. Is what still seems to "work" in some places and at some times wholly wrong?

Undoubtedly, the operational approach flourishes partly because the newer theories are not yet well enough known. Yet in

[17] The formalizer of operational analysis was the physicist P. W. Bridgeman in his *Reflections of a Physicist,* Philosophical Library, Inc., New York, 1950, pp. v, 1–35; "Operational Analysis," *Philosophy of Science,* vol. 5, p. 114, 1936; and "Some General Principles of Operational Analysis," the *Psychological Review,* September, 1945. See also P. M. S. Blackett, "A Note on Certain Aspects of the Methodology of Operational Research," in his *Studies of War,* Oliver & Boyd, Ltd., Edinburgh and London, 1962, pp. 176–187; and Ernest Dale, *The Great Organizers,* McGraw-Hill Book Company, Inc., New York, 1960, chap. 1.

cases where they are known, the operational approach is still important.

The trouble with the principles is not that they are "wrong principles" but that they are not really principles, except in cases where they are too obvious to need stating. Fayol himself called them principles merely for convenience. He wrote: "There is nothing rigid or absolute in management affairs; it is all a question of proportion. Seldom do we have to apply the same principle twice in identical conditions; allowance must be made for different changing circumstances. . . ."[18]

They might rather be called diagnostic guides for examining an actual or a proposed organization and determining how it can be improved. It is absurd to say categorically as Gen. Sir Ian Hamilton did: "The average human brain finds its effective scope in handling three to six other brains"—even if one specifies, as Graicunas does, that the functions the three to six other brains are handling are interrelated. But there is a limit to the span of control, though it may differ with individuals and with their positions, and if it is increased indefinitely a good many important matters will—as Alvin Dodd used to say—"fall between the chairs."

Similarly, the principle of unity of command does, as Herbert Simon suggests, conflict with the principle of specialization, and instances may be cited in which companies have disregarded it not only without disaster but with preeminent success. For example, Shell Oil during many of its years of most successful growth had a duarchy of Marcus and Samuel Samuel, neither of whom could act independently under the terms of their partnership:

> They had to reach agreement, but never did so, on any single subject, without a violent quarrel. Members of the staff remember the sounds of terrible combat, anger, and recrimination . . . that could be heard through the door of the office that they shared. Sometimes a clerk would be summoned to bring information, and while he waited the two brothers would always go to the window, their backs to the room, huddled close, their arms round each other's shoulders, heads bent, talking in low voices, until suddenly they would burst apart in yet another dispute, Mr. Sam with loud and furious cries, Mr. Marcus

[18] *General and Industrial Management,* Sir Isaac Pitman & Sons, Ltd., London, 1949 ed., p. 19.

speaking softly, but both calling each other fool, idiot, imbecile, until suddenly, for no apparent reason, they were in agreement again. . . . Then Mr. Marcus would say: "Sam, speak to him on the telephone," and would stand at his brother's shoulder while the telephoning took place.[19]

In the United Nations, we oppose (and probably rightly) a "troika" approach to the distribution of the powers of the Secretary General which would provide for execution by three diverse nations, yet we use this very approach among our three joint chiefs of staff because we want diversity of views in policy making.

But, like the principle of the span of control, the principle of "unity of command" does have diagnostic or explanatory value— too great diversity does produce confusion, frustration, and inefficiency.

For example, at Westinghouse in the early 1930s, the company seemed to be losing more heavily than comparable firms. This was particularly so in the heavy (and important) turbine division, where there were, in addition, many customer complaints, poorly attended to. Now undoubtedly this may have been due in part to human relations shortcomings, but an organizational analysis revealed (more quickly probably than a morale study could have done) that the managers of the Westinghouse plants had a considerable number of bosses who were too busy (by span of control) to coordinate quickly and effectively enough. Hence the formal organization was changed so that each manager had only one superior to whom he was acountable. The reorganization paid off in terms of profits (and, according to some of the participants—in terms of personal goals).[20]

Then there is the argument that while companies built along the operational model may be doing well (though not as well as they might be doing if they did *not* follow classical lines), they are nevertheless to be condemned because they are straitjacketing their people into organization men. Chris Argyris writes:

[19] Robert Henriques, *Marcus Samuel: First Viscount Bearsted and Founder of the "Shell" Transport and Trading Company, 1853–1927*, Barrie and Rockliff, London, 1960, p. 53 (the recollections of a Mr. X, a pensioned employee of the firm, who preferred to remain anonymous).

[20] Dale, *The Great Organizers*, pp. 169–174.

"There is a lack of congruency between the needs of healthy individuals and the demands of the formal organization. . . . The resultants of this disturbance are frustration, failure, short time perspective, and conflict."[21]

But whether or not one is disposed to accept this point of view surely depends on the values pursued. If an organization's primary aim is greater profit, then requiring that people become organization men may be the lesser evil as compared with going downhill or even out of business.

In any case the sophisticated operationalists do not consider organization in a purely mechanistic way—they appear to welcome and benefit from the other disciplines. In practice, it is not a matter of black and white (though it may appear so in some of their writings when they are trying to make a case), but the degree of gray.

After all, even the President of the United States has a job description that puts limitations on him (through the Constitution, the acts of Congress, and the decisions of the Supreme Court). The job description is not changed each time a new President is elected; however unhappy he may be personally, his fulfillment of certain objectives for the country as a whole is considered more important.

Does the operational theory make predictions possible? Not, perhaps, in the form in which the principles are generally stated, but one may, through comparative analysis, draw some generalizations that will be, if not applicable to all organizations everywhere, at least commonly applicable to many business organizations.

For example, take the principle of delegation, i.e., increasing the responsibility or authority of subordinates should result in greater profits through better decisions, better training, improved manpower utilization. This thesis was tested in a quantification of the Westinghouse reorganization,[22] and possibly a more sophisticated thesis resulted, as follows:

The first impact of delegation was an increase of profitability,

---

[21] *Personality and Organization: The Conflict between the System and the Individual,* Harper & Row, Publishers, Incorporated, New York, 1957, p. 233.

[22] *Ibid.,* pp. 169–174.

partly probably because increased unity of command resulted in less diffusion (and confusion), partly because of improved accountability, and partly perhaps because the impact on morale was good.

After a time, however, administrative expenses began rising faster than profits because the increase in delegation necessitated more *net* hiring in the plants and at headquarters as well, since greater audit activity was needed to check on how well the delegated authority was exercised. Infighting for position maintenance and improvement probably affected profits adversely as well.

Still later a third type of impact became noticeable. Relations settled down, and there was a decrease in the number of people required both at headquarters and in the field. In the third and longer-lasting stage, profitability tended to be greater than it would have been if the original centralized system had been continued.

The Westinghouse thesis has been checked qualitatively with a number of other firms, which have stated that their experience with decentralization was similar.

Human Relations

The rise of the human factor as a vital element in management theory goes back to some of the pioneers of scientific management.[23]

However, the pioneers did not fully meet the first requirement of scientific work as stated in Henri Poincaré's book, *La Science et l'hypotheses*,[24] which started a revolution in scientific

[23] Lillian M. Gilbreth, *The Psychology of Management* (her Ph.D. thesis, University of California), Sturgis & Walton Company, New York, 1918; H. L. Gantt, *Industrial Leadership*, Yale University Press, New Haven, Conn., 1916; R. G. Valentine, "The Progressive Relation between Efficiency and Consent" in E. E. Hunt (ed.), *Scientific Management since Taylor*, McGraw-Hill Book Company, Inc., New York, 1924, pp. 203–211; R. F. Hoxie's great work, *Scientific Management and Labor*, D. Appleton & Company, New York, 1918; the famous paper by E. K. Hall, vice-president of A.T.&T., "New Objectives in Personnel Relations," which describes the gradations of methods by which leaders direct; Mary Parker Follett, *Creative Experience*, Longmans, Green & Co., Inc., New York, 1924.

[24] E. Flammarion, Paris, 1918.

thought. This is the requirement that general propositions enunciated by scientists (where they are not mere definitions or disguised conventions about the use of language) were hypotheses designed to crystallize and organize further thinking and be subject to verification, modification, or refutation. (This cannot be said about those human relations propositions which can be evaluated only subjectively, such as the "happy problems, happy people, happy solutions" approach.)

The first to tackle the role of personality in organization scientifically in terms of Poincaré's requirements were, of course, Elton Mayo, F. Roethlisberger, and W. J. Dickson in *Management and the Worker*[25] and Kurt Lewin in *Topology*[26] (and possibly Freud in *Group Psychology and the Aanalysis of the Ego*).[27]

The new concepts the first three authors introduced had a profound effect in improving the explanation of the behavior of employees and in changing managerial attitudes. They showed that there is an "informal" organization structure as well as a formal one; that the formal organization is only like the visible part of an iceberg; that the administrator is dependent on the efforts of every member of the organization, and that his power of control and command is limited; that the employee has feelings and sentiments that can vary greatly; that he needs to be consulted; and that he has objectives and relationships outside the mechanical structure.

Thus the most rational mechanical structure can rarely be introduced without extensive consultation.[28] But some of the authors of this school have shown that as a rule more is required than consultation, persuasion, and teaching of those who are to fit into the (economically) rational structure; i.e., more factors,

[25] Harvard University Press, Cambridge, Mass., 1939.

[26] McGraw-Hill Book Company, Inc., New York, 1949.

[27] The Hogarth Press, Ltd., and the Institute of Psycho-Analysis, London, 1949.

[28] See the pioneering works of the Tavistock Group on Human Relations: Elliott Jaques, *The Changing Culture of a Factory*, Tavistock Publications, London, 1951; *The Measurement of Responsibility*, Tavistock Publications, London, 1956; and particularly Cyril Sofer's *The Organization from Within*, Tavistock Publications, London, 1961, a comparative study of a family business, a technical school, and a hospital based on sociotherapeutic approach.

psychological and social factors especially, have to be taken into account.[29]

E. Wight Bakke[30] carried the explanation further by pointing out that the individual employee or manager hopes to use the organization to further his own goals (the "personalizing" process), while the organization attempts to use the individual to further its goals ("socializing" process). In a fusion process, the organization to some degree remakes the individual and the individual to some degree remakes the organization.

The human relations theories also helped to provide better explanations of why people in organizations behave as they do by stressing and exploring the role of the group. Classical theory had rested too unilaterally on the individualistic approach to management, following J. S. Mill's dictum that "Men are not, when brought together, converted into another kind of substance."[31] Of course they are not, but as the playwright Pirandello has said, "The individual apart from the group [apart, that is, from birth] would be both speechless and mindless."

Going a step further, Rensis Likert's controlled studies have demonstrated the importance of providing improved interaction between groups, through the "linking-pin" method.

The possible shortcoming of the human relations theories (apart from the fact that many of them were already known to the manager) would seem to be their underlying value assumption of the desire or drive for harmony. As the great philosopher Kant had already pointed out, perfect harmony would be possible only under a "system of eternal peace" in which the world was a vast cemetery. Certainly the individual's adaptation to the group may reduce freedom of discussion and innovation after a certain point of homogeneity is passed, and if the goal is other than unanimity, the results are likely to be bad.

The theories need to take into more account not only the existence of conflict situations but the irreconcilability of some conflicts and the impossibility of successfully "adjusting" everyone. In one large and well-known organization, two vice-presi-

29 See, for example, Chester Barnard, *The Functions of the Executive,* Harvard University Press, Cambridge, Mass., 1938.

30 *The Fusion Process,* Labor and Management Center, Yale University, New Haven, Conn.

31 *A System of Logic,* VII, I.

dents competed remorselessly for the presidency, and when one won out, he ousted the other. In another organization, the chairman and president had equal powers and each fought tooth and nail to eliminate the other because their personal and corporate goals were utterly antithetical. When the chairman asked the board to hire a psychoanalyst (his own) to "evaluate" the organization, his rival was able to win the board and oust the chairman.

Thus, even though everyone in the modern organization experiences the joys and pangs of the power struggle, most of the human relations theories and writings avoid them as the Victorians avoided mention of sex.

Not much of predictive value appears to have come from the human relations front in terms of the likely behavior of actual people if one of the human factors is changed, though some work has been done with simplified models. For example, there is Likert's useful finding that a "good supervisor, i.e., one who gets higher production, is likely to be one who is thought to have more influence with his own superior. Supervisors whose influence with their superiors was slight or nonexistent did not get as good results with the same "good supervisory practices."

Some work useful to the practitioner has also been done by analyzing the role that an executive plays or expects to play, and thereby predicting his likely behavior. For example, Bakke notes that "for one man to play successfully the role of benevolent superior, another has to play the role of grateful subordinate."[32] This may eventually lead some practitioners to realize that they cannot play the role of "paternalistic employers" successfully unless others will play the roles of "child-like employees."[33]

But none of the human relations theories so far has much value in attempting to predict behavior arising out of highly complex situations or behavior at the top management level.

Management Science

The vast and fast-developing management science approach is likely to have a broader application in the future. Applying the criteria to it at present we find:

[32] E. Wight Bakke, op. cit., p. 21.
[33] Ibid.

In the *selection* of facts, there is certainly a real contribution to many fields, since many more facts may be included if a computer is used, and many more different courses of action stimulated (and quicker reaction to change brought about). One of the dangers, however, is that the management scientists who select the facts may be ignorant of the subject on which they are working, which is why computer installations are increasingly supervised and even programmed by company personnel rather than by outside management scientists—unless the latter spend considerable time familiarizing themselves with the corporate problems.[34]

Another problem is that some management scientists are guided in the selection of facts by wrong assumptions and prejudices. For instance, a machine tool manufacturer is told that his tools must be run by tape rather than by men so that, in case of a nuclear war, a duplicate tape would be available in another part of the country. But part of the value of the machines is that they make it possible to allow for the fact that each piece of metal is different, and this requires the use of a human brain— at present at least.

In the *explanation* of the reasons why one strategy rather than another should be used, the simulation of a large number of different conditions can be very useful (e.g., in advertising and pricing policies). But the problem here is not only the likely absence of basic facts, but the more serious one of the pretentious pouring of "old wines into new bottles," for example, the construction of an intricate accounting matrix to replace the traditional T accounts, which not only makes understanding more difficult but can be misleading in some respects.[35]

In *prediction* management scientists have scored superior results over traditional problems in middle management decisions—inventory turnover, reordering, and queuing problems,

[34] Ernest Dale, *The Decision-making Process in the Use of High-speed Computers,* an unpublished research study for Cornell University, 1962–1963.

[35] "Toward a General and Axiomatic Foundation of Accountancy—With an Introduction to the Matrix Formulation of Accounting Systems," *Accounting Research,* Cambridge University Press, New York, October, 1957, pp. 328–355.

etc.; but they have not done much in the area of top management problems[36] except "on the fringe" as reporters and analysts of some market research problems.

Some of the reasons for the management scientists' lack of involvement and lack of results in predicting and guiding top management decisions include:

1. Lack of many basic data and inability to substitute experience and intuition for them.

2. Changing parameters while study is in process and decisions are being carried out.

3. Inability to take account of nonquantifiable factors. (Though some work has been done in combining estimates and facts.)

4. The expense and time involved. (One capital investment feasibility study cost over a half million dollars and the final recommendations—months later—were the same as those of the department manager concerned.)

5. Inability of most programmers to handle esoteric OR (operations research) approaches.

6. The fact that negotiating out the scale and priority of investments is more common than "computerized" results.

Conclusion

After such a lengthy, and I realize a largely inadequate, test of the uses of the three principal approaches to functional management, the question may well be raised whether they can be successfully integrated. Again lack of space prohibits using more than one example, which while not perfect does seem to be operational in terms of long-term increase in profits, despite occasional interruptions and checks, as well as in terms of survival and industry leadership over a comparatively long period.

It is the General Motors Corporation which appears to have combined the three approaches quite felicitously. The contributions were made by many who include:

[36] Dale, *op. cit.* For example, CEIR, one of the largest and most-publicized management science organization, has been losing increasing amounts of money since 1958, and the price of its stock in 1962 dropped by 92 per cent.

In management science, Donaldson Brown,[37] A. E. Bradley, F. C. Donner, S. du Brul, A. Court, C. F. Roos, and Victor von Szeliski.[38]

In the *operational approach,* J. E. Mooney,[39] Donaldson Brown, and Alfred P. Sloan, Jr., in their organization memorandums.

In the *human relations* approach, C. E. Wilson[40] and Donaldson Brown,[41] as well as the recent work on organization done by the General Motors Institute.

The "Fusion Process" of these three approaches was perhaps best explained by Donaldson Brown in his privately published *Some Reminiscences of an Industrialist.* Developed essentially in the 1920s and 1930s, the GM group started out with management science; the multiple breakeven analysis of GNP in relation to variations in industry sales, company sales, and company profits before and after taxes. The investments in plants were then planned on a standard volume at standard prices. In each fiscal year, prices would vary on the marginal principle designed to maximize return on investment. For each year also, plans were made on optimistic, average, and pessimistic bases. Many individual studies used mathematical techniques and models, but the principle of Occam's razor, or use of the simplest approach, might be applied to some of the most complicated problems, for example, postcards were used to study some aspects of consumer demand and simultaneously to promote it.

The operational approach as developed at Du Pont by H. M. Barksdale and his associates[42] was elaborated and made to work at GM by Donaldson Brown (who had been one of the co-

[37] "R = T × P," "Pricing Policy in Relation to Financial Control" in *Some Reminiscences of an Industrialist,* Port Deposit, Md., 1957, pp. 26–44, 130–157.

[38] *The Dynamics of Automotive Demand,* Detroit, Mich., 1939.

[39] *The Principles of Organization,* Harper & Row, Publishers, Incorporated, New York, 1939.

[40] "Five Years of Industrial Peace," National Press Club, Washington, D.C., 1950.

[41] "Industrial Management as a National Resource," *The Conference Board Management Record,* April, 1943.

[42] See Ernest Dale and Charles Meloy, "Hamilton MacFarl and Barksdale and the Du Pont Contributions to Systematic Management," *Business History,* pp. 127–152, Summer, 1962 (Newcomen prize essay, *Harvard Business Review,* 1962).

authors of the organization criteria of Du Pont) and Alfred P. Sloan, Jr., who had written his own organization memorandum in 1919.

The human relations approach was partly based on the rigidly honest and "common sense" code of the du Ponts, partly on a highly sophisticated anticipation of human relations theory (e.g., P. S. Du Pont's insistence that the formal organization be adapted to personalities[43] and the use of Likert's "link-pin" idea through the GM policy groups, and the emphasis on cooperation).

These three approaches were then "fused" through the system of "coordinated control"—which was partly a product of management science (Donaldson Brown's rate of return investment analysis, responsibility accounting, and linkage of rewards to performance); partly operational in that increasing profits was the goal and audit was independent of operations; and partly human relations, e.g., Donaldson Brown's system of two-way communication.

True, General Motors is not perfect. It has probably not ever succeeded in enlisting the kind of the cooperation on the lower levels that the social scientists have visualized. But in terms of its own objectives—constantly improving the utilization of its investments and maintaining leadership in its industry and the economy—it has been immensely successful. It has, in fact, fulfilled John J. Raskob's famous prediction of 1918:

After this war the greatest economy in the world will be the U.S.A.; the greatest industry the automotive industry; and the greatest company, General Motors.

True, there is still much more to be done. The theories of the functional approach will have to be much improved. But I believe that the empirical foundations to achieve improvement are there, and the practitioner stands ready to help the theorist integrate these three and often seemingly contradictory approaches.

[43] Dale, *The Great Organizers, op. cit.*, p. 61.

B CONTRIBUTIONS OF THE BEHAVIORAL SCIENCES TO A GENERAL THEORY OF MANAGEMENT

Fritz J. Roethlisberger

Were my task just to state the influence of the behavioral sciences on managerial practices, I would feel easier, because at that level I believe a fairly simple and brief story can be told. But when my task also involves their contributions to a general theory of management, I feel that I face some formidable problems. I cannot rid myself of the notion that a theory should be able to predict and explain as well as to influence. Moreover, the behavioral sciences are not yet one. I cannot do justice to all the contributions of each of the disciplines that comprise them, and I am not capable of synthesizing their findings by stating a set of general propositions about organizations from which under specified conditions the practice of management can be derived. This would be my ideal of a general theory of management, and short of it, any synthesis that I propose I cannot help but think will be guilty of slanting their contributions in some way or other.

WHAT I PROPOSE TO DO

All these qualms became intensified when during this past summer I read the current literature on organizational behavior in preparation for this assignment. I was impressed with how far in one direction and how little in another we had gone in the past two decades. Although new avenues of research had developed and new schools of thought had arisen, many of the problems remained the same; and around these problems the same issues were being raised.

In reading the current literature it seemed to me, for example, that among those of us who have chosen *organizations* as a fruitful place in which to study man's behavior, there was less agreement about just what it is that we are or should be trying to study there. In fact it might be said that during the past two decades, the more we have agreed about the place where we should study, the less we have agreed about what it is we should be studying there, i.e., what our unit of analysis is: (1) man, (2) organizations, or (3) man-in-organizations.

In spite of this situation the illusion still persists that because we are all studying in the same place, we must be studying the same thing and hence that our findings should be capable of being easily related to one another, that is, that our common place determines our common subject matter. But when we try to relate on this assumption, the illusion becomes quickly shattered, the distinction between where and what we study becomes only too evident, our differences become more painfully revealed, and we find that what and not where we study determines our subject matters.

As this is the first problem that faces me, I want to tell you how I propose to deal with it. I have little skill for synthesizing results from different approaches that are trying to explain different things. General theory building is not my particular forte. In view of these limitations, therefore, I have decided to do something for which I feel I am better fitted and which at the same time I hope also will facilitate the purposes of this conference.

I want to present one particular approach toward the study of organizational behavior and administration that was carved out from the behavioral sciences. It represents a long-term research strategy to which I have been committed for many years. I do not think it is the only approach nor do I think that it is uniquely my approach; I think that it is shared by many other investigators. Nevertheless I will not press this point as I do not want to commit anyone to it. It will therefore be a highly personal account of my problems and those of others who, as I see it, are engaged in a somewhat similar pursuit.

What I want to do is to look at this approach from the point of view of a twenty-year perspective and to review its early formulation with its associated hopes and aspirations, its contributions, and its problems and limitations. It will be primarily the story of those persons in the behavioral sciences who, in spite of serious terminological difficulties, were essentially concerned with trying to carve out a new disciplinary entity around the focus of an empirical study of man's behavior in organization and what this meant for administration. They had come to organizations in order to study the problems that organizations presented for administration in particular and not for society in general.

As I am not multilingual, I will tell this story in my own language system. This will create very probably the impression that I am making a case for just one school of thought. I wish I could get around this problem, but I just do not know how. I would like to believe that if I had the skill I could tell essentially the same story in another language system.

Although I shall be borrowing ideas from others freely, and in this sense there will be nothing original in my account, I shall quote no names. This is not because I should not like to acknowledge my personal indebtedness but because I would like us to look at the ideas for themselves and not in terms of the people with whom they tend to become associated. Moreover, many of the ideas that I will be discussing have been expressed by so many different persons, even though in different ways perhaps, that it would be difficult for me to ascribe them to one particular person.

THE EARLY FORMULATION

Following World War II there was a strong movement in the direction of breaking down some of the artificial barriers that it was felt existed among some of the disciplines in the social sciences, particularly those of social anthropology, social psychology, clinical psychology, and sociology. Among some of the members of these disciplines it was felt that in certain respects their respective subject matters overlapped, and hence that in certain areas they could make more hay by getting together than by going it alone. Although there was never anything like complete consensus on this point, nevertheless there was a sufficient number of members from those different disciplines who felt this way to warrant the formation of new interdisciplinary combinations for purposes of teaching and research. In time the name "behavioral sciences" came to be applied to these disciplines, and labels such as "social relations" and "human relations" came to be attached to their combinations.

Among the many different places in which these different disciplines could fruitfully meet there was one which seemed to hold promise, namely, in purposive organizations. These purposive entities had not been overly cultivated by any one of these disciplines separately; no strong claims had been staked out there by any one of them alone. It was obviously the most neutral territory in which to meet, but more than this it provided an excellent place in which they could meet in order to study some of their common concerns.

Two important concerns loomed fairly high. For many behavioral scientists the balance between the rational and nonrational elements of human behavior was one of the critical issues of modern life. Since organizations provided some of the best examples of man's successes and failures to achieve rational behavior, where could this concern be better studied? And also for many behavioral scientists organizations provided a fruitful place to study some of the most important problems of a democratic society: the problems of order and freedom, control and initiative, and the centralization and decentralization of authority.

But there were also other ideas associated with this new focus for the study of man's behavior, in which there was considerable intellectual excitement at the time and in which I became involved and in time committed. This excitement arose from the fact that organizations could provide a concrete setting where all the elements of behavior that the individual disciplines traditionally sought to explain singly were present together. There was, for example, both institutional behavior and individual behavior going on. Both what was expected of man and what he wanted were present and could be empirically studied together in their relation to each other.

Although this idea of studying together these two important aspects of man's behavior seemed to make sense, it was also clear that this new empirical investigation could be achieved only if each discipline would renounce the search for immediate explanation in the important determinant of behavior with which it had been traditionally concerned, and instead would seek first for uniformities in the actual behavior that followed from their interactions. If this could be done it was felt a new level of understanding and knowledge might be achieved.

How We Drew Our Lines

But how was this to be done? To put it oversimply, we would try to do this by drawing an arbitrary and imaginary line around an organization and treating the actual behavior that went on inside as the phenomena to be first observed and in time to be explained. All the important elements of behavior that the individual disciplines traditionally sought to explain would be there, so to speak, but as givens or boundary conditions of the actual behavior to be first observed and in time explained.

For example, the different values that the various persons in the organization brought to the organization would be treated as givens, i.e., as something lying outside the line which we would undertake to explain. This did not mean that we would ignore them as important determinants of behavior. Obviously they were one of the important determinants of the behavior we would be observing and of course we would have to identify what these values were. But why people had the values that they did we would not be concerned, as such, with explaining. This did not mean that we could not explain them or would not accept or make use of the explanations that common knowledge or the individual disciplines concerned with their explanation provided. And moreover, if in particular situations we needed to know, we felt that we knew where to look, i.e., in the personal histories and social backgrounds of the particular individuals involved. But this was not to be our chief concern.

Likewise with the rules of and the activities required by the organization, these too, although not ignored as important determinants of behavior, would be treated as given and as constant during the period under investigation and not as matters to be explained. They too, like the values that different individuals brought to the organization, we would treat as one of the boundary conditions under which the actual behavior evolved. Again let me state that it was not because we felt that we could not explain the proliferation of rules and requirements that seemed to develop in organizations as they grew larger and entered into the world of science and technology. If necessary we felt that we knew in what direction to look; but this is not our first order of business.

A Natural Social System: Formal and Informal Organization

Underlying this way of thinking was the notion of a natural social system. Organizations were to be conceived fundamentally as natural social units, but they differed in one important respect from other kinds of social groupings and social organizations that emerge whenever men are living together and that sociologists generally try to explain. They were different in the sense that they were social units that had been established for the explicit purpose of achieving certain goals. Built into them by the goals to be achieved and the means by which they were to be achieved were certain prescribed and planned relations that had not spontaneously emerged in the course of social interaction. We used the term "formal organization" to refer to these prescribed rules as well as to the required activities and interactions and their coordination that have been established for the explicit purpose of achieving certain prescribed goals.

But this official plan and prescribed ways about who should be doing what and where, when, and how it should be done we did not think were to be treated as descriptive propositions of the actual behavior that was going on in organizations. Nor did we think that they should be treated as higher-order general propositions—principles so to speak—from which the actual behavior could be deduced and thereby explained. If so, we were out of business. Our job was done, and no empirical investigation needed to be made in order to find out what was going on; this could be learned by reading the official manuals and job descriptions. But as no empirical investigations that had been made thus far had come up with this finding, we felt that instead of treating them as simple descriptive propositions of actual behavior or as general propositions from which actual behavior could be deduced, it would be more apropos to treat them as normative propositions about what behavior should be. As such they were influencing what the behavior was, but they were not the behavior itself nor did they explain it.

To the emergent patterns of behavior that evolved within this formal framework we gave the name sometimes of "informal organization" and sometimes of "social structure." It referred to the practices, values, norms, beliefs, and unofficial rules as well as to the complex network of social relations, membership patterns, and centers of influence and communication that developed within and between the constituent groups of the organization under the formal arrangements but that were not specified by them. These patterns of behavior could not be obtained from books; they could be obtained only from observing and interviewing the members of the organization. Although they developed within the framework of the formal organization, they were not all completely determined by it. But neither were they completely independent of the formal organization. Many of them seemed to be nurtured by it.

However, this question about just how the formal and informal organization were actually related in particular cases, it seemed to us, was an empirical question, to be decided by the results of the investigation and not before it. For purposes of investigation, therefore, we would treat the formal organization as constituting one of the important dimensions of the immediate environment in which the actual social structure of the organization developed, and we would collect our data accordingly. Just as there was only one organization so there was only one social structure; formal and informal were analytical concepts to refer to two different dimensions of the territory and not to two separable things in it. It was this concrete social structure which emerged from what was *put there* by the formal organization and what was *brought there* by the individuals who came there that we would be trying to observe, identify, and diagnose and from which we would obtain the elementary descriptive propositions that we would finally have to explain.

Structure, Function, and Equilibrium

In its earlier formulation this new conceptual focus for the empirical investigation of man's behavior in organizations had also associated with it, besides the notion of social structure, the notions of function and equilibrium, as they were then being used by social anthropologists, before the concept of "functional analysis" had been refined by sociologists to refer to something more disciplined in nature. As these ideas have been the source of so many disputes and misunderstandings, I hesitate to add anything now that will help to increase their number; certainly nothing that I can say now briefly is going to clear anything up. But as they are matters which we may wish to discuss later, I will put them on the record and make a few general comments.

It has been said that scientific investigation begins and ends with theory; it has also been said that it begins and ends with observation. Be this as it may, it has also been said that the scientific investigator in any particular field starts with a theory that is quite different from the theory which he later develops. For some scientists this difference is sufficiently great to warrant the use of two different words to refer to them. Sometimes the words "conceptual scheme" (for investigation) are used to refer to the former and the word "theory" (of explanation) is used to refer to the latter. Although there is no general agreement on the use of these words, this will be the way I shall use them.

It has also been said that in order to be fruitful for investigation conceptual schemes do not have to be too precise and clear. Why? Because their function is not to explain but to fix attention upon what is to be first observed and in time explained. Their attributes are utility and convenience for purposes of investigation; not truth or falsity or clarity for purposes of explanation.

So from this point of view I am putting to bed for now (but not for later discussion) these notions about structure, function, and equilibrium by placing them in the category of conceptual entities which in themselves may not explain and perhaps in time may need explaining themselves, but which nevertheless, in the first instance, because we cannot do everything at the same time, may help to produce findings that are well worth explaining. By such a cavalier disposal of these very important ideas I do not think that I am downgrading them or misrepresenting the use that was made of them by the early investigators. Because of their empirical leanings these investigators were more interested in the heuristic value of these ideas than in their logical consistency and metaphysical implications.

Moreover, it seemed to them that in purposive organizations —because of their goal orientations—the notion of function could be used without implying any great mystique. What was going on in a firm, for example, could be viewed from the point of view of the function that it had for (1) achieving the goals of the organization, (2) maintaining the ways of life of the constituent groups of the organization, and (3) satisfying the needs of the individuals comprising these groups. In this sense the functional point of view did provide a framework or rationale for understanding what was going on. It could easily be seen that what was functional for one might not be functional for another, so there was no built-in preestablished harmony in this way of looking at things. There was plenty of conflict around, as all the early investigations showed.

But no final pronouncements were made about the inevitability of these conflicts. Rather they were viewed as characterizing the setting in which the administrator worked, made his decision, and exercised his authority. What could provide a better opportunity to look and see how he went about it?

The Development of Knowledge and Practice Together

So associated with this new conceptual scheme for the empirical investigation of man's behavior in organization was the notion that this behavior could be more concretely observed from the point of view of the problems that it presented for the people who were responsible for administering organizations. By doing this it was not our intention to slant things in the direction of management values or of being exclusively practical, although these dangers did exist.

It was another idea that captured our imagination. In this way we felt that we could develop theory and practice together. We would be looking at organizations, not from the point of view of the problems that they presented for society in general, but from the point of view of the problems that they presented for persons who were doing something about them or could do, if they so chose, something different about them. Knowledge about the behavior of people in organizations would be developed hand in hand with knowledge for someone who could utilize it in a professional way.

Any idea has associated with it certain imagery and, as I remember it, the medical analogy was often used to make this idea vivid. The clinical practice of medicine was often compared to the clinical practice of administration. Just as the descriptive laws of physiology could help in the improved practice of medicine, so these descriptive laws about the behavior of persons in organizations, when found, could help to improve the practice of administration, and from them more competent professional management would more likely emerge.

A Situational Orientation

One other element—and it will be the final one upon which I will comment—was associated with this early conceptual scheme for the empirical investigation of man's behavior in organizations. Many of us had gone through a period of "wild psychoanalysis"; we did not wish to go through another period of "wild functional analysis," i.e., of speculating about the possible functional benefits to some system or other of every piece of behavior that we looked at.

While this danger existed we felt that it could be best contained by being situationally and clinically oriented, i.e., by being oriented to the functions of certain pervasive patterns of behavior that appeared in concrete situations that we were studying and for which we could obtain some firsthand clinical evidence. This dictated for many of us in the beginning a field research and a single case approach to the study of organizations. This raises some methodological issues that I will return to later.

Summary

In summary, then, let me comment briefly in general about some of these early ideas that I think set the stage for many of us who were starting an empirical investigation of man's behavior in organizations.

1. There was nothing new about any one of the ideas. They had all been borrowed from the behavioral sciences; for example, the notions of social structure, function, and equilibrium.

2. Although isomorphic to the territory, these ideas were not defining what in particular the territory was; they were more ideas of how it might be investigated in order to obtain the data and in time the propositions upon which a more scientific explanation could be built.

3. We drew our boundary lines between what we would treat as givens and what we would try to explain so that neither traditional psychology nor traditional sociology could preempt the field and so that a premature reduction of one to the other could be avoided.

4. These ideas constituted a long-term step-by-step research strategy for empirical investigation; the payoff was not going to be immediate because there was nothing to be explained until the findings were in.

I think that I could have made many of the same above statements had I been using the conceptual and terminological system of "force field theory" and stating it as a tool for investigation and not as a system of explanation. Anyway, it was this new long-term research strategy embodied in a conceptual scheme for investigation that captured the imagination and created the excitement for many of us at the time. It was far from being sheer empiricism. As I have tried to show, a set of explicit ideas were being brought to the investigation. It was hoped, however, that they would carry with them the least amount of preconceptions, i.e., the least amount of metaphysical notions about what organizations or man's relation to them should be. It was hoped that they would help to get results that in time would throw a new light and perspective on some of the traditional problems of management and labor, to break through some of the old distinctions and traditional concerns and ways of talking and thinking about these matters, and even to cut across the traditional distinction between pure and applied research.

It was hoped that this empirical investigation could be developed together in the direction of obtaining both improved knowledge about organizations and improved administrative practices on the part of responsible people in them. Improved knowledge would come by establishing first the simple descriptive propositions about man's behavior in organizations. These propositions would come slowly by patient, pedestrian effort in the field and well-documented case studies. When more carefully tested and verified, they would provide the basis for improved knowledge and practice.

SOME FINDINGS AND APPLICATIONS

I have spent some time on these ideas—which I have called the conceptual scheme for the empirical investigation of man's behavior in organizations—because they set the stage for two decades of research around two aspects of organizational behavior: (1) morale and employee productivity, satisfaction, and motivation, and (2) leadership and supervision. In these two areas not only were the findings the greatest but also the direction in which they pointed for the improvement of administrative practices was the clearest. As this development has been well documented in the literature, let me review it very briefly.

Some General Findings That Were Checked by Many Different Investigators

It seems to me astonishing how at one level of analysis the findings of different investigators checked. Again and again they pointed to:

1. The inadequacy of the motivational assumptions underlying the traditional principles of management
2. What little influence the employee was supposed to exercise, what few interpersonal transactions he was supposed to have, what little two-way communication there was supposed to be and how doing what he was told and being obedient to authority seemed to be the sole integrative force under the traditional principles of management

3. The conflict between the principles of scientific management on the one hand and the determinants of cooperation on the other, i.e., how the application of these principles seemed to be at odds with the way members of an organization became identified and committed to its goals

4. The more a supervisor managed in terms of what he was supposed to do in accordance with the principles of management, the less he seemed to be doing an all-round, long-term job

5. How supervisors and managers who seemed to get the best overall, long-term effect seemed to be displaying a leadership style quite different from those who did not

6. How supervisors and managers who were displaying a leadership style different from what they were supposed to be doing received little support from (a) their superiors, (b) the traditional theory, (c) any accepted new theory, or (d) any feedback of results, other than those of the traditional kind, that would reflect the good overall long-term job that they were doing

7. How, under the traditional principles of management, informal leaders tended to appear in many work groups in order to take care of the maintenance functions that the task leaders failed to perform

8. "The restriction of output syndrome," i.e., how under the principles of scientific management, employees tended to develop a concept of a day's work that was not too high or too low to get them into trouble

9. "The man-in-the-middle syndrome," i.e., the different ways supervisors resolved the conflict of trying to get the cooperation of their employees while at the same time trying to get them to do what they should be doing at the proper time, place, and with the proper methods; and as a result, the different leadership styles that tended to emerge or not to emerge, such as, for example, institutional, autocratic, laissez-faire, accommodative, personal, production-oriented, person-oriented, group-oriented, democratic, permissive, supportive, and transactional

10. "The staff-line syndrome," i.e., how staff people, who were supposed to be helping line people by setting standards for evaluating the results of employees, tended to be regarded by the line people more as a source of interference than as a source of help

11. "The distributive-justice syndrome," i.e., the many complaints that took the form that it isn't fair or just that what I'm getting is not proportional to what I should be getting in terms of my age, seniority, education, sex, etc.

12. "The vicious-cycle syndrome," i.e., how the unintended dysfunctional consequences of the traditional methods of control tended to encourage a continued use of them, e.g., the breakdown of rules begot more rules to take care of their breakdown or the breakdown of close supervision encouraged the use of still closer methods of supervision and as a result, the continuous search and invention of new control systems to correct for the limitations of previous ones

13. "The specialist-generalist syndrome," i.e., the sharp difference of outlook, skill, knowledge, and influence required and acquired by those who do the work of the organization (whether they be workers, salesmen, clerks, technicians, or scientists) and by those who are responsible for facilitating that the work gets done, well illustrated by the differences, for example, between the optimizing of this *or* that and the "satisficing" of this *and* that

14. "The frozen-group syndrome," i.e., the kind of static accommodation which many work groups seemed to make to the organizational environments in which they had to survive

15. "The underdeveloped-individual-development syndrome," i.e., the amount of apathy, uninvolvement, and uncommitment which existed among some members of an organization, particularly at the work level, and the needs for belonging, competence, self-development, and identity which were not being tapped by management and which could not be tapped by the traditional principles of management

The Development of Human Relations Training

For many investigators as well as practitioners who wanted to do something, the action prescription to which these findings pointed was relatively clear: supervisors and managers needed to have a better understanding of cooperative-conflict phenomena in order to do a better job of supervision and management. This educational development of supervisors and executives has proceeded in ever-increasing stages of sophistication which I will review very briefly.

1. At an obvious manifest level, these findings pointed to the need for more participative management, two-way communication, and permissive leadership. These ideas were not entirely new to some managements, and to those who were interestd in going in this direction, these findings helped to give support. But to those who were not, these findings had little impact, and so exhortations to be more

participative, permissive, and "two-wayish" fell on deaf ears. Anyway, for many of these managements, how you become this way presented for them a difficult question.

2. Even to the investigators it became obvious that although more participatory methods needed to be utilized, these methods were not capable of being abstracted and learned apart from the concrete behavior of the persons who were to practice them. The development of new styles of leadership involved a reeducational job. In order for the supervisor to be able to understand and to deal with the phenomena of cooperation and conflict that the institutional type of leadership ignored, he needed more fundamental training.

3. From these ideas, the beginning of human relations training at the supervisory and foreman levels developed. In many early programs this training took place at a persuasive and anecdotal level, going little beyond that of urging supervisors to treat their employees more like human beings. But among the better programs—at least in intention and ignoring for the moment the question of how well they were doing it—there was an attempt to reach a more cognitive level, and through case materials, discussion, and lectures, to give the supervisor an understanding of the nature of cooperative-conflict phenomena and the skills that were associated with them.

4. In some programs a further refinement took place that I think is worth underscoring. It became clear that the fruitful ways of thinking for empirical investigation, outlined earlier, could also be utilized for the improvement of practice. If supervisors could be taught these ways of thinking and learn to explore their problem situations in terms of them, better diagnoses of particular situations could be made. And from better-diagnosed situations, better actions it was hoped would follow. Not only would the utilization of this way of thinking direct their attention to matters of feeling, sentiment, social structure, and informal organization—matters which the traditional principles of management ignored—but also it would counteract the supervisor's search for the one right way and the one right answer. It was more important for supervisors to have the spirit and tools of situational investigation than to have assigned role prescriptions. (This development probably took place more in courses that were being developed at business schools for potential executives than in training programs for supervisors in industry.)

5. As these programs developed the clinical psychologist came more and more to the fore. He had been present from the beginning as one of the important contributors to the interdisciplinary combination involved in the empirical investigation of man's behavior in

organizations, and if I have neglected to mention his contributions earlier, it is only because I have been cutting corners in order to cover a large amount of material rather quickly. Anyway, his methods of interviewing in helping persons to talk about matters that were important to them had been borrowed and utilized freely during the period of investigation. But they were equally useful for the development of practice in trying to help supervisors to listen more intelligently and understandingly to the members of the work groups that they were supervising.

6. As time went on, however, some unanticipated problems began to appear. One of them appeared around the question: "Were these programs not being developed under some rather unrealistic assumptions?" For example, they were being addressed mainly to the supervisory-foreman level. How could new styles of leadership be developed among them while their bosses continued to manage in the traditional way? How unrealistic could you get? Supervisors were not free agents and independent variables, and yet human relations training seemed to be making this assumption.

7. Another set of problems appeared around the relation of knowledge to practice. It was felt that supervisors did not readily change their behavior from reading books and being told about the determinants of behavior or even from discussing case materials about the experiences and problems of others. Changes were more likely to take place when they became sensitive to the particular feelings and sentiments (values) that *here and now* were influencing their own behavior in a supportive setting which would allow them to re-evaluate their perceptions of themselves and others. Although these ideas were coming from the clinical insights of psychotherapy, they were also receiving a great deal of support from the results of many training programs where it had been found that it was easier to get the supervisor to talk about the new styles of leadership than to practice them and where it was difficult to get them to feel the difference between the intent and the consequences of their behavior.

8. To take care of these problems many different modifications were introduced. Programs began to appear at higher echelons of management; executive development became the new thrust. Trainees were taken away from the organizational environments in which they worked and placed in new and more unstructured situations where they could "unfreeze" their old ways of doing things, experiment with new roles, get some confidence in becoming more role-flexible and reflect upon how they could apply this new learning when they got "back home." This kind of learning emphasized the need to examine

more "here and now" data and less "there and then" data, i.e., to look more at the data (group processes) that were being generated and were taking place *here and now* in the group while it engaged in discussions about its task and to be concerned less with prefabricated materials in the form of "written cases" about somebody else's experiences.

9. This development, which is known as laboratory training or T group or group dynamics or sensitivity training, aims to reach a much deeper level of understanding of cooperative-conflict phenomena than any other previous version of human relations training. It is heavily influenced by social psychology, group dynamics, and psychotherapy; it is deeply concerned with humanizing bureaucracy; it has become the newest and for some behavioral scientists the most exciting instrument for organizational change; and around it has developed a new professional group of "change agents" and a new field of "change agentry."

10. As can be seen, human relations training has traveled a long road from its early days of trying to urge superiors to treat people as human beings to the present sophistication of the T group. But, it would be incorrect to believe that this is its final or only version; revisions are continually being made; different combinations of theory and practice are being sought and tried in different programs of human relations training.

11. Nor would it be correct to believe that the present T group version is not being criticized by some behavioral scientists. One question that keeps cropping up is: "Has it not gone too far down the road of psychotherapy?" On this question, although the intent of its practitioners is clear (i.e., "T" in T group stands for training and not for therapy), the evidence is not clear because the line between certain aspects of social learning and psychotherapy is not clear. But more serious still for some is the question: "Can bureaucracies be humanized and democratized?" How successful has the T group been in achieving its own aims? What do the results show? Here again the evidence is difficult to obtain. Testimonials do not provide too good evidence, but also because these questions cannot be easily made operational, they cannot be easily tested.

12. As a result two doctrinal positions have arisen in the area of organizational change, and the underlying tone of the current literature on the subject reflects them well. There is one school of thought which, while willing to admit that bureaucracies are strongly resistant to change and that there are "bugs" in their position, nevertheless believes that it is worth trying to do something and that in time the

bugs can be removed. They support their position with evidence and insights from psychotherapy and clinical psychology, and this evidence, although not quite germane to the point, is nevertheless difficult to discount completely. Then there is another school of thought which says in effect, "it can't be done," that bureaucracies are bureaucratic for very good functional reasons, and hence that human relations trainers who are trying to humanize bureaucracies are "incurable romanticists" and deluding themselves.

13. So this is the stage at which one development of the findings has reached. Although each side of the above dispute can cite some evidence in favor of its position, it is doubtful that these doctrinal positions can ever be resolved by this method. So I should now like to turn to other developments which to some behavioral scientists not only are equally promising and exciting but also need to take place before some of the problems raised by human relations training can be resolved.

SOME UNFINISHED BUSINESS

Let me return to the findings. Some behavioral scientists have raised questions about these findings that were quite different from those questions with which the human relations training group was concerned. They were asking questions such as: (1) Had the findings been contaminated by the conceptual scheme? (2) Had they been sufficiently tested and were they in the form to be tested? and (3) Did they not themselves need to be explained? The first question has raised considerable discussion, some of which I feel has not been too fruitful; the second and third questions have stimulated a great deal of fruitful research and speculation.

Problems of Slanting

Many criticisms have been made of the early formulation. Although I shall list some of them below for purposes of our discussion later, I will not attempt to consider each of them. Rather I will raise a more general question which to me underlies many of these criticisms.

It has been said that the original formulation, which I have called the conceptual scheme for empirical investigation, slanted things in the direction of (1) irrationality or nonrationality, (2) harmony and conservatism, (3) the organization's internal environment, and (4) management values. It tended to overlook (1) the more rational problem-solving behavior of organizations, (2) conflict, (3) the organization's external environment, and (4) union values. It had basically an antieconomic, antiscientific management, antiengineering, antilegislative, and antiformalistic bias. These biases have so contaminated the findings that they can not provide a solid foundation upon which to build.

If we remove from these criticisms any implications of a lack of intellectual integrity on the part of the investigators—and this is the assumption upon which I will proceed, namely, that there was no deliberate slanting in terms of the investigators' ideological beliefs and that this issue is not being raised by the criticisms —then we are left with a problem that has never ceased to intrigue me.

Any conceptual scheme slants; this is what makes it useful. Because one cannot look at and talk about everything at the same time (a most unfortunate human predicament), a conceptual scheme says, "look *here*," instead of (or as well as) "there." And in a certain sense persons who use it will find what they are looking for. But this is not as serious as it sounds, as long as one understands why this is so and how it can be corrected.

The conceptual scheme that I stated earlier, for example, was saying in effect (1) don't just look at actions; look also at interactions and their associated sentiments; look at the interactions between persons and groups and in the organization; (2) look for both the intended and unintended consequences for some involved system (e.g. personality, small group, formal organization) of certain pervasive patterns in the organization; (3) look for the patterns of behavior that keep recurring, that have seemed to settle down in some kind of practical equilibrium, i.e., that are expressing some long-term accommodation to the environmental forces about them; and *above all*, (4) seek for descriptive propositions—not *normative propositions* about these pervasive phenomena that are being observed.

The Confusion between Descriptive and Normative Propositions. I wonder how many persons realize what a serious slanting this was. Organizations, and business organizations in particular, are highly normative worlds. They are bristling with normative propositions about how things *should be* and *should* be done and what rational behavior *should* be. The world of organizations, as any field worker knows, is teeming with these notions of what is "right" and "wrong" and what is "good" and "bad," what is "rational" and "irrational," and what is "good sense" and "bad judgment." Many of the propositions of traditional management theory and scientific management are of this sort. They are the kinds of propositions that the practitioner wants.

As a result many difficult problems are encountered when one tries to slant things in the direction of stating descriptive propositions about man's behavior in organizations which involve as one of its very important elements these normative propositions about how people should behave. The introduction of descriptive propositions into this highly normative world is as welcome as a "hole in the head." For this reason it may have unanticipated dysfunctional consequences that far outweigh the functional consequences that are intended. Among those who have tried it, this problem is understood, but among those who have not, the underestimation of the importance of this problem never ceases to astonish me.

One of the problems is that these propositions which are intended to be descriptive from the point of view of the speaker do not remain descriptive very long from the point of view of the listener. How often have we underscored, when using words such as "bureaucracy" (in relation to a certain kind of formal organization), "democratic" (in relation to a certain style of leadership), and "nonlogical" (in relation to a certain kind of behavior), for example, that we are using these words in a descriptive and not an evaluative sense? Does anyone hear this? Even words like "group," "conformity," or "deviance" do not remain descriptive very long. For many persons statements to the effect that "democratic" (good) styles of leadership may have sometimes some dysfunctional (bad) consequences; that "nonlogical" behavior (bad) may perform sometimes some highly useful (good) social functions; and that "rational" behavior (good) may sometimes have some dysfunctional (bad) consequences imply for them some very serious contradictions.

Even the form of the findings previously stated, although

intended to be descriptive of certain clinical uniformities in organizational behavior, can easily generate sentiments which will involve evaluative judgments and metaphysical suffering, such as for example that management people are not too bright; or that there is an irreconcilable conflict between the demands of organizations and the creative, self-developmental needs of man; or that bureaucracies are unfortunately a necessary evil in this world, etc.

In view of these problems which exist in my experience among ourselves as well as among businessmen and laymen, I am not assigning a very high prior probability that anything I can say now will clear them up. But as in these matters of conceptual clarity, hope springs eternal, let me repeat what has been said over and over again in one way or another by many, namely, that the concept of "function" does not make behavior thereby "irrational," "nonrational," or for that matter even "rational." It is not stating how people should behave according to some normative model of behavior. Rather it is providing a rationale for behavior, a model for the analysis of behavior that can be applied to managers as well as to workers.

Applied to any individual, it is stating what benefits a person is getting from behaving the way that he does. Hence from *his point of view,* even though his behavior may not be rational from the point of view of an outside observer; even though his behavior may land him in a "looney bin"; even though his behavior does not coincide with a normative model of how under conditions of uncertainty he should behave in order to maximize his expected monetary value, his behavior is not thereby nonrational. What this means is that from the functional point of view one can make some sense of it. So it is possible that from some normative point of view the behavior is nonrational and still from the functional point of view one can make some sense of it, if one so chooses.

The Confusion between External and Internal. Equally slanted was the way in which we sliced our cake for the purpose of investigation, and which in turn determined what became for us "external" and "internal." As I have stated before, we chose to treat as boundary conditions for what we would be observing in the organization (*a*) the values that people brought there and

(b) the prescribed ways in which things should be done in order to achieve the organizational goals. Thus, for us a and b became the environment for the actual behavior that we were observing. As a result the actual behavior (social structure) that emerged from these environmental conditions became the internal environment of the organization. This was *not* the organization's external environment in which the organization had to survive, such as the marketing environment in the case of a business organization.

Obviously this formulation slanted us in the direction of looking at and trying to understand the organization's internal environment, i.e., how the actual on-going structure operated and was administered in order to survive in its external environment. This did not mean that we ignored the organization's external environment; we were very interested in any changes going on there that would have consequences for the social structure and the way it would cope with them. But why these changes were going on "out there," we were willing to leave to the economists and the sociologist to explain. We were interested in trying to explain how the internal system, i.e., the organization from within, was going to assimilate and cope with this external environment.

Although in theory it is recognized that these ways of slicing cakes for certain investigatory and explanatory purposes have nothing God-given about them, in practice this is sometimes forgotten. When someone treats as given what someone else wants to explain or vice versa, bitter disputes sometimes occur, even among those of us who are theoretically sophisticated about these matters. But among those of us who are not and who believe that some higher authority settles these questions, the confusion in my experience is very difficult to straighten out with words—no matter how clearly we try to define them.

Anyway, it was this way of slicing the cake that allowed us to obtain an understanding of the executive's behavior that ran counter on almost all points to what the traditional principles of management said that his behavior should be. Let me illustrate this sharp contrast.

a. According to the traditional principles of management, the internal environment contains only the explicit control mechanisms that the manager and his experts put there. Once these controls have been set up so that everyone knows what is expected of him, the executive spends the remainder of his time making decisions that affect directly the organization's relation to its external environment. This way of thinking emphasizes the external environment as the executive's chief concern. It is the external environment to which he should be paying the most attention, toward which his fundamental posture should be directed, with which he should be acquainted and about which he should have knowledge. In the case of a business organization, for example, his habitat becomes the marketplace. According to this point of view, a general theory of management would be derived from a knowledge about this external environment.

b. According to the way we sliced the cake, the internal environment is populated with the values and norms that have been *brought there* as social precipitates from the backgrounds and experiences of the individuals comprising the organization as well as the standards, controls, rules, and programs that have been *put there* for the purposes of achieving the organizational goals as well as the practice, norms, and values that have *developed there* under these conditions. This environment is not solely the executive's creation; it is not something independent of him; he both affects and is affected by it and in it he is highly involved. According to this view, the executive's job is not in the marketplace, buying and selling. This is the work of the organization and the executive's job is not to do the work of the organization but to facilitate the getting of it done. His job is not to make all the decisions himself but to see that the proper resources are being brought to bear on the making of them. These decisions have to be made within the internal environment of which he is an involved member. It is this insight upon which the human relations training programs have been built. How does the executive secure changes in the internal environment under these conditions of involvement?

Moreover, the internal environment not the external environment is an important referent for many of the executives' most important decisions: e.g., Where do I want to go? What do I want to be? What business do I want to be in? What share of the market do I want to have and what price (not only economic) am I willing to pay for it? Toward all these questions the external environment is neutral, except to state the conditions under which these goals can be realized, i.e., the price which would have to be paid for their realization. But the involved executive—not the external environment—has to decide what price (not only economic) he is willing to pay. According to this point of view the executive's natural habitat is the internal environment and from an acquaintance with and a knowledge about this internal environment, the professional competent manager as well as a general theory of management would be developed.

Problems of Verification

Let me return to the findings again, because besides arguing about them, there have been some behavioral scientists who have tried to verify them. But this has presented some difficult problems, and I will cite only some.

1. A reexamination of the previously mentioned findings will show that they consist mostly of clinical uniformities which were obtained from field research of single case studies. A single case may help to reveal this uniformity; it does not verify it. For this, not evidence from one case but evidence from many independent cases is needed.

2. But in order to do this, social categories have to be created, in which it is often difficult to include the network of social relations between individuals and groups, that is, the social context under which these uniformities revealed themselves in the first place.

3. Moreover, many of these uniformities are not stated in the form which allows them to be verified easily. The anthropological-sociological concept of "function" (i.e., x fulfills function c for system y), for example, is not the same as the mathematical concept of "function" (i.e., y is a function of x), and it is often not easy to translate functional statements of the former into functional statements of the latter, although some of them can be.

So the verifiers have had plenty of trouble, but as these troubles involve difficult technical problems upon which they are diligently working and in time will make some headway, let me pass on to another problem.

Problems of Explanation

As may have been noticed, throughout this paper I have been concerned with questions of explanation: e.g., What are we trying to explain? What constitutes explanation? Is there not an important difference between investigation and explanation? May not the confusion between the two underlie some of the arguments about our classification schemes and terminologies? By confusing investigation with explanation may we not be trying to do two different things at the same time and thus misusing the instruments of one for the purposes of the other?

Recently in the literature I have detected a school of thought about scientific explanation which interests me because I think that it could be used to help us not only to reduce the amount of our disputes about words, concepts, and classification schemes but also more importantly, to get on with the job of explaining our findings. If I understand this school of thought correctly it is saying something like this:

1. Let us stop being so concerned with differences in conceptual schemes; with looking for logical inconsistencies in them, with torturing ourselves with their metaphysical (ultimate, final, irreconcilable) implications and with trying to make them logically consistent and metaphysically impregnable.

2. When things get tough and our findings seem paradoxical or contradictory, let us stop trying to seek for explanations by means of new words, labels, and concepts that are more logically consistent, psychologically appealing, or culturally attractive.

3. Instead let us concentrate upon the findings that our conceptual schemes have helped us to obtain. Let us keep looking at these findings for the simple uniformities which they may reveal in the form of "x varies with y." These simple empirical propositions are our most enduring possessions. With them explanation begins; without them there is nothing to be explained.

4. Let us look for the boundary conditions under which these simple uniformities reveal themselves and if under condition A, our colleague has found that they result in state P while under condition B we have found that they result in state Q, let's not rush to give the lie to our colleague. No contradiction is necessarily involved. This result, if A and B are understood correctly, may help to confirm and not refute them.

5. Once these simple empirical propositions have been established, let us search for a set of more general propositions of the same order, from which under specified conditions the simple descriptive propositions that we have observed—as well as others that we may not have as yet observed—may be derived.

6. Let us state clearly what we are treating as given and what we are trying to explain. This is not the problem of just one school of thought or one investigator; it is a problem for all investigators of any school of thought.

7. Let us not try to reach *deductively* the general propositions by which our simple propositions are to be explained; these general propositions are arrived at *inductively*.

8. The deductive way that a theory (of explanation) looks *when completed*, (i.e., as a set of higher-order general propositions from which under specified conditions the lower-order descriptive propositions can be deductively derived) is not the way this theory is *arrived at*.

9. The simple descriptive propositions are reached in many ways; field research is a good way, although not the only one; the simple propositions are confirmed by survey and experimental methods, but the general propositions from which they are derived are inductive creations and inventions.

10. This is why it is futile to try to repatch our conceptual schemes in order to seek for better explanations. It doesn't go that way. The processes of investigation are not to be equated with the processes of explanation. Let us not confuse them.

I find these statements both reassuring and exciting. They say to me, "Let's start making an inventory of our simple descriptive findings, and let us search for more general propositions to explain them." To me this approach, if done explicitly, offers some hope of cutting down our interminable conceptual arguments and of making some progress in explaining our findings.

SOME CONCLUSIONS

The underlying theme of much of what I have been saying has been something as follows:

1. Some interesting clinical findings have been obtained about man's behavior in organizations; some of them have been checked by statistical procedures.

2. In securing them no canons of scientific methodology were violated which make them unworthy of explanation. Many of these findings do not need to await further refinement before we try to explain them.

3. They were obtained by focusing (*a*) not upon man per se, (*b*) not upon organizations per se, but (*c*) upon man-in-organizations. They are therefore limited to this domain or subject matter.

4. These findings have been clinically checked by many different investigators from different schools of thought. Although they have

been argued about and different ultimate meanings have been attached to them, they still remain relatively unexplained, i.e., in the sense that there exists no set of more general propositions which explain them.

5. These findings are begging for explanation. Few investigators would argue that they are unrelated. But up to very recently their explanation has been sought for more in a set of more logically inter-related concepts than in a set of more general propositions.

6. There is no reason why any investigator should try to explain these findings if he is interested in explaining something else. But likewise, there is nothing in science which says that if he is interested, he should not try to explain them or that he should be explaining something else.

7. For those who are interested, then, let's get on with the job of trying to explain our findings. Let us not keep rediscovering America over and over again; let's begin to try to explain what we have discovered. If and when we do, we may have the beginning of what we are looking for—a general theory of management.

C DECISION AND THEORY MANAGEMENT THEORY

Robert Schlaifer

In a sense, I believe that I am here under false pretenses, since our announced objective is to contribute to the unification of the theory of management and I am convinced that decision theory is not and never will be a *part* of a theory of management. Professor Koontz has recently written, quite correctly in my opinion, that a theory cannot develop unless its domain is defined closely enough to make it teachable and researchable; but on the one hand the subject matter of decision theory itself—or better, normative decision theory—is barely small enough to meet this requirement, while on the other hand a theory of management in any ordinary sense of the word "management" must clearly include a very substantial number of subjects which are not part of the subject matter of normative decision theory. At least I for one cannot imagine that the expression "theory of management" will ever exclude substantive matters relevant to human beings and organizations in order to encompass normative decision theory.

NORMATIVE DECISION THEORY

I shall have to justify my presence, therefore, by a different argument, namely, that we are all interested in education and research which will improve business management or business administration; and I do believe that normative decision theory has something to contribute to this goal. The subject of normative decision theory is really the logic of deliberate choice under uncertainty. It therefore has no direct relevance to the vast majority of decisions made by managers in the ordinary course of managing since application of a system of formal statement of the decision problem, and any manager who stopped to make a formal statement of more than some very small fraction of his decision problems would clearly have no time left for managing. What we hope is that education in subjects other than decision theory will lead him to make most decisions correctly even though the problems are never stated formally, and perhaps the study of formal methods of choice will also make an indirect contribution to this goal; but the real case for decision theory in the curriculum and in the research program of a business school has to be based on the argument that even though it is rarely applicable, it promises to pay off handsomely on those occasions where it is applicable.

Perhaps I should now make a little more clear exactly what normative decision theory is; and I shall start by trying to make clear one thing it is not. It has nothing to do, at least directly, with the study of the way in which decisions are actually made by individuals, groups, or organizations. This class of problems is the subject matter of descriptive decision theory, and for all I know the methods which prove valuable in descriptive decision theory may or may not have anything to do with the methods of normative decision theory. Normative decision theory starts by considering the problem of the decision maker who is consciously aware that more than one course of action is open to him and who wishes to make a conscious, reasoned comparison of the advantages and disadvantages of each of these courses of action before choosing one among them. Observe that I have *not* said that he wishes to consider all possible courses of action and pick the best; a man could devote his whole life to developing the best of all possible buggy whips and never come to a solution.

WHERE DECISION THEORY IS WORTHWHILE

In most decision problems, the decision maker will regard only one course of action as worth serious consideration, and in such problems he will have no use for decision theory; in others he will not feel sure what action is best, but he *will* feel sure that the problem is not worth much analysis, and in these problems too he will have no use for decision theory. I believe, however, that enough problems are left over to make decision theory worthwhile. These problems are of two general types.

1. Those where the problems are complex and the stakes very high, so that analysis which promises to be of real help is worth virtually whatever it costs in the way of effort on the part of the decision maker. Many capital investment problems are of this type.

2. Those where the problems are complex but formal analysis costs the decision maker relatively little effort because most of the factors involved in the problem can be dealt with by technicians and only one or two really require the attention of the responsible decision maker himself. Many inventory problems are in this class; so are many problems of experimentation and sampling where the essential problem is to decide when to postpone final action until more information has been collected, and when to stop collecting and act.

What exactly does decision theory have to offer in such situations? Essentially, it allows the decision maker to break his complex problem down to a number of very simple problems, the solutions to which logically imply the correct solution to the complex problem. The decision maker himself must solve those component problems which in his opinion require the exercise of his judgment; both the solution of the remaining simple problems, and the working out of the implications of all the simple problems, can be carried out by a technician or technicians using a computer if necessary, and the decision maker can be sure that the results of the computation will reflect every one of his own relevant judgments as expressed in the solution of those simple problems he chose to solve.

To be more concrete, let me begin with the second class of problems I mentioned above, those where formal analysis is useful because it costs the decision maker very little effort, whereas a direct attack on the complete problem would cost a tremendous effort. Let us take as an example a businessman who ultimately must choose between package A and package B for his product. Package B is more attractive, in his opinion, than package A, but it costs more. The businessman may choose here and now between the two packages, or if he likes he may decide to do some store testing before making up his mind finally.

I think none of us here would be very surprised to hear a businessman in such a situation say, for example, that if he had to choose now, he would choose B despite its higher cost because he thought there was an even chance that it would increase sales by at least 20,000 units and one chance in four that it would increase them by as much as 30,000 units. The businessman is much less likely, however, to be clear regarding the desirability of store testing, and even less regarding the amount of store testing needed; and it is here that decision theory makes its contribution. It shows that judgments already expressed in the form of an even chance and one chance in four, and a few more judgments of the same sort, imply not only that B is the best choice, if the choice must be made immediately, but also that there is a definite "best" amount of store testing to do before actually making the choice. This right amount of store testing will of course depend, not only on these judgments, but on the cost of testing, the size of stores available for testing, the week-to-week variability of sales in each store, and so forth; but all these are factors which the businessman's technician can determine on his own and which need therefore take none of the businessman's time or attention.

PROBABILITIES AND DECISIONS

Some of you may object at this point by saying that things are not so simple as I make them seem, that statisticians are by no means in agreement that the right decision of the businessman's problem can be found as easily as I have said, and that my whole position rests on some hidden assumptions. There are indeed some assumptions involved in my conclusions, but I think they will stand up very well under close inspection. The crucial one is that the decision maker can bring himself to say and mean such things as that the chances are even that package B will increase sales by at least 20,000 units. That businessmen will in fact quote odds on an unknown event is of course a well-known and easily observable fact; the important part of the question is whether they *mean* these odds in the sense that they are willing to bet their company's money in accordance with them, or simply quote odds to justify decisions already reached. As to whether businessmen *can* quote odds that they really mean, I would answer that if a horseplayer is capable of examining the horses and their previous performances and then coming to the conclusion that he will bet on Shooting Star if he can get two to one, but otherwise he won't, then a businessman ought to be able to make a similar effort if he thinks it worth his while.

Whether he will think it worth his while depends, of course, on a comparison of alternatives. In our example, he can either solve his problem by assigning the required probabilities and then delegating all the remainder of the analysis to others; or he can call for figures on the cost of store testing, using statisticians to tell him something about the reliability of store testing and how it varies with the size of the test, try to understand the statistician's answers, and on this basis compare reliability with cost and cost with the risks involved in wrong decisions—which in turn depend of course on how wrong the decision is, that is, on how much better the other package would have been. Remember that if he chooses this latter alternative, then after duly weighing all the information he has collected, he must assert that in his opinion the company should do twenty weeks, say, of store testing, since either more or less than this would be less reasonable than exactly twenty weeks. I do not mean that he must defend the proposition that twenty is better than nineteen or twenty-one; but I do mean that he must defend the proposition that twenty is better than five, or zero, or fifty.

While I have no real evidence to go on, my guess is that once the businessman understands these two alternatives, he will usually do one of several different things: say that marketing experiments are never reliable, and pick the package he likes; run an experiment of the same size he ran the last time he had a similar problem; hire a consultant or tell a subordinate to decide on the right size of experiment without bothering him further; find out how big an experiment his chief competitor used recently and do the same; or finally, assign the required probabilities or betting odds and delegate the calculation of the size of the experiment which these probabilities logically imply. I doubt very much indeed that any business executive will really prefer the second alternative mentioned before, namely, to try personally to make a decision which takes genuinely reasoned account of all the factors affecting the proper size of an experiment. In a very real sense, then, it is not decision theory versus something else; it is decision theory or nothing. I would guess, furthermore, that it is not going to be very much harder to train businessmen to use decision theory in this sort of application than it was to train them to use linear programming in applications where that technique pays off.

PROBLEMS REQUIRING SYSTEMATIC ANALYSIS

In the other and more exciting class of problems where decision theory may some day be of use—problems where a systematic analysis seems called for because the stakes are so high —much more is naturally demanded of the responsible decision maker. The ultimate payoff of the chosen course of action will usually depend, not on one or two unknowns which require judgmental evaluation, but on a great many; and evaluation of all the factors by probability assignments clearly places a heavy burden on the responsible decision maker. The problem does not really lie so much in the sheer quantity of evaluations, since insofar as the important unknown factors are independent it is scarcely possible to argue seriously that it is easier to take reasoned account of all of them together than to take reasoned account of them one by one; but a very real problem does arise because the unknown factors will not in general be independent. Quantification of judgments concerning interdependent factors can be very tricky indeed, and I agree wholeheartedly with those who say that attempts to apply decision theory in such situations may lead to a result which is less in accordance with the decision maker's true judgment than a result reached by intuitive analysis of the problem as a whole.

We have thus reached an area where the immediate task of business schools is not training in the use of decision theory but research in how to apply decision theory—specifically, in how to phrase questions concerning interrelated unknowns which will make it as easy as possible for the decision maker to come as close as possible to expressing his true judgments. On the other hand, I have no doubt that such methods *can* be found—it seems to me simply paradoxical to assert that no matter how a complex problem is divided into parts, the sum of the difficulties of the parts must always be greater than the difficulty of the whole.

Let me also mention briefly another aspect of decision theory which at present is more in need of research than teaching. In discussing the store-testing example, I said that once the decision maker had expressed his judgments by assigning probabilities to unknowns, a mere technician could analyze all the implications. What the technician can certainly do with the available data is calculate the probability distribution of the profit which will result if the decision is made immediately, the probability distribution of the profit which will result if the decision is postponed until twenty more weeks of testing have been carried out, and so forth; and from these distributions he can certainly calculate for each amount of experimentation the expected profit—roughly speaking, the profit which would result on the average if that amount of experimentation were carried out in each of a large number of apparently identical decision problems. Now in a problem of a choice of package design, I think it will generally be true that a decision maker will in fact want to choose the course of action with the highest expected profit—to play the averages, so to speak; and I tacitly assumed this to be true when I said that after making certain probability judgments the decision maker could delegate the entire problem to the technician.

When the stakes are very high, however, this will virtually never be true—for the same reason that a man who prefers an even chance at ten dollars to four dollars for certain will generally prefer forty million dollars for certain to an even chance at a hundred million. Now decision theory offers what in principle is an excellent way of taking full account of such attitudes as the analysis of a decision problem. In fact, a method for taking systematic account of attitudes toward risk was developed quite some years before people began to work on methods for taking account of judgments concerning unknowns. To apply this method, we can start by asking the decision maker to imagine that he is involved in a venture which has a chance of resulting in either a ten million dollar profit or a five million dollar loss, and we can then ask him to decide for how much cold hard cash he would be willing to sell his rights in this venture. Given the answers to a few such questions, we can determine what is called the decision maker's "utility for money," and we can then show that to be logically self-consistent, he "should" solve any real high-stakes decision problem by choosing the course of action which has the highest expected utility rather than the highest expected monetary profit. Observe that this allows the decision maker to make a clean separation in his thinking between the problem of forming and expressing his judgments about the unknown in his problem and the problem of deciding upon and expressing his attitudes on risk as such.

RISKS AND HUMAN ATTITUDES

The trouble with this method of separate analysis is not that it is not logical; the trouble is rather of the same nature as the trouble I mentioned in connection with formulation of judgments concerning interdependent unknowns. Because the businessman is not really used to thinking about buying and selling ventures which will have one or the other of just two possible consequences, his answers to the very simple hypothetical questions we ask him may actually reflect his attitude toward risk much less accurately than his answers to more complicated problems of a type with which he is thoroughly familiar. As an example, people will often state quite reasonably that as their assets increase, they would be willing to pay a smaller amount for insurance against a fixed dollar risk, but they will then go on to answer questions about hypothetical gambles and risky ventures in a way that is inconsistent with this more basic attitude.

Once more it seems to me that our conclusion should not be that the theory of utility is useless, since it is only by use of this theory that we can separate the problem of judging what risks are involved in a given course of action from the problem of deciding how we want to react to these risks. On the contrary, we should in my opinion conclude that the method of analysis has so much to offer that it is worth expending considerable effort in research aimed at learning how to phrase questions that will elicit something very close to a person's true basic attitudes toward risk.

DECISION THEORY AND MANAGEMENT THEORY

In closing, let me point out that if I am right about these two needs for research, then decision theory is no more sufficient unto itself than management theory. The research I have mentioned is primarily psychological in nature, rather than mathematical or logical, and if it is to be done successfully, it will need all the help psychologists and psychological theory can give. I would guess that, however it is defined, management theory will find itself similarly intimately related with other disciplines, and that it will be an independent subject only in the sense that it constitutes a teachable and researchable part of a very large whole, not in the sense that it is the key subject in education and research for the improvement of business management. Perhaps we need to think of the business curriculum less in terms of an organization chart, where a large number of subsidiaries dangle from a clearly defined head, than in terms of the Olympic symbol, where a number of links form a closed, circular chain.

D APPROACHING THE THEORY OF MANAGEMENT

Herbert A. Simon

I have been asked to describe the "management systems" approach to management theory. Unfortunately, I do not really know what that phrase means. If it is meant as a label for whatever approach it is that I take, I find great difficulty in distinguishing it from the approaches of Professors Dale, Roethlisberger, and Schlaifer. We are all concerned with human behavior in organizations; hence our work is, whether we call it so or not, behavioral science. We are particularly concerned with managerial behavior—hence with management functions. Since most of the behavior that occurs in organizations involves the choice of courses of action, we all take a decision-making approach. Several of us use quantitative techniques from time to time, although not exclusively; hence we represent the mathematical approach. Human behavior in organizations produces complex interactions and indirect consequences; hence all of us, in striving to understand that behavior, represent a management systems approach.

Consequently, I cannot take seriously as our goal here the "synthesis" of these approaches. It is impossible to do serious research in the field of management without synthesizing them, and all of us—together with our many colleagues in the field of management—have perforce done so. There is nothing antithetical about being interested, at one and the same time, in management functions, behavioral science, decision making, systems, and mathematics. Indeed, I recommend such a combination of interests to anyone who wants to take part in the exciting task of advancing the science and art of management.

I am aware that Professor Koontz has presented the contrary case in a recent article in the *Harvard Business Review*. I find his description of the "semantic jungle" of management theory unrecognizable. If the sample of persons assembled on the platform is supposed to provide a microcosmic sample of the species that grow in that jungle, then the jungle must have been planted in rows. I am irresistibly reminded of a surrealist poem that begins:

> They must be curious trees indeed
> Where the great elephants go walking
> Without bumping each other . . .
>   Without bumping each other . . .
>   Without bumping each other . . .

Nothing would be served by my taking up my time bickering with Professor Koontz or saying why I disagree with almost every assertion in his article. I mention it because it expresses the point of view that appears to underlie the structure of our program and I want to be unequivocally on record as not agreeing with that point of view.

THE DIVISION OF LABOR

As a management theorist, I understand that there must be a division of labor in any elaborate enterprise. So there must be in the field of management research. But a division of labor is different from "approaches" to be "synthesized." There was, at one time, an Aristotelian, a Cartesian, a Leibnitzian, and a Newtonian approach to mechanics. They were not synthesized; they were liquidated in favor of the Newtonian, which turned out, in the crucible of observation and experiment, to be the one that best represented the facts. This does not mean that there is no division of labor among physicists. There are experimental physicists and theoretical physicists; high-energy physicists and low-energy physicists; atomic spectroscopists and molecular spectroscopists; and specialists in mechanics, heat, light, sound, and electricity.

Similarly, there are scientists in the field of management who seek to make their main contribution through the careful observation of events in real organizations, or through the analysis of historical records of such events. There are others who think that controlled experiments, whether in field or laboratory, can contribute much to our understanding of human behavior in organizations, and who devote their major efforts to this end. Still others tend to specialize as theoreticians, and some of these use rather esoteric tools drawn from mathematics, or the even more modern black magic of computers.

There is specialization also along substantive lines. Some investigators have paid particular attention to leadership style. Others have sought to discover the determinants of employee morale and its relation to productivity. Some are most concerned with the cognitive aspects of the decision-making process—either with describing how human rationality is brought to bear on decisional problems, or developing new and more powerful decision-making techniques.

It is important that we think of ourselves and of all these men as participants in the same enterprise, not as representatives of competing or contradictory approaches. The synthesis, if there is to be one, grows out of the continuing task to which all of us address ourselves, of making theory relevant to empirical observation and observation relevant to theory.

THE PROGRESS OF MANAGEMENT SCIENCE

Far from being dismayed by semantic confusion in the field of management, I am exhilarated by the progress we have made in our generation toward creating a viable science of management and an art based on that science. What are the benchmarks of that progress?

Empirical Data. A generation ago, our factual knowledge about human behavior in organizations was proverbial and anecdotal. It consisted of folk wisdom and the unchecked observations and conclusions of participants. Now I do not discount the value of folk wisdom or of experience, but they are the forerunners of scientific knowledge, not the foundations of it. Knowledge in science is to be objective and public. It must be checkable so that disputes of fact are settled by fact, and not by the 'tis's and 'tain'ts of debate. Science is not a set of findings, it is a body of techniques for discovering and testing facts and generalizations of fact.

Within this generation, we have begun to learn how to observe human behavior in organizations, objectively and by testing. Perhaps more remarkable, we have learned to perform controlled experiments with organizations and organizationlike groups. Professor Roethlisberger was a principal in one of the first of those experiments—the Hawthorne studies. A decade later, I participated in another, in a welfare agency here in Los Angeles. And a decade after that, in this same city, I observed the experimental method carried into the laboratory on an organization-wide scale, in the air defense studies of the systems research laboratory at RAND—now the Systems Development Corporation.

It hardly seems necessary to add that the sum total of facts we have accumulated about human behavior in organizations is still a pail of water in an ocean of ignorance. But if you don't like the way things are, it is sometimes cheering to look at the direction in which they are moving. In the field of management theory, we can say that we have today quantities of objective, relevant facts several orders of magnitude greater than were available to us a generation ago. We have made a good start on the great work of buttressing folk wisdom where it was right, correcting it where it was wrong.

Theories. A generation ago, such organization theory as we had consisted largely of lists of unrelated "principles." Within this generation, we have begun to build up bodies of interrelated propositions that describe the complex systems that are organizations, and propositions that predict the ramifying consequences of acting on those systems in particular ways. The ability of the management sciences to do this has depended heavily upon the parallel rapid progress in theory building in social psychology and sociology. So, to cite an example, we find work in psychology on the mechanisms of aspiration levels illuminating the goal-setting process in business firms, in particular, the notion of "satisfactory profit." But the conversation is two-way. Simultaneously, we see observations of behavior in business firms providing an increasing part of the evidence on which rests our acceptance of general psychological mechanisms like the aspiration level.

Analysis of Decision Making. Within this generation, sociology, social psychology, management theory, and some parts of economics have begun to develop a common vocabulary to express their common interests in closely related phenomena. The growth of common language has hastened the breakdown of the isolation of management theory from the other behavioral sciences. Central to this new vocabulary is the concept of decision making and terms descriptive of the decision-making process. This is perhaps most obvious in the work that is normative and prescriptive. For most such work, whether under the label of business economics, management science, or operations research, is aimed at aiding and improving the decision-making processes.

But a decision-making point of view is almost equally pervasive through the descriptive parts of management theory. A man's choice of job, the determinants of his work pace, the interaction of personal and organizational goals as decision premises, the unanticipated consequences of organizational calculation, programmed and nonprogrammed aspects of decision making—these are typical topics to which the management theorist addresses himself. To be sure, *what kind* of decision theory best describes behavior in organizations is still a matter of lively dispute. It is a dispute that is going to be settled in the not-too-distant future by our rapidly expanding empirical knowledge about the ways in which decisions actually are made in organizations. I shall spare you my prediction of the outcome—which you would not find difficult to guess.

Quantitative Tools. A generation ago, management and mathematics were worlds apart. The standard mathematics course in the business school exposed students to the arithmetic underlying double-entry bookkeeping and to the esoteric mysteries of the compound interest table. Today management makes use of linear programming—without understanding how it works—as unconcernedly and frequently as the housewife makes use of her automobile—without understanding how it works.

The fear has been expressed—Professor Koontz, for one, expresses it—that those entranced with the new developments will confuse the tasks of management theory with general sociology, or psychology, or economics, or mathematics. The danger seems to me slight. It seems to me slight on the purely empirical grounds that I don't see much confusion existing in the minds of the management theorists of my acquaintance, or in the research publications that appear in our journals.

The progress of management theory today is inextricably interwoven with techniques of observation and experiment, with sociology, psychology, and economics, and with the sharp tools of mathematics. In this respect, there is no more confusion than exists in other areas of scientific endeavor that has its observational techniques, its bodies of general theory, and its tools of analysis. Confusion, by another name, is progress to which we have not yet become accustomed.

Gathering empirical data about behavior in organizations, building and testing theories in collaboration with the other behavioral sciences, using decision making as a central concept for organizing the analysis, employing quantitative and mathematical techniques—these are not "approaches" to the science of management, much less "intellectual cults," as Professor Koontz charges. They are the warp and weft of the increasingly successful endeavor to create a genuine science of management, and an art based on that science. The only synthesis that is required is an understanding of their respective contribution to the pattern. I think that synthesis has been largely achieved over the past generation.

ORGANIZATIONS AS COMPLEX SYSTEMS

Within this general context it makes perfectly good sense to talk of the "systems" *aspects* of management science. Measured by almost any common-sense criterion we might want to apply, organizations are complex systems. The tools of scientific inquiry that suffice for our exploration of simple phenomena may prove entirely inadequate in the face of complexity. The term "systems" is being used more and more to refer to methods of scientific analysis that are peculiarly adapted to the unraveling of complexity.

Management science is not alone in its concern with complexity; biological organisms are complex systems. So are the control and communications systems that guide missiles, provide defense against hostile attacks from the air, and govern the operations of modern automated chemical plants. So is the human brain and nervous system. So are digital computers and the programming languages and monitor systems that are employed with them. In all these areas of pure and applied science—biology, engineering control systems, psychology, computers and programming, and management science—there is a growing awareness that complexity itself is one of the central problems, and that much of the research effort must be directed toward developing powerful tools for handling complexity.

This concern with complexity is leading today to the establishment of systems programs in our universities. At Carnegie Tech, for example, we now offer a doctoral program in systems and communications sciences. Students in the program take their degrees, with a major in "systems," in any one of four departments, representing four of the five areas of science mentioned above: electrical engineering (engineering control systems), psychology (the human information processing system), mathematics (computer programming system), or industrial administration (organization systems). We propose soon to have a graduate biology program that will represent the fifth area.

The systems major at Carnegie is defined by a common core of courses and a common examination. The content of those courses indicates pretty clearly what the concern with "systems" is all about. The common courses are largely devoted to techniques for analyzing and synthesizing complexity. All the participating disciplines contribute the techniques they have been developing, putting them in the common pool. From electrical engineering, we get, for example, servomechanism analysis and information theory. Psychology contributes techniques for simulation of cognitive processes and adaptive networks. Mathematics offers probability theory and the rapidly developing theory of computation and programming. Industrial administration provides the tools of operations research—linear and dynamic programming, for example, and systems simulation.

Management theory, then, is both beneficiary of and contributor to a growing body of techniques especially adapted to the study of complex systems. It is further evidence of the progress of management sciences in our generation that we are, in fact, major contributors as well as beneficiaries. Today the methods of linear programming, developed largely by management scientists, are being used by biochemists to study oxygen exchange in the lungs, and by civil engineers to design structures. Dynamic programming methods, developed in the management sciences, are being used by electrical and chemical engineers to design process control systems. Programming techniques for the simulation of systems behavior, developed in the management sciences and psychology, are being adapted to the tasks of simulating biological and physical systems. I hope you will pardon this excursion. I could not resist the temptation to point with pride to this partial reversal of the traditional peck order of the sciences.

Why did a burgeoning of systems techniques occur at this particular moment in history? I do not know the whole story, but it is pretty obvious that half the answer lies in the digital computer. Much of the history of science can be written in terms of its tools. The telescope gave science a tool for viewing the immense and distant; the microscope a tool for probing the minute; and the calculus a tool for capturing the fluent.

The modern electronic digital computer gives us a tool for grappling with the complex—a tool whose powers, present and immediately prospective, are commensurate with the presumptuousness of the questions we are now asking of nature. We are asking about the processes of the human mind, the interior of the atomic nucleus, the transmission of hereditary information, the unfolding development of the individual organism—and questions about interacting human behaviors and decision-making processes in organizations. The computer, particularly the computer used as simulator and not just as statistical workhorse, is providing new ways of modeling these complex systems, and, by modeling them, predicting their behavior.

The term "systems," therefore, does not denote an approach

to management theory that is antithetical to, or even distinct from, empirical observation, development of behavioral theories, use of a decision-making frame of analysis, or application of mathematical techniques. It denotes a concern, in the conduct of all these activities, with complexity and with the necessity for developing tools that are especially adapted to handling complexity. No one who has observed closely the developments of the past decade can avoid, I think, the optimistic conclusion that we now have some powerful tools of this kind, and the promise of more.

From this conclusion, the prediction must follow that the coming decade in the management sciences is going to witness even more rapid and exciting progress than the decade just past. In the course of that progress, the various kinds of activities that go into the building of management theory and practice will, without too much difficulty, find their appropriate synthesis, as they have in the past. Science, like all creative activity, is exploration, gambling, and adventure. It does not lend itself very well to neat blueprints, detailed road maps, and central planning. Perhaps that's why it's fun.

...
111 TERMS, METHODS, AND CONTRIBUTIONS: CAN THEY BE SYNTHESIZED?

After the initial presentation of the papers outlining the basic approaches to management theory and research, the symposium adjourned for syndicate discussions. The hope was to focus attention on the terms, methods, and contributions of the various approaches to management to see if progress could be made toward synthesizing them. The results of these syndicate discussions and selections from the general discussion of this subject are presented in this chapter.

While one afternoon of discussion is hardly enough to expect significant progress on such an important and complex subject, the syndicate discussions did show various areas of agreement and disagreement, understanding and misunderstanding. The results of these discussions are summarized by Professor Tannenbaum. In order to show the flavor of the symposium discussion and the subjects dealt with under the general problem of synthesis, the following three major subjects in this chapter deal with problems of synthesis in development of a theory of management, a discussion of the classical approach theory, and the discussion of decision theory as a basis for developing a theory of management. While there has been no attempt to put the entire record of the symposium in this chapter, the more provocative and summarizing remarks made by various participants are presented in their own language.

A

OBSERVATIONS ON
LARGE GROUP AND
SYNDICATE DISCUSSIONS[1]

Robert Tannenbaum

I have been asked to take a look at the conference up to this point (and particularly the syndicate discussions) and to provide a bridge from the previous papers and discussions to those which lie ahead. We started with the general conference theme of "Approaching a Theory of Management," and this session is now focused on the more specific question: "Terms, Methods, and Contributions: Can They Be Synthesized?"

I think that as conference chairman, Professor Koontz initiated a grand conversation involving all of us—a conversation that will continue on throughout. This conversation has already taken place in various places and in various forms. It began with the papers already presented, followed by discussion in the total group. It continued in small group discussions. There have been many informal discussions dealing with the key themes. I will try to report what my colleagues and I have heard; and, in doing so, I will interpret, draw tentative conclusions, and raise questions.

[1] These observations were originally presented extemporaneously from notes. The presentation was tape-recorded. This chapter is an edited version of the tape transcription; it is not a paper prepared in advance of the conference.

I suppose all of us are aware of the tremendous differences represented by the participants in this room—differences in academic preparation, in interests, in values, in types of work, in modes of research, and in other characteristics which no doubt have a considerable effect on what we are trying to do here. Even to try to capture the full richness and diversity in one discussion group is quite difficult. In fact, I have increasingly been feeling that perhaps our planning committee's expectations were overly optimistic. To expect such a large and diverse group to come to some meaningful agreements about management in such a brief time period is perhaps hoping for too much. Yet by no means am I discouraged about what has thus far been accomplished; I think much of real value for many of us has emerged.

What seems to be the key areas on which we have been focusing our attention? *First,* there has been much discussion around science itself, a type of discussion that would be as relevant if this were a conference of biologists, physicists, or astronomers. But I have been wondering whether as much time would have been spent on these basic issues of science and scientific procedure if we were representatives of a longer-established professional field.

What are the issues we have discussed in this area? There has been a focus on issues around the philosophy of science as such. We have asked ourselves the question, "How is theory built?" and have compared notes on how we go about moving from impressionistic kinds of approaches to data to the possible evolution of a general theory of management. We have discussed the problem of separating the givens—the things we take for granted in the work we do—from that which we are trying to explain.

There has been quite a bit of discussion around the issue which Professor Roethlisberger first raised, that of differentiating between concepts, definitions, and the like on the one hand and propositions which help us explain on the other hand. Professor Roethlisberger left us with three concerns of his on which he hoped we would focus (to some extent we have and to some extent we haven't)—the problems of slanting, of verification, and of explanation; and there was Ernest Dale's emphasis on the problems of selecting facts, of explanation, and of prediction.

There have also been questions about the criteria of a good theory. One discussant in the group suggested that we ask these two subquestions: Is it logically consistent and is it testable? But perhaps most frequently discussed, at least in some of the groups, was the broad question of what is truth? How do we judge what is truth? What are our methods of validation? When do we accept a proposition, and when do we reject it?

As has already been said, these questions could have been raised in any scholarly setting; they are certainly not peculiar to our present concern with management theory and research. Yet, the amount of attention we have devoted to them must say something about this conference. Perhaps they say something about the recency with which many of us have been involved in precise scientific investigation.

The *second* main area of discussion has been around the broad question of management theory itself—the announced focus of the conference. In one way or another, this question has been asked: What should be included in a theory of management?

As I listened to the various small group discussions, I wondered if we here would, in fact, see ourselves as management theorists as against, for example, decision theorists or small group theorists or systems theorists. I have wondered what our own identifications are in this research area; my hunch is that there are relatively few of us who would see ourselves as management theorists per se. How many individuals here are really broadly and deeply interested in the subquestions raised by Professor Koontz: "Can we integrate? Can we synthesize? Do we have a common terminology? Do we have a basis for a broad explanation of management and of organizational functions?"

Another issue in this area with which we have toyed around in various ways—and this is perhaps the fault of those of us who planned the conference—was first mentioned by Professor Simon. Previous papers often implied that the work of decision theorists, behavioral scientists, and so on, represents different approaches to management theory (whatever that might be). From the way the discussion has gone thus far, a more meaningful focus would have been in terms of *contributions* to management theory rather than in terms of various *approaches* to it. More than a semantic difference is here involved. To me, at least, the main emphasis of Professor Simon's paper was on the varying contributions that different specialists among us are making to a better understanding of management. The notion of approaches did give rise previously to considerable discussion. A general impression that seemed to emerge from these discussions was how vague most of us are on what the different approaches really are. Much ambiguity is present here. What do we mean by the classicists, by the functional approach, by decision theory, by behavioral science, by the systems approach, and by the others?

As we talked about possibly moving toward a theory of management, there was much give and take around the issue of synthesis. Some individuals were saying, "We need synthesis, it's highly desirable." Yet others were saying (using the words of one participant): "What we really need is unsynthesis to avoid being excessively hemmed in, being caught in narrow constrictions that limit the most fruitful, the most productive and creative unfolding of the work that we are doing."

Also there were real doubts expressed by some—even by those who may feel that some kind of synthesis is desirable—as to whether we are yet ready for it. Perhaps it is too early in the game, we know too little, and there is much more detailed and specific work yet to be done in all these different areas of contributions before we can begin to move toward a general theory. On the other hand, assuming we are ready to move toward a more general theory, what is the best strategy to use in moving from specifics to such a theory?

A point worth underlining made by Professor Simon in his presentation is that at this stage of the game those of us working in the field are beginning to make contributions to some of the more basic sciences from which for such a long time we have primarily drawn. The process that is now occurring involves a two-way exchange, in which useful contributions are flowing in both directions.

We continually kept wondering about the nature of management theory. What are we striving for here? What do we really want to achieve by a theory of management or by a science of management? Perhaps if we could be more clear on our objectives, the answers to many other related questions would fall more readily into place.

The *third* main area of discussion directly relates the previous presentations and discussions to those to follow. This has to do with the problem of the relations between the work of the scientist and that of the manager or practitioner. In the small discussion groups, it seems that there was a frequent request from practitioners for a theory which would have broad applicability in providing useful guidelines for practice—that would provide answers to some of the really difficult questions facing managers. On the other hand, the academicians seemed to resist being too general in their formulations or in moving toward a broad synthesis. This statement, for example, was made by one: "We need a lot of small-think results, and these must be developed." Another said, "I'm restive about the discussion today. We should be content with biting off small pieces." It appears that the primary preference of the researchers and academicians is for rather specific, limited foci of work, while that of the practitioners (the managers) is for useful generality in results.

Perhaps we need to move from "the scientist *versus* practitioner" to "the scientist *and* the practitioner." And there seems to be a great need for specialists who can perform a bridging function between the two—an individual who can understand what the scientist is doing and talking about and who can interpret this to the practitioner, and vice versa.

At least one discussion group pointed up this important thought: the relationship between practitioners and scientists should not be one-way—a relationship in which the full responsibility falls on the scientist to make what he is doing intelligible and useful to the practitioner. The practitioner, it was emphasized, has a responsibilty to reach out in trying to understand the terminology, the methods, and the results of the scientist. Furthermore, the practitioner may have some responsibility not only to make his own organization available as a research setting, but additionally to do research himself or to foster it in his organization.

The *fourth* main area of discussion is the one Professor Koontz spoke so much about. It involves the problem of semantics. This certainly cuts across some of the other areas I have previously mentioned, but I think it warrants specific mention here.

One academician in a small group said, "The terms used were so fantastic I could not understand them." However, Professor Simon, stressing the positive side in his comments, expressed the feeling that we have been making real progress in understanding each other, in using terms that communicate. I suspect that a comparison with where we were in this regard five or ten years ago would certainly support this kind of conclusion.

My own impression is that we still face major problems in semantics. We did have great difficulty really understanding each other. As specialists, we use quite different terminology. There are few here, I suspect, who have even some familiarity with many of the specialized terms that are frequently used by others of us in our different fields of specialization.

The recorders report that our terminological difficulties extended in many directions. They were present with scientists in relation to scientists: decision theorists with behavioral scientists, systems men with functionalists, and so on; we had great difficulty talking across our scientific specialities. The difficulties were also present when scientists or academicians tried to talk with managers or practitioners—and vice versa.

There were other semantic difficulties that perhaps were not so explicit. It was reported that even practitioners with different backgrounds and from different organizations at times had difficulty talking with each other. And there were barriers as we attempted to cut across national or cultural boundaries. It was reported that graduates of different schools with different majors who find themselves working together in a given organization have difficulty not only communicating with each other, but also with the managers with whom they are associated in work. What responsibilities might we have in our training of students to facilitate their later collaborative efforts?

An experience in one group is I think worth highlighting, for it suggests one possible answer to our difficulty with semantics. The first half of this group's discussion was on a very general and abstract level. When the discussion was at this level, the members of the group had great difficulty in understanding each other. The second half of the meeting dealt with a case that was presented by one of the practitioners. After this case was presented and everyone began focusing on specific data and a specific problem area, a much more useful and meaningful vehicle was available to the diverse group members for reaching some common ground. From one phase of my own experience—the area of training, we have often found in our staff discussions that when we are talking in general or abstract terms about our theories or methods of training, we often encounter great difficulty. But when we get to specific operational issues, we are able to talk with each other much more effectively. Also—and this is a matter that intrigues me very much—we find that what an individual tends to do in practice is often markedly different from that expected judging from the position he took when he was talking abstractly and generally.

The *fifth* main area for discussion first raised by Prof. Keith Davis is the general area of values and ethics. It seems that there are at least two different ways in which concern about values and ethics have entered into our discussions. One involves the values or ethics of the researcher himself; for example, how do his values affect his choice of research problems and of methods? The other (and perhaps more frequently discussed one) involves a concern about the values of the organizations the researcher is trying to study. What about their purposes or ends? How do the existing organizational purposes or ends affect what we are studying and the conclusions we draw from what we study? To what extent are these values or ends subject to change? What is the process by which they can be examined and changed? Is the process by which values or purposes are assessed a scientific one or is it something else?

The *sixth* area, dealing with management education, leads to the session on education in business schools for management research and theory. There was some discussion of whether we really should be schools of business or whether, in effect, we are moving in the direction of becoming schools of management or schools of organization. This is perhaps tied to the question of a general theory of management: to the issues around synthesis and to the issue raised by Ernest Dale concerning the universality of management. To what extent is what we are teaching relevant to people going into the management of a variety of organizations (public and private), and to what extent is it primarily relevant only to business organizations?

These questions were raised: What do we now know that we can actually teach? What is (or what should be) the relationship between management theories and a management curriculum? What should a management curriculum look like? What is the process by which we educate or train managers, not only those now in our schools but also those who return to the campus?

In focusing on the research function of our schools and our responsibilty in developing researchers, certain group members expressed considerable concern about the quality of research that has been emerging. There is a feeling among some that much of the research that has been coming out of our schools of business has been relatively poor, and that better research has come from specialists associated with the more traditional academic departments.

I would like to close with a personal observation which is more interpretive and therefore more subjective. I was interested in the general social processes that were going on, both in the small discussion groups and in this large group. As I said previously, we have spent much time thus far discussing research strategies, methodologies, procedures, etc. And yet, we have given little attention to the sociology and psychology of science, including the personal and interpersonal processes involved in our "scientific" deliberations.

Each of us, I suspect, comes from training and experiences that have been relatively narrow with reference to what is encompassed by the broad notions of management theory and research. Many of us must feel fairly secure in our own bailiwicks. Yet as we face people who have different specialties than we, we feel rather uncomfortable. As we have tried to talk with each other here, there has been a lot of sparring. There has been much evidence in the large group and in the smaller groups of the need on the part of a number of us to give the other person the needle—to strike out against individuals who are different from us, who see things differently, who work differently, and who speak differently. There is perhaps a feeling that "my" approach and "my" goals are more meaningful or useful than "yours."

It seems that as we interact with each other, there is an implicit strategy on the part of many of us to avoid the areas in which, if exposed, we will feel uncomfortable in the presence of our colleagues, and to use those opportunities which present themselves to expose ourselves where we will look our best. I have wondered to what extent the nature of our joint enterprise (as Professor Simon referred to it) leads us to protect ourselves when we feel we might be exposed and to make our impressive interventions only when we safely can do so. Perhaps our need to "play it safe" has had a major role in determining what we have talked about and how we have talked about it. And perhaps this need has overshadowed our frequently expressed desires to illuminate the problem areas which we have been discussing. To what extent have we been involved in one-upmanship, and to what extent in scientific discourse?

I thought I saw—and this I feel less confident about—a pecking order emerging in some of the small discussion groups. Very often the individuals who were doing most of the talking were individuals who represent what would generally be seen as the more prestigeful, the "harder-science" areas. The pecking order seemed to go on through those that do not fall into this first category but are still scientists or academicians, and then down to those who are practitioners. I have been wondering to what extent this implicit pecking order helps to explain the patterns we have followed in our efforts to communicate with each other.

One conferee said, "I keep going to conferences—and then go home and work the way I want to." In closing, I wonder how representative this point of view is. If it is, in fact, a widely shared view, what does it tell us about ourselves as researchers and practitioners, and about the relevance of a conference such as the one in which we are now participating?

B THE PROBLEMS OF SYNTHESIS: A DISCUSSION

The major problems of synthesis were discussed under the heading of the nature of a theory of management, whether or not a theory of management is even needed or possible; the problem of semantics in management; and whether a synthesis of approaches and research and investigation in the field of management is even desirable. In order to deal with the discussion along the lines of these subjects, the editor has taken the liberty of extracting the comments of various seminar participants and arbitrarily placing them within the subject matter outlined.

THE NATURE OF THEORY

Professor Schlaifer: Before I start, I think I ought to make clear in a few words, if I can—or rather to suggest in a few words— what decision theory is. I am not sure that everybody knows what decision theory is or particularly what we are in the habit of calling normative decision theory, although anybody can choose his words.

First of all, it is not a theory in the sense of the kinds of theory that Professor Roethlisberger was talking about earlier, because it is not intended to predict anything, and it is not intended to explain anything whatsoever. It has nothing to do—

frequently, at any rate—with the way that decisions are actually made. That is a subject—a worthwhile subject of study. It can possibly be that the subject that I am interested in could be of some small use in connection with a descriptive or predictive study of theory making, but it is, certainly, at most, a peripheral interest, a peripheral use of normative decision theory.

Normative decision theory starts by looking at the problem of a decision maker who is consciously aware that he has a decision problem, who is consciously aware that there are a number of alternative actions that are open to him, and who wants to make a reasoned choice among these courses of action. I want to be careful of one thing. I am not saying that he wants to pick the best possible course of action. I think this is a totally illusory goal. I don't suppose anybody can ever pick the best possible course of action in even a trivial set of circumstances, let alone a complicated set of circumstances, but theory starts to apply if there are a number of courses of action and a person wants to make a reasoned evaluation of them and choose one in the light of this evaluation.

Secondly, normative theory is not strictly normative in another sense of the word which implies in some way or the other that this is the way that decisions *ought* to be made. I want to be very clear that I assume the vast majority of decisions are, will be, and even should be made without the use of normative decision theory. The mere task of formulating a decision problem in a way that makes it possible accurately to apply normative theory means that you could not even state decision problems completely, let alone solve them this way in most cases.

Professor Simon: Let me first be very brave here and state what nobody else has undertaken to state in answer to the question: What is a theory of management? Or what would a theory of management be if we had one? I guess the latter is the way some people would ask it. I wouldn't ask it that way. I will ask it the first way: What is a theory of management?

Professor Schlaifer has already indicated that a theory of management might be either of two things. One is descriptive. How do people, including those people we call managers, behave in organizations? What do they do? How do they do it? If certain situations arise, how do they react to those situations?

What is human behavior in an organizational environment like? That is what I understand the descriptive theory of management to be about.

Then there is a normative theory of management. The distinction here is a familiar one to all of us. It is the distinction between physiology and medicine; it is the distinction between physics and engineering. There is a normative theory of management: If I want to accomplish such and such results in an organization, then what do I do? What should I do? Fritz Roethlisberger emphasized the descriptive theory of management.

I don't mean that these do not have implications for each other; I simply mean that you can distinguish a proposition of the descriptive theory of management from a proposition of the normative theory of management.

The relevance of one to the other again was illustrated by Professor Schlaifer's paper, where he pointed out that if we were to develop further the normative aspect of management decision theory, one thing we might do is to carry out some real behavior research about the circumstances under which people could give meaningful answers to questions about their preferences. Now, I think I can turn that into a perfectly operational question about behavior. I gather you thought so too, Professor Schlaifer. An answer to that kind of question is predictive of what their answers to other questions will be about their preferences, or predictive about their behavior. Such predictions are, of course, of great importance to a normative theory of management.

Likewise, statements about people's behavior: what will a man do if a foreman cusses him out—a matter that concerns Professor Roethlisberger and his colleagues—these are descriptive propositions. Although they are descriptive propositions, they may and do have a great deal of bearing on the normative questions of how *should* a foreman behave if he wishes to accomplish such and such results in a factory. This is why we call both of these a theory of management. Anybody who is interested in management will need to be interested in both the descriptive and normative theory.

Professor Roethlisberger: I was interested in Herbert Simon's optimism, expressed in his paper, because I think it follows from a normative-theory way of looking at how people *should* behave in relation to ambiguity, uncertainty, etc. I think he expressed it beautifully.

That is exactly the way we should behave in relation to the confusion we are in, but those of us who are interested in the descriptive, in how people do behave under conditions of uncertainty and ambiguity, are not so optimistic.

I certainly agree that both these theories, both normative and descriptive, are needed by management. But I did not use the word normative only in the sense that Herbert Simon did as to how a person should behave—in order to reach a certain goal— what would be the "best" means to achieve it and so on? For some of us, particularly among business- and laymen, normative implies a value judgment about the way people should behave which those of us, at least, who are trying to influence the behavior of others, bump into over and over again.

I am interested in the way that any descriptive statement of behavior, or what we intend to be descriptive of it, can be switched into a normative role model for behavior. Notice it was done in the whole human relations approach—in a way human relations became a kind of role model for the way the manager should behave, regardless of circumstances. No matter how clear one tries to be about this distinction in his communication to students, I find this confusion between normative and descriptive cropping up.

Mr. Brown: We have talked about this theory of span of control. I know it very well, and I remember the men in my company having conversations concerning it. I said at the time, "This theory is of no use to me and I'll tell you why, because you haven't defined your terms." Among other things, I would want to know this: When you say span of control of a manager should be only such and such, do you include in the term manager the foreman or don't you, because if you do include foremen in the definition of the word "manager," then the average number of subordinates of foremen in British industry is thirty and you know it. That's a fact; so obviously your theory is a bust. If you do not include the foremen in the class of "manager," whom do you include, because before I can understand a theory about the span of control, I must know these things. As you will understand, I am in a different position than managers are, in contrast to the people who think about these things in universities.

If I'm going to use a theory and make the decision to use it, I may be committed to thousands of pounds of expense in doing it. I must be certain that I've understood it quite thoroughly before I implement the proposal to apply it. I am not prepared to use any theory unless I understand precisely what it means

Dean Jacoby: As I have listened to the conversation that's gone on here and thought about it, it seems to me that however we define this thing we are discussing management and the set of abstractions that constitute its theory, we could agree that at least two kinds of activity are involved on the part of the manager. In the first place, making decisions or choices regarding what to do and, secondly, methods of getting the job done. In other words, implementing the decisions.

At the risk of a little oversimplification then, I would say that management is the sum of these two types of activity, decision making in a broad sense and decision implementing. Now, for economists like me, to the extent that we have anything to contribute to knowledge, our expertise lies mainly in the first aspect because our basic magic lies in resource allocation.

DO WE NEED A THEORY OF MANAGEMENT?

Mr. Kemble: As the managers for whom I am speaking view their bafflement, its basis is the need for living with social theories, social theories that emanate from our universities as to their responsibility and as to the place of business in the general culture. Yet these theories don't seem to jibe with the viewpoints of reality as we find them from customers and other employees in the company. It was for this reason that I picked up from a very excellent article by Professor Koontz the point which I paraphrased a little that the theory of managing must recognize that it is but a part of a larger universe of knowledge and theory. It seems to me that practicing managers would agree with that statement. More importantly, they'd expect the managing theory would be consonant with more general theory, but here is the rub. In the development of management theory, should there be uncritical acceptance of general social theory, or is it possible there is need for adjustment in popularly held theories? By popularly held theories, I do not mean those that the real scholars hold. I'm talking about the ones of the man in the street or the senator who is leading an investigation committee.

Is it possible that there is a need for adjustment in such theories as well as some adjustment on the part of managers themselves? I think I have implied even more than this in my article—and I have just said it several times—to what extent are the viewpoints that have been developed by managerial experience a possible focal point for considering changes in traditional social theory—the way we understand our social institutions and as we understand them as they are being taught at educational institutions?

Mr. Neuschel: It does seem appropriate to ask to what end, for what purpose, for what good are your efforts as researchers expended? And if the real objective of your efforts is to improve the management process, then it seems clear that the contributions of management theory have to be made in terms of what has been referred to here frequently as normative propositions. These quite frankly from the viewpoint of the practitioner are still in pretty short supply.

I say this without in any way meaning to contradict Professor Simon's statement in his paper which said, "I am exhilarated by the progress we have made in our generation toward creating a viable science of management." In absolute terms, I would certainly agree that this exhilaration is warranted unequivocally, but I submit that in this whole area we are shooting at a moving target and our real progress must be measured not so much by how far we have come in relation to our own past capability as by where we stand today in relation to the growing need for greater management excellence on a great many different fronts.

Now, in this context, the practitioner can judge the work of scholars and researchers in the whole field of management theory only in terms of its imediate usefulness. He is quite unlikely to know about it until it reaches a point of application and he is equally unlikely to have any background or vision that would enable him to evaluate research programs or projects that are still in process. It's not surprising, then, that many businessmen believe there is little of real use to them in the outpourings of management theory and research. At the same time, while a manager may not be able to point to a long list of advances that he can ascribe to theory, he can't nevertheless reject theory because, you see, he really has nowhere else to turn.

THE PROBLEM OF SEMANTICS

Professor Simon: Within this generation we have had a tremendous advance in the sophistication of our theories and ways of talking about decision making and about the decision-making process. We have, in fact, gone a long way toward developing common vocabularies to talk about administrative processes and managerial processes, these vocabularies in considerable part focusing around the notion of decision making and viewing the management process as a process of decision making. Along with that vocabulary of decision making, and ability to talk about the process, about how alternatives are discovered, about how alternatives are selected, or how they ought to be in terms of normative theory—along with this we have a rapidly expanding body of empirical knowledge about how decisions are actually made in organizations, including, in recent years, successful attempts to simulate some kinds of middle management decision-making processes quite accurately with digital computers.

Now I would like to insert a word at this point about the vocabulary we use to move ahead. We are sometimes accused, in developing a science of management, of developing a vocabulary (more often called a jargon) which is not quite understandable to the practitioner and, therefore, must be wrong. It is argued that, somehow or other, we must be able, as the science develops, to express everything we have learned in the language that was the man in the street's language a generation ago. I put that in the past tense, because, of course, as science develops, and particularly as the science of human affairs develops, the man in the street's vocabulary changes. You can talk to the man in the street today about a lot of things that Mr. Freud was interested in and he will understand what you are talking about. The growth of any field of knowledge involves a growth of vocabulary. We are just going to have to learn a lot of new words, and some of them are going to be big words.

I do not want to defend all the jargon used in the other sciences because, of course, other sciences do have jargon. (Mine just makes clear distinctions where distinctions are needed.) I should point out that medical men today still learn all sorts of strange Latin names for things we know as elbows and shoulders; and lawyers today still learn all sorts of strange technical vocabulary for things which I am sure, with a certain amount of circumlocution, could be expressed in English. Well, I know and you know that they do this in part to impress us. I don't think perhaps we ought to be too sensitive about doing a little bit of it on our own part to impress others.

My real defense of jargon here is not its social status advantages, however. My real defense of jargon is that, as a field of knowledge develops, it necessarily begins to look at the world with different eyes; it begins to make different distinctions about the phenomena of the world than common sense did before. It therefore develops a new vocabulary to describe the new distinctions it is making. Wittgenstein was earlier quoted as saying that everything that can be said can be said clearly. There is some dispute as to whether everything he said in his major work, the *Tractatus Logico-Philosophicus,* was said clearly; but, at any rate, he didn't assert that everything that can be said be said in four-letter English words. He didn't deny the need of technical vocabulary.

Professor Jackson: It seems to me the problems in the semantic jungle—as I believe you called it, Professor Koontz—is not that people use words in different ways but that they don't bother to define the way they are using them.

Scholarly reading is, generally speaking, difficult in every field. That's as true in the ancient established sciences as it is certainly true in psychology, and I think it's going to be true in business.

The gentleman who spoke a minute ago referred to a sequence of things that I'm sure Professor Simon would agree that he and I would both consider part of the decision-making process. I think that we have not defined what we consider the decision process to be well enough so that this misunderstanding with us will not arise, but I think that the important point that I'm trying to get at is that people should not be diffident about stopping a minute and saying, "What I mean by this word is this," and explain it in terms that they think other people will understand who haven't read their book just published.

Mr. Brown: Now, look at the history of electricity. I'm sure it started when somebody defined an erg and a dyne and a joule, and they proceeded from these very simple definitions to the definition of more complex things like volt, amp, and ohm; and as history went on, on the basis of this clear definition, there was no doubt about these terms very rapidly becoming international words upon which somebody constructs a theory. If someone were to immediately examine his theory about the way he uses his word "volt" or something like that, the whole theory is in a temporary state of collapse until you make quite sure he is using "volt" in the same way that everybody else uses it. In other words, you can't start up here without the definitions that initiate the process.

Now, the British Institute of Management, the American Management Association, and the business schools of America haven't any definitions, gentlemen. You haven't even a definition of manager. How can you construct a theory about management when you haven't got a definition of the word—of the role of the manager? This is the point that's been nagging away at me the whole time this discussion is going on.

You may say, "Oh, that's very well but how does one construct definitions?" We have been working in our company in collaboration with a very brilliant man, a sociologist, and we have been trying to see what is the definition of a definition. We have a rough one which we use and it's this, that a definition: (1) must be based on data or phenomena, facts or assumptions that are accepted by the people who want and use the definition; (2) must be a logical inference from those assumptions; and (3) must be stated in terms in which any reasonable person can decide what lies within or without the definition.

SYNTHESIS: DESIRABLE OR UNDESIRABLE?

Professor Dubin: May I start with a very facetious comment? I want to accuse many of the people here of being collectivists, if not communists! I want to do it in the following manner: It seems to me that the insistence that we bring things together, that we synthesize, is another way of saying we all must have a common line of some sort—in which we say, "These are the facts," and we all take an oath that these facts will be forever agreed to. The common line must deal with a theory or theology to which we all subscribe.

I happen to be an intellectual free enterpriser. I would like to put in a plea for free enterprise in perhaps one area where it still can exist; namely, in the affairs of the mind, in the affairs of the intellect.

It seems to me therefore that Professor Simon really hit the keynote when he implied, "Let's not worry about being collectivists. Let's not worry about being intellectual communists or communizing our intellectual life." He implied, "Let's be happy in our diversity," and this I think is very essential.

Professor Fox: First, I'd like to say that I am only partially "Simonized"! I think one of the problems that we have had, those of us who have followed Professor Simon's work with great interest and great profit to ourselves, has been perhaps the unfortunate fact that his declaration of solidarity made in his paper did not appear in the first part of his book *Administrative Behavior*. I think that the desirable course is to build upon what is good and best in so-called orthodox or classical theory. I think that, if anything, much of Professor Simon's very real contribution has been perhaps misunderstood or dulled by the impression which some of us got that the baby (of orthodox theory) was thrown out with the bath water by him.

I do feel that he has made some very real synthesizing contributions, and I am glad to hear now this declaration of solidarity.

Professor Miller: It would appear that one of the basic questions which this meeting was called to answer is the question of when synthesis is a euphemism for eclecticism.

We have had a great many different areas of approach to

this one subject. Professor Simon has suggested that confusion is a good thing. When someone says that, you immediately think of cases in science where it was. It is equally easy to think of cases where it wasn't, for instance, in biology where they used to have seventeen different classification systems. Now, there was never any synthesis of these seventeen. There was a discovery that one of them was the best and an attempt to utilize that one and discard the other sixteen.

It appears to me that one of the basic questions, which no one undertook to answer, is the question of what is a science. The one distinction that is made repeatedly is that somehow a science consists of observing facts and then attempting to explain them. I would say that without really trying very hard you could think of those, over the last forty years, who, I think, proved beyond any shadow of doubt that you cannot make this distinction, that there is no such thing as a fact without a theory and, therefore, you are on the wrong approach.

Professor Simon made some remarks about the old Thomistic system. While I certainly would agree with him, the Thomists did make some distinctions when they talked about sciences. They talked about theoretical science, practical science, theoretical art, and practical art. They made some very important distinctions along these lines, none of which seemed to enter into the fiber of the discussions that we have heard.

One of the distinctions they made was that you had to define a science by its approach, not by its subject matter. Probably one of the great tragedies is that everyone takes physics as the example. Is jurisprudence not a science? It appears to me that one has great difficulty in distinguishing between synthesis and eclecticism without knowing exactly what is the scientific method or thing which you finally want to achieve.

C THE CLASSICAL
APPROACH AND THEORY:
A DISCUSSION

Much of the discussion of the symposium dealing with the contributions of the various approaches to the theory of management dealt with the classical and the decision approach to management theory. As will be noted, the so-called classical approach to the theory of management generally refers to the observations and principles made by such noted practitioners as Frederick Taylor, Henri Fayol, James C. Mooney, Lyndall F. Urwick, and others of the relatively early scholars who attempted to bring out of management practice and experience certain explanatory concepts and fundamentals which, from their experience, seemed to explain the nature of the managerial task. Although other scholars of management might refer to these approaches as "the management process" or "an operational" approach to management, many who refer to the classical approach appear to have in mind only the contributions and analyses of the early writers who gained prominence prior to World War II.

Prof. R. C. Davis: I was interested in Professor Dale's paper. He says there is little, if any, agreement with much of the validity of the classical approach as outlined by the pioneers of scientific management: Taylor, Gantt, Fayol, Mooney and Reiley, Gulick, and Alvin Brown. I just wondered if he would outline briefly what this classical approach is and what evidence is there that these gentlemen would have recognized it had they been here.

Professor Dale: The classical approach, I would say, is one that takes account only of purely rational factors, and takes it for granted that human beings will act rationally in their own best economic interest. It also tends to consider each part of management and each person in the organization as a discrete unit, and pays little attention to the more complicated reactions that actions of one kind or another may produce.

I have tried to take over from the classicists what they have developed in terms of, let's say, criteria, which are often valuable in diagnosing what is wrong with an organization. They did try to be overuniversal, but I think I would be a little more charitable to them than Professor Simon was. As you know, from my own writings, I have given a good deal of credit to what the classicists have done because they have surely tested their criteria, if I may use that term, very widely by experience.

Of course, I don't know what the group feels is the real test of the work we are doing. To me it is very largely the test of experience, as shown by comparative analysis. Certainly there has been some real testing of the classical ideas in, for example, the work of Fayol, who was at once a great thinker and a very successful practicing businessman.

Experience is needed in thinking about management as it is in any other discipline because you can't think without having something to think about, namely, facts. Experience is also essential in the execution which follows the thinking out of a hypothesis.

So I believe we have been a little too critical. I agree with Professor Davis that the classicist of today is a sophisticated classicist rather than the old-line industrial engineer. And in the light of his use of experience he should be called "operational."

Look at the consultants, who, after all, have to live by what they do—and there are some very able ones represented here. They probably would not disagree with my statement that quite a considerable part of the body of wisdom they are still using in their recommendations to management of large and small corporations might be referred to as "classical" or rather "operational" theory.

The trouble with the classicists, it seems to me, is, first, that they have not gone far enough in refining their theories and have perhaps been a little too dogmatic in their attitudes. Second, they haven't done enough in the way of getting acquainted with the tremendous additional body of knowledge developed largely by the group represented here.

The difficulty with the newer approaches is that they have not been sufficiently recognized by business managers to receive a real test. Perhaps, therefore, their potential effectiveness has been somewhat exaggerated.

It would be very helpful if the other schools of thought would give us a great deal more than they have in the past regarding values, principles, and theories that they have not only developed but *tested* as well. In that way, our body of knowledge might be greatly enlarged.

Simon and March explained some of the new theories very well in their book. So here is a fine opportunity for a foundation to give some money to make possible the testing of the propositions set forth. That would spell real progress.

Professor Simon: I really think the classicists are much worse off than you make them. They are worse off largely because there was no procedure provided (I can think of some individual exceptions to this in the work of Taylor) in most of the work we now call classics for making the science objective and public.

Where would medicine be today if we relied on the fact that we believed such and such because so and so was a darn good sawbones, and when he cut a leg off, you know it was cut? What you are saying about Fayol is that I ought to believe Fayol because he ran some coal mines, or whatever it was that he ran, very well. I see no reason to conclude from this that he is a man who can state propositions of organization theory that will stand up under the tests of evidence.

What I think is the "new look" that we have learned over the last decade is how to begin to gather objective, verifiable, testable, and reputable evidence about propositions in management. I find, except for some of Taylor's earlier experiments—the most impressive ones on such things as the cutting of metals, rather than on the human aspects of organization—except for this, I find very little of this in the literature we call "classical." I am just not prepared to accept propositions because they are uttered by a guy who is a skillful practitioner in a field.

Prof. R. C. Davis: I would like to take exception. I think he is in worse shape than he thinks he is in this respect: After all, these people have done this. They didn't just talk about it. Their error was, I think, that they developed a doctrine or theory based on their personal experiences.

But Professor Simon overlooks the fact that those who followed them have synthesized the experiences of these people and have drawn common propositions which integrated the experiences of these people. In that sense it is a broader basis of experience than the ones he sets up, which usually have to do with some rather narrow experiences under some local conditions.

I think you underestimate, possibly, the contribution that these people have made. They have not set up a proposition which says, "You must believe Fayol," or "You must believe Taylor," or you must believe anyone. All they said is that these people went out and did things. They were not stupid. They must have learned something.

What seems to be the common thread of truth that goes through it? Let's synthesize them from the point of view of the writer, who may be far from perfect and usually is.

Professor Koontz: I am a little bit concerned when we talk about the classics. It has been a long-time sport for everybody to hit the so-called classics. We overlook the fact that we are really name-calling. We are taking certain of the pioneers, the Fayols, and Taylors, and others, and we are trying to say that anybody today who is interested, as I am, in a management process approach is therefore a classicist.

This is almost like saying to you people in the human relations field that the research on social psychology ended with Lillian Gilbreth's book and Walter Dill Scott's early works. Personally I don't like to see the kind of name-calling involved in trying to compare the findings of someone in the early 1900s or even the 1930s with the findings in the 1960s.

D DECISION THEORY AS A BASIS OF MANAGEMENT THEORY AND RESEARCH: A DISCUSSION

One of the most widely used approaches to the study of management, particularly among those in academic ranks, has been to regard decision making as the central function of the manager and, therefore, to analyze the nature and implications of this process. Decision theory has varied in concept, among those who use it as a point of departure, from a narrow analysis of rational choice to a very broad analysis of all the factors involved in reaching and implementing a decision in an organized enterprise. The discussions of the symposium indicated considerable interest in decision making as an integrating approach to management theory.

Professor Dubin: Somebody asserted that the real heart of management, indeed all management theory, should center on decision making. This may very well be, but I want some proof of it. The studies we have—and they are pitifully meager—as to what executives do show that when you ask them what functions they are performing, they say that about 20 to 25 per cent of the time they are making decisions. When you go and observe their behavior rather than ask them to estimate it, this falls to something around 15 to 20 per cent of the time. Thus, if you get some measure of actual executive behavior, you discover less than a quarter of their time seems to be devoted directly to making decisions.

As a sociologist, my simple question is: What are they doing the other three-quarters of the time?

Mr. Brown: If you ask how much time an executive takes in making decisions, you have to be pretty clear about the meaning of the question. For example, to me a decision is made often after much cogitation, discovery of information, reading, and discussion; and then the decision itself may be made in almost the flash of a second. I eventually come to a conclusion; if you think of a decision in that way then I should think it takes about 0.001 per cent of an executive's time; but if, on the other hand, you think of decision making as being the whole process leading up to that choice, then that is quite a different matter.

Thus, it all depends on the way you look at the question as to what answer you give to the question: "What percentage of time does an executive spend making decisions?" In my terms I would say that the main burden of work of an executive is making decisions but, of course, I refer to the whole process leading up to the moment of choice and not just the mere process of choice after the exploration has been done.

Professor Bach: Well, I think here we are back in the old terminological argument. You can apply the term decision any way you wish, and the main point here is, you must be clear about what you mean. It would seem to me to be very nonsensical indeed to suppose what we are interested in is only that instant of choice. Surely what we are concerned with is in some broader sense the managerial measure of behavior which involves what Mr. Brown has pointed out as a long process of searching out what is the problem. This, it seems to me, has to get into the act long before you come to the question: "How do you make up your mind on the problem?" What is the problem you are making your mind up on anyhow?—which I think is one of the big problems the manager faces in this whole process of accumulating evidence: accumulating a feel for the problem many times in the subconscious fashion. And then beyond this certainly is the problem: What do you do with the decision? How does it get carried out?

Professor Dubin: (To Mr. Brown) Can you delineate for me where the decision-making functions are while you are building and maintaining morale? What are you deciding? What is the nature of the decisions you are making when you are building and maintaining morale among your staff?

Here you have got an operating problem. A department or division somehow or other is low and you have got to raise it up. You have mentioned this in your book. Now, are you deciding things? Are you engaging in decision making or are you doing some operating acts in order to build up morale which may be low?

Mr. Brown: That is a very difficult question indeed. I will try to answer it. You refer to a situation where a person is worrying about the morale of his organization. What I would at once begin to consider are the following matters: the physical conditions of work, the output of work itself, the extent of the authority and the responsibility of the people who are exercising that authority and responsibility, and so on. I would also want to look at the sources of the authority of the managers involved in the situation, and to do this I would want to look at the power groups involved in the situation, that is, the shareholders, the consumers, and the representatives of those employed in the organization. I would want to see how these power groups invested managers with authority. May I call attention to the fact that although managers may possess, from their personal characteristics, some personal power, broadly speaking, it is the authority of a manager with which we are concerned. There is a difference between these two things, power and authority. Power is that attribute of an individual of a group which enables him to impose his will on others. Authority is something attached to a role. You talk of authority when you take up a role, and when you resign from the role, you lose the authority. Therefore, I would want to look at the sources of the authority in the role of the managers concerned in the situation because this stems from the power groups in the situation, and one of the most important of these, from the morale point of view, is the employees of the company.

Professor Marschak: The question was whether you make decisions about, for example, delegation of authority, firing a man, and firing the head of a department—whether these are all decisions or whether they are some other exercises of your organization.

Mr. Brown: All that I have described just now is, to me, a process of decision making in the broadest sense of the word because I regard the analysis of organization and of the particular problem and the consideration of all the data which that process provides as being a necessary prelude to the making of decisions.

Professor Simon: As I have listened to this discussion about decision making, it has seemed to me that the important question is not terminology. The reason why decision-making terminology has become popular is because it has suggested a way of getting on with research. If you stop thinking about terminology and start thinking about a decision-making process, then I think you begin to develop a conceptual apparatus for studying management process. You think of the manager—at least on his cognitive side—you think of him as an information processor who is capable of learning certain things in his environment, who is capable of cogitating about these things and as a result of this, taking certain actions and emitting certain streams of symbols to others in the organization. This suggests immediately that you ought to go into the organization and begin to record and analyze this ingestion and emission of streams of symbols. As far as I can see, the reason why decision-making terminology has been steadily expanding in research on organizational behavior is that it does suggest this first step toward the empirical study of behavior. It also begins to suggest a second step, and that is the analysis of these streams of verbalizations, in terms of the program inside the manager, that produce them, if I may use some computer terminology.

Professor Marschak: I think it's quite important to point out some differences between the interests of Professor Simon and those of Professor Schlaifer. Both are interested in decision. Presumably both are also interested in improving, and not only in describing, the decision practices of business managers. After all, this is what the business schools are for! But Professor Schlaifer is more concerned with improvement, i.e., with the establishment of decision rules, or norms, that should be followed by those practitioners who want their decisions to be, in the long run, successful.

We must look forward to a time when Professor Schlaifer's (and others') normative approach will make fuller use of the result of Professor Simon's (and others') descriptive work. At present, normative decision theory usually assumes, as a legitimate first approximation, that the decision-making instrument—a human brain or a computer—has unlimited capacity, can be acquired and operated at no cost, and does not make errors. Under these assumptions, a best decision rule, e.g., an optimal inventory control policy or an optimal production schedule, is worked out, given the data of the physical and social environment, such as the physics and chemistry of a production process and the psychology of the consumers. But there are still other kinds of data, collected by Professor Simon, but so far neglected by Professor Schlaifer: data about the costs, capacity limitations, and errors, which characterize, not the environment, but the decision-making instruments themselves, be it men, machines, or complexes of machines and men called organizations.

A set of decision rules that ignores human limitations is not efficient. We must hope that a future decision theory will become more efficient by incorporating the knowledge of frailties of decision makers (and also the knowledge of how to select and train decision makers) gathered by descriptions of ongoing organizations.

Prof. R. C. Davis: We approach decision making from the standpoint of time, and we also approach it from the standpoint of scope and also as a factor in research and a subject for research. It would seem to me that from a pragmatic point of view, it is obvious that the importance of decisions and decision making depends on the results that flow from the decision; and some of them amount to nothing, and some of them are at the top of the organization, but not now—two years from now; so I should think you'd have to take into account additional small other things for consideration: the echelon and the quality of devotion to attention which makes it possible from the decisions that are made.

Mr. Brown: Speaking as a manager I would say this. If you want to improve decision making, then you must make clear to people occupying particular roles the types of decisions that they are called upon to make. I perceive that the normal situation in industry is that managers, and others too, are placed in a position where every time a situation arises which seems to call for a decision, then the first thought that must occur to them is: "Am I responsible for making this decision or not?" In other words, they have a subdecision to make first, of that order. If, on the other hand, you delineate the types of decisions that belong to particular roles—not in a static way but in a dynamic way—by stating the prescriptions which bound these roles, then you have got over some of the problems of decision making. I would regard that as priority number one in an attempt to improve decision making.

If a man does not know the type of decisions which he is paid for making, then I do not see that the same abstruse considerations arising as to the process of thought in which he should indulge in making them, the effects on other people, and all the rest of it, come in. They arise after you have cleared up the primary situation.

Professor Roethlisberger: I don't know if this would help, but it seems to me that I differentiate between two different kinds of decisions—a business decision, that is, a decision involving the firm's relation to its external environment, from what I would call an administrative decision, that is, a decision involving the internal environment of the firm, that is, involving the relations of people to each other.

I wonder if what Professor Dubin was saying, when he asked what were the decision-making processes in which Mr. Brown indulged when he tried to maintain morale in his organization, was that somehow—and maybe this is semantics—the word "decision" does not quite cover that domain. The word "commitment" is more what we think about.

Professor Dubin: I want to use an illustration of a situation we have all been part of. Professor Tannenbaum said, "In observing the small discussion groups, there was a status factor operative in the participation," and he described who participated most, who participated next most, and who participated least. He presumably is giving us an accurate description of the behavior of people in quasi-administrative groups.

My question is this: What kinds of decisions were the participants making, and even if you knew these decisions, would it tell you anything about status and status relationships in the small discussion groups? Do we need other dimensions, other variables, to really describe the meaning of status to us? This is Professor Roethlisberger's point about changing this into other variables so we can really understand the problem.

I think it would be totally trivial to say that each of us sat in these meetings, made decisions about our personal status, made decisions about whether this was a status-oriented situation, and then proceeded to act. I think there is something more involved here if we are to understand status, and the decision-making approach doesn't seem to me to be the most central or crucial, though it contributes some trivial insights into the situation.

Mr. Parkhurst: I use the word "decision" to encompass both these fields. I think that's unimportant except that we ought to do enough defining to understand each other; but I would like to submit that in my judgment, in my guess, these two types of decision making, as I would call them, are of somewhat near equal importance. I think it's most important to distinguish between the two—whatever you call them—but I don't think that decision making narrowly defined as Professor Dubin is defining is trivial at all. I think it's very important, but I think this other type of decision—if I may use that word again—is of comparable magnitude.

Professor Wagner: The reason decision theory has become fruitful and challenging is that, using this approach, it is possible to abstract the important elements of an organizational problem without having to assume a particular organizational structure. Consider business decisions relating to marketing, production, inventory, employment, or finance. By means of the modern approach, these decisions can be studied in their elemental form. Furthermore, their interactions and impact on other decisions can be analyzed. Hopefully as a result, it will be possible to argue rationally the way lines of authority and power ought to operate within specific companies. Such is the emphasis on decision making in current business research. Unfortunately, we have very little scientific knowledge about how consistently to make good decisions in a complex system. There remain many significant and fundamental questions to be solved before decision theory will lead to any cohesive theory of management.

Professor Le Breton: I just want to say one small thing here. It seems to me that if we overly concentrate on decision theory, we somehow imply that we are not concerned with how these decisions are carried out unless we cover this concept under decision theory. I think I see at least a few organizations which find it comfortable to differentiate between those groups having a major responsibility for the major decisions or the feeding of information to a decision maker and that large part of that organization which is preoccupied with what we might call the implementation. One could comfortably say: "Why not talk about a model of planning and implementation, not necessarily done by one person in all cases but increasingly done by groups, those who may tend to do the planning and those who receive the master plan from others?" The second group is asked to implement decisions, and although they, in turn, make decisions relative to implementations, their major responsibility is to implement.

Prof. Keith Davis: I wonder if I'm understanding correctly some of what is being said. As I understand this broad area of decision making, I can't distinguish it at all from a similar thing called management. In other words, I don't see what management would cover that decision making wouldn't cover. Is that right?

Professor Koontz: I think that's what Professor Bach would say, too. He wished he hadn't even called it decision making.

Professor Davis: In other words, we are looking at the same thing or encompassing the same area but looking at it from a different framework and a different method of analysis.

iV THE PRACTICING MANAGER AND MANAGEMENT THEORY AND RESEARCH

In the development of the seminar program, those responsible for it properly regarded management theory and research as tools for improved practice. It is difficult to believe that anyone would deny that the ultimate crucible in which management theory and research must be tested is practice. Just as medicine, engineering, and architecture are arts which depend upon underlying sciences and upon disciplines developed especially for them, so is management. Unless theory and research in management do aim to improve ultimately the art of managing, it is difficult to see how these activities can be justified.

In order to obtain contributions from those discerning and

able practitioners who have been responsible either for actual managing or for the improvement of managerial practice, the following four papers were presented. They range from the development of significant management concepts in practice by Wilfred Brown and looking at management theory as a tool for practice by Dr. William Ballhaus to the expectations of the practicing manager from management theory and research covered in Edward D. Kemble's paper and the very discerning summary of management's needs in the area of theory and research outlined by Richard F. Neuschel.

A MANAGEMENT THEORY FROM MANAGEMENT PRACTICE: THE CONCEPT OF CONTRACTION

Wilfred Brown

The main contention of this paper is that the vocabulary and the concepts which we use in thinking or talking about industrial organization are lacking in realism, with the consequence that much of our thinking as managers is not as constructive as it could be. This unrealism is evidenced by the lack of a language about organization which has been defined in boundary terms. By "boundary terms" I mean in a manner which enables any reasonable person to ascertain what falls within or without the ambit of the meaning of the word. Lack of such a vocabulary leaves us unable to define even our problems with clarity, with the result that when we discuss them with others, our conversation often turns into a semantic confusion. It is noteworthy, for instance, that neither the British Institute of Management nor the American Management Association has yet defined the meaning that they attach to the word "manager."

In the company with which I am associated we have, over the last fifteen years, in collaboration with a social scientist, carried out research work which has led to the emergence of a conceptual scheme which, as a result of practical use, seems to us to fit the reality not only of our own operations but of organization as a whole in industry. This is a bold claim, but I shall attempt in this paper to support it by taking, as an example, a fragment of ongoing happenings in industry and, using the relevant parts of our conceptual scheme, to illustrate the extent to which our findings have been of assistance in seeking a solution.

The problem which I select is concerned with conflict between the management of a company and its employees represented by shop stewards or union officers. This sort of conflict, I think you will agree, is altogether too commonplace. Its sources are complex and numerous, and I have no intention of discussing them all. If, however, research can define one source of this conflict and point to means whereby trouble arising from that source can be reduced, then a contribution to the solution of this problem will have been made.

In order to be able to discuss this problem in precise terms, I must start by defining the meaning we give to a number of words, both for the sake of clarity and as an example of the usefulness of the practice.

Executive system. This system comprises the network of positions to which the company's work is assigned. It is made up of positions which shall be called "executive roles." The executive system includes all members of the operating organizations, a member being in his executive role while he is carrying out his job responsibility.

Managerial role. This is the role of a member who has subordinate to him authorized roles into which he can appoint members and determine their work; he is accountable for his subordinates' work in these roles.

Managerial authority. The term is used to refer to the minimal authority attached to a managerial role which has to do with control of work by subordinates, i.e., that a manager must have subordinate roles into which he can appoint members, from which he can remove members, and within which he can set terms of reference and determine differential rewards.

Immediate command of a manager. This command comprises that group of members which he makes *immediately* accountable to him.

Extended command of a manager. The extended command comprises all the members under his control.

Crossover point. In relation to any two or more rules, the crossover point is the most junior manager whose command comprises these roles.

Representative system. This system comprises constituents, elected representatives and elected committees, and electoral units and constituencies.

Representative role. This is any role in the representative system which a member takes up by election and in which he acts on behalf of the constituency or electoral unit which elected him.

Constituent role. This is any role in the representative system in which a person takes part in the election of a representative.

We have used all these definitions for many years, and our managers have found them well related to the reality of everyday activity. In what follows I am using all the words defined above in an exact sense.

There is a widely held assumption in industry[1] that sound organization precludes a manager giving instructions to any except his immediate command. This leads to some absurd situations. A plant manager may decide, for example, that everybody in his extended command who has been absent through ill health must present appropriate medical certification in order to be eligible for sick pay. Now, in many companies the convention is that the plant manager will instruct his superintendents, they in turn—in their own name—instruct the foremen, who instruct the operators. Everybody knows the real source of the instruction because, as it applies to everybody in the plant, it could only have come from the crossover point manager—the plant manager.

One can multiply the above example many times over in connection with the issue of any type of instruction which seeks to set up uniform conditions in the extended command of a manager. It is clear, therefore, that the nature of organization is such that managers frequently do issue instructions which are directed at subordinates who are not immediately responsible to them. Despite this obvious fact, a high proportion of managers continue to believe that to issue an instruction to their subordinates' subordinates is wrong.

Let me now generalize the point made by my example:

[1] When I refer to industry or business, my reference is to conditions in Britain. I have insufficient experience to know whether such comments are valid for the situation in the United States.

4	Plant manager
3	Superintendent
2	Foreman
1	Operator

If rank 4 gives an instruction to rank 3 (his immediate subordinates), which leaves rank 3 discretion to give differentiated instruction to rank 2, then that is what I will call a 4/3 instruction. But if rank 4 gives an instruction to rank 3 which leaves no discretion to rank 3 in its application to rank 2 and rank 1, then I designate that as a 4/3-2-1 instruction. My example about medical certification is a 4/3-2-1 instruction. The quality of the 4/3-2-1 or a 4/3-2 instruction which makes it applicable to people below the level of a manager's immediate command, we in Glacier call "contraction." We had to choose a word because none is in general use to refer to this property of an instruction which is frequently implicit in a manager's instructions but often not explicitly recognized. The word "contraction" was chosen because a 4/3-2-1 instruction does in a sense "contract" the line of communication under a manager. It conveys the idea of a manager communicating directly with those more than one removed from him down the executive system.

I now define the meaning of the term contraction as follows:

Contraction. That property of a communication issued by a manager which makes it applicable not only to his immediate command but also to other members of his extended command is a contraction. It can occur in individual cases where a manager telephones a junior member of his extended command to obtain information, or when a manager issues a policy or instruction which applies not only to members of his immediate command but to others in his extended command.

This property of contraction is of great importance in a situation where negotiation is taking place between a manager and representatives of those in his extended command.

I now wish to describe what I hope will appeal to you as a typical situation in the life of a manufacturing plant; to describe the problems which arise; and to point to one of the causes of such problems which might be eliminated by more disciplined thinking.

The company is nearing the completion of some large contracts; new ones for somewhat different types of work have been negotiated, and this new work is about to be put into production. These changes in work load entail alterations in plant, tooling, reorganization of departments, switching of men from one department to another, change of type of work for a proportion of the working force, etc. Details of the way in which the changes are to take place begin filtering down the executive system. Considerable anxiety is already beginning to build up, and this is exacerbated by the usual rumors that there will be a payoff or that wage rates will be affected, etc.

Representatives of those affected ask to see the plant manager, and a meeting takes place. The plant manager explains in detail the changes that are planned and their effect on jobs, pay, and conditions. The representatives refuse to accept some of the changes and propose others. A state of disagreement emerges. The meeting closes, and the representatives go back to their constituents, discuss the situation, and, in the light of their discussions about what the plant manager has told them, formulate a series of "demands." The plant manager, concerned about the apparent resistance to the changes which he feels are reasonable and necessary, reconsiders the whole situation, sees the general manager in charge of manufacturing, and decides with his concurrence to put forward a somewhat modified plan in an attempt to reach an amicable settlement.

A second meeting of management and representatives is arranged, and the plant manager puts forward in precise terms his compromise plan. The representatives state that they will consider it and sound out "their people" about it.

At a third meeting the representatives state that even the compromise plan is quite unacceptable, and threaten strike action unless their original demands are met. These, to the plant manager, seem quite unrealistic, and, additionally, he feels that to accept them would seriously weaken the authority of management on the grounds that if he gives way in the face of threats of strike action, then the threat of resort to force will be used constantly in the future. The following day the working force goes on strike and the plant stops.

A number of significant characteristics which seem to be

fairly common to most strike situations now begin to emerge as follows:

1. There is considerable reluctance among many operatives to the walkout!

2. Many of them have no very clear idea about the objectives of the strike and, accordingly, would have stayed at work were it not for the fact that stopping work merely means loss of pay, but staying at work as a minority can bring catastrophe.

3. They know that there have been discussions with management but know little of the compromise offered. In view of the prevalent rumors about payoff or transfer to less acceptable work, they rationalize their doubts about the situation by the assumption that because their representatives have called for strike action, therefore management must be trying to put something over which is not to their advantage.

Eventually, higher management in meeting with trade-union officers work out some further modification of the original plan. The strike is over, but everybody has lost a week's wages or more, and the company has lost considerable output.

There is a whole field of reasons for such happenings: the previous labor relations history in the plant, the personalities of managers and representatives, the actual details of the plans and proposals made about them, etc. There is, however, one source of the trouble which is seldom seriously considered, and this involves the notion of contraction.

It is commonplace to hear managers in these strike situations make statements such as:

The company's proposals are thoroughly reasonable—nobody is going to have a raw deal. The trouble is that you cannot rely on shop stewards to present them accurately or fairly to the labor force. Every time there is a strike in this plant it is because people have a completely unrealistic picture of management's intentions. We need representatives who will convey proposals accurately to the rest, instead of these fellows with a chip on their shoulders who distort everything we say.

Let us consider again the second meeting where the plant manager presented his compromise proposal. This proposal was a contraction communication. It was intended for an entire strata of his extended command at a level separated from him by his superintendents and foremen. There were two viable courses open to him. He could have made his proposals clear to his immediate command (his superintendents) and instructed them to see that they were communicated equally clearly *in his name* by some means to each operator whom they affected. Or, he could have stopped the plant for half an hour and presented his proposals in person. This would have given every operator an opportunity to ask questions and thus to clarify the proposal. But the plant manager did neither of these things; *he relied on representatives to convey his message for him.*

Such reliance upon representatives is symptomatic of widespread confusion about representative systems. Representatives are not responsible to managers but to their constituents. If representatives keep within their roles then they speak on behalf of their constituents, and they convey such aspects of anything that managers say as may seem germane to the interests of those constituents. They are often emotionally highly tuned people and elected as much for their courage as for their intelligence. In a situation where there is tension about reorganization, such representatives will often pick out from any proposal made to them the implications and possible threats which they can project into them. Accuracy of communication is very much at a discount. A manager cannot instruct a representative to do anything because, when the latter is in his representative role, he has laid aside temporarily his executive role, i.e., he is not performing the work of his executive position for which he is paid. Thus, for a manager to rely on the representative system as an accurate means of communicating his proposals is quite unrealistic.[2]

In British industry this type of reliance upon representatives is widespread. It is, indeed, uncommon for a plant manager, a general manager, or a managing director to realize the contraction content of his communications, and to route them appropriately through the executive system or to make executive contact personally. It is my opinion that many of the strikes which

---

[2] I am aware that labor legislation in the United States contains provisions which limit the sort of communications which senior managers can make to their extended commands. The question I would ask is this: "Would the legislation have been so worded if the whole subject had been conceptualized as in this paper?"

take place could be inhibited if this simple point were appreciated.

I am interested in the sources of this unrealistic behavior. One of them, I think, is the extent to which we unconsciously model our industrial behavior on the democratic nature of our social life. If a government desires its proposals to be discussed and commented upon, it submits them to representatives of the people such as members of Parliament, county councils, town councils, and others. In short, such matters are routed through representative systems. This is appropriate, but what managers overlook is the fact that our social life is different from our work life. We are born into the role of citizen or constituent with the eventual right and responsibility to choose a government and to elect representatives who form a legislature. This legislature and government not only makes laws but appoints and controls the executive systems which implement those laws. Note that as citizens we have not got an executive role in society. Industry is very different, for we individually decide to contract into an executive role. We undertake to carry out the instructions of a manager and the policy of the company in return for specified pay and conditions. Once we have assumed such an executive role we take on another role as a constituent and also, perhaps, as a representative, but we lose these latter roles when we lose our executive position. Much could be written on the distinction between the two situations, but all I want to do is to say enough to make it clear that they are not analogous, and that, therefore, industrial democracy is not another form of political democracy but is a completely different thing, whatever it may be. Personally I think that the use of the term "industrial democracy" should be dropped because it can only lead to confusion. It implies that the mechanism of association in both political and industrial life is the same, and this is not so.

Because we want to be good "democrats," we are misled into behaving as managers in industry in a manner which is not compatible with the nature of the social systems which constitute industrial organization.

A second reason is compounded, in my experience, of fear and confusion. The fear is often simply that concerned with talking straight to a large body of people who may be in a somewhat emotional condition. The confusion arises from lack of a precise idea about what the purpose of such a meeting would be, and anxiety about the prospect of arguing with hundreds of people simultaneously. It seems a great pity that these inhibitions should exist, for they are largely unreal. Senior managers in industry are often unpopular figures not because of what they really are as personalities, but because they remain unknown quantities to the rank and file if they never talk to them as a group. Being unknown quantities allows people to project into their image all the negative ideas which the ordinary anxieties of work life generate.

A third reason why managers fail to communicate directly with members of their extended command in their executive roles in stress situations is because union officers and shop stewards are equally confused about the situation. Most representatives, on being informed by a senior manager that he will call his extended command together and inform them directly of his proposals, would object in the most vehement terms.

I have had experience of such objections from both shop stewards and union officers, and the conversations which ensued had the following content:

Representatives: If you talk in person to a general meeting of our members it will be a breach of accepted negotiating procedure. It is utterly illogical to negotiate with us who are elected to speak on behalf of our members and, at the same time, to discuss the issue with our members behind our backs. We are not going to allow it.
Manager: I must make certain that those who are responsible to me and for whose work I am held responsible will clearly understand the full import of my detailed proposals. There are two possible channels of communication: the first through the representative system and the second through the executive system. If you wish me to use the first, I must have some means of making certain not only that the precise communication I want to make reaches members of my extended command, but also that the answers to any questions about my proposals are the ones which I would give myself. Now to accomplish this end through the representative system involves certain conditions. Are you prepared to agree to say to your constituents precisely what I tell you to say, to report back precisely any questions they ask, and to convey my answers to those questions in the form I give them? Furthermore, I must have some means of checking to make sure that

you are precisely carrying out my instructions, and, therefore, I would have to insist that an observer, chosen by me, was present at your discussions to make certain that you reported with accuracy.

Representatives: That is a ridiculous suggestion. Shop stewards certainly cannot take instructions from managers. Their job is to look after the people they represent and to defend them from managers. The idea of someone on the management side supervising our discussions with our constituents is unthinkable.

Manager: Fair enough. I too agree that it is a ridiculous suggestion. I only wanted to demonstrate the complete impracticability of asking a manager to rely on representatives as a means of making his proposals clear to his own extended command. Do you, however, agree that a manager must have at his disposal some means by which he can make quite certain that his specific proposals are understood by his extended command?

Representatives: Not necessarily. We do not understand what all the fuss is about. It is custom for managers to present proposals to representatives, and the extent to which the detail is conveyed to the rank and file is a matter for our judgment.

Manager: Well, now the cards are down on the table. I am responsible for the operation of this company to those who own it. If it is not operated efficiently, I am fired. If my policies and plans are not communicated clearly and directly to those whom they affect, then they become the subject of speculation, rumor, and distortion; and efficiency will suffer. I am sure you have all had plenty of experience of that. Yet you defend a situation where I am to be denied free communication with my subordinates and must leave what is said to them to be the subject of your individual discretion. To be consistent you should equally try to deny me the right to post notices or to instruct my superintendents or foremen to speak directly to their commands.

Representatives: You do not understand our attitude. We are not objecting to a manager talking to his men; we are objecting to two sorts of negotiations going on at the same time; one with us, the men's representatives, and the other between you and all our constituents.

Manager: But I have no intention of negotiating with all of my extended command together. That would be impossible in such a large gathering. Negotiation involves two parties coming together, exchanging views, separating to consider what is in their best interests, modifying their attitudes, and coming together again. Such a process, repeated if necessary many times, eventually leads to proposals which are acceptable to both parties. If that is negotiation then it would be rendered impossible if it involved thousands or even hundreds of people. Representative systems are essential in large companies because they make negotiation of changes in conditions of work possible. If I were to attempt to negotiate with all the men at once I would undermine the status of the representatives, and that would be detrimental to the company.

Representatives: Well, we are glad to know that you have some sense of realism about our function, but we are not yet satisfied. Suppose our members start discussing a settlement of the problem with you when you meet them, then you cannot stop them. There is always an element of stupidity among those in a large meeting. They might well start on a process of negotiation with you along lines which are quite inconsistent with the long-term interests of the majority of our members.

Manager: *My* meeting with *my* extended command will be an executive meeting, held in working hours, and those present will be paid for the period of attendance. I shall then, as the crossover point manager, issue a contraction instruction to them to attend. You will also be present, but in your executive roles, not as representatives. The rest will not be there as constitutents who elect representatives, but in their executive roles. I shall make it clear that the purpose of calling them together is to present my proposals and to have such questions and answers as are required to make them quite clear. As it is an executive meeting I, as crossover point manager, have control of it.

Representatives: But how can we be sure that the whole thing will not turn into one vast confused negotiation?

Manager: You will be present, and I am prepared to sign an agreement with you which will preclude me from such mass negotiation. You will then be in a position, at such a meeting, if things go wrong, to assume the role of representatives and draw attention to the breach of agreement.

This narrative of the sort of conversations which have taken place is not a verbatim account, but it contains the substance of points which have been discussed at considerably greater length. I will abandon this style of presentation now because it is inappropriate for the remainder of the points which I wish to make.

Sometimes a manager says: "This demand which the representatives are making is unreal, not only because it simply cannot be granted, but also because I know perfectly well that my people are pretty satisfied with things as they are and are not prepared for a lot of trouble over this issue. Outside influences are at work, or a few of them are trying to make trouble!"

Here is a manager assuming that his assessment of the aspirations of his extended command is more accurate than the apparent assessment made by the representatives of the desires of their constituents. My experience suggests that it is very difficult indeed for managers to make such judgments. There is little doubt that at times representatives do get out of role and make demands that have little to do with their constituents' real wishes. But it is exceedingly difficult to know when this is so. I am, therefore, very much alive to the danger of making assumptions (as a manager) that I know the views of my extended command better than their representatives do. For a manager, the words, "I know that my people are not prepared to support what their representatives are demanding," can be "famous last words."

Thus, in my view, a manager would be well advised, whatever he believes, to act on the assumption that the description of the views of his subordinates put forward by their representatives is valid. I suggest that a manager is out of role if he says to his extended command: "Your representatives say you want this, but I can hardly believe that they are accurately representing your wishes. What is it you really want?" etc. By saying such things he is involving himself in matters which are not his responsibility.

If some strata of a manager's extended command is pressing, say, for a wage increase which he considers to be quite unreal, then when he meets his command at an executive meeting, his appropriate comment is: "You seek a wage increase of so much," or "You seek a change of working conditions of the following sort." Some members of his command may respond: "That is not so—we are pressing for something different." The manager's reply will then appropriately be: "Your representatives have so informed me—as far as I am concerned I shall continue to act on the assumption that their description of your views is correct. If you discover that your representatives are not presenting your wishes, demands, views, etc., accurately, then that is a matter between you and your representatives, but it is not my business."

We call this "working through" the problem. We do not feel we have achieved anything very constructive if we solve just the problem in hand. We want to extract in generalized form the principles that have, in fact, been accepted so that they will govern behavior in the future and thus avoid a continued series of discussion each time the problem appears.

Our project[3] has been described as a "research" project, but the term can be misleading. Managers and others in our company do not ask our social consultant to do research. When they have a problem they ask him to come and help to solve it. I think it may be of interest to you to describe just how he does help them to do this. I shall continue with my example of contraction.

A meeting was held by mutual consent on the subject of negotiations. It included myself, as chief executive, my deputy, and five shop stewards and trade-union officials of the unions concerned. All present agreed that we should invite Jaques to help us. The degree to which he had established his consulting role as an entirely independent one was evidenced by the decision that he should take the chair and should also undertake discussions with each of the individuals present at a later date. After the initial meeting, he held discussions with a meeting of the shop stewards and union officials, with the stewards as individuals, and with myself and my deputy. In each case he attempted to state to each of the groups or individuals with whom discussions had taken place their own views in conceptual form. These reports were presented back to the people who had supplied the material and, after discussion and much amendment, they were, with the agreement of the individuals concerned, reported back to a full meeting with management, union officials, and stewards, together with his own analysis of the facts which had emerged.

It was on the basis of such reports and analysis that a series of policies emerged. These were discussed, worked through in a further three meetings, and finally agreed upon. At this point the proposals were put before a factory works council and adopted.

For those interested in the detail of time expended, the facts

[3] The project has now been in operation for fifteen years. The first three years were on a collaborative basis between the company and the Tavistock Institute of Human Relations, aided by a government grant. The last twelve years have been in collaboration with Elliott Jaques, who led the original Tavistock team.

are as follows: In addition to the four big meetings of all concerned, each of which took two or three hours, he held three meetings with myself and my deputy, thirty individual discussions with shop stewards, and ten meetings with groups of shop stewards and trade-union officials of various composition. These meetings were spaced out over nearly two years, although this length of time is not typical of his work and came about due to the need to involve five trade-union officials and the difficulty of fixing dates when such busy people were all simultaneously available.

The policies which emerged are stated below. These policies form part of a much larger document known as the "Company Policy Document," but I quote only that section which concern the subject of this paper.[4]

RESPONSIBILITIES DURING NEGOTIATIONS BETWEEN REPRESENTATIVES AND A DETERMINING MANAGER[5]

During negotiations, the structure of communication on the matter under negotiation between the determining manager and the subordinates represented in the negotiations is changed from the normal two-way pattern to the following:

1. The elucidation of the official executive point of view remains a direct executive relationship between managers and their subordinates.

2. Communication for purposes of negotiating is between the determining manager and the representatives.

3. Communication of the group consensus is from the members as constituents to their representatives, and from the representatives to the determining manager.

A determining manager who communicates directly with his subordinates during negotiation (whether by face-to-face con-

[4] See Appendix of *Exploration in Management*, published in 1960 by John Wiley & Sons, Inc., New York, for full Company Policy Document. Unfortunately, it does not contain the particular policies discussed in this paper because the book was written before this particular "work-through" had been finalized.

[5] A determining manager is one who has been given discretionary authority to make decisions about the subject under discussion on behalf of the company.

tact or in a written or other type of communication) shall recognize that it is an executive communication for the purpose of elucidating the official managerial point of view for his subordinates, and not for negotiation or soliciting views and information:

1. He shall communicate with his subordinates in their executive roles only (but if any of the official representatives acting for the members are not members of his executive command, he may allow them to be in attendance as observers).

2. He shall make such communications as he decides to be necessary to ensure that his subordinates are sufficiently informed, recognizing that to contract during negotiations is a serious matter and that to do so unnecessarily or in the wrong manner may cause unrest in his command.

3. In a contraction meeting, if his subordinates try to draw him into negotiations, he shall call to their attention that the meeting is his executive contraction meeting and that he cannot entertain on such an occasion members opening up negotiations with him or otherwise changing the channel of negotiation.

Employees shall recognize that in electing representatives to negotiate on their behalf, they are responsible for:

1. Arriving at a constituent group consensus taking into account the various viewpoints and trends of opinion among themselves, having given due consideration to the information communicated to them in their executive roles by managers

2. Subordinating their individual views to the group consensus, once a group consensus has been arrived at or has been revised

3. Communicating their consensus as a group to the determining manager only via their representatives

4. Continuing to use their representatives to conduct the negotiations on their behalf so long as those representatives continue to have their mandate

Representatives are responsible for:

1. Assisting their constituents to arrive at a consensus or to reconsider it, by information and advice based on their experience, their knowledge of company policy and procedure, and the special knowledge and assessment of the situation they have (by virtue of their representative position) of both management attitude and opinion and the interests and desires of their constituents

2. Presenting the constituent group consensus to the determining manager on the basis of the consensus among their constituents

3. Negotiating with the determining manager on the basis of the consensus among their constituents

4. Reporting back to their constituents their own view and interpretation of the course and content of the negotiations, and not purporting themselves to convey the official views of management

Managers, and employees in their representative and constituent roles, shall reconsider their standpoint as may be necessary in the light of the progress of negotiations in order to facilitate the discovery of new or compromise solutions of the problem.

I have already commented on the paucity of the vocabulary and concepts available to managers to describe organization. You will have noted the value we place on definition of concepts. A word of explanation on the way words and the concepts they stand for emerge in our "work-through" sessions may be of interest to you.

The word "consensus" appears in the policy. Its use signifies an important advance of insight. In our discussions repeated reference had to be made by all concerned to the process which goes on when representatives mix with their constituents, listen to them, discuss issues and argue with them, and form intuitive impressions of the group's aspirations. The shop stewards in our meeting spoke of the uselessness of the whole negotiating procedure unless all their constituents were prepared to accept the results of negotiations, and of the heavy responsibility which they carried in deciding what proposals to accept or reject on behalf of their constituents. They pointed out that it was not a question of them acting as mere messengers between the management and their constituents and taking a series of votes, for this would not be a viable manner of negotiating.

The word consensus is a common enough English word, but how many people use it in industry to refer to this very complex social process of discovery of group aspiration? Thus it was that our discussions dug deep into the processes that necessarily had to operate in a negotiating situation, and when at last we shared a common insight into their nature, we had to choose a word to refer easily to this shared perception. We began talking about representatives discovering the *consensus* of opinion of their constituents. Once the concept and its label has thus been established, it becomes possible to use it vigorously and to teach others in the company what we mean by the word and thus to spread the insight which has been gained. When one has this clearer picture of the sort of processes which form part of negotiation, then the superficiality of much of the normal opinion and comment about negotiating and strike situations can be recognized, and it is essential for managers in particular to be able to do this.

That is the process which has led to the vocabulary we now use. People meeting in discussion dig deep, discover a closer approximation to reality, and then a word emerges to label what has been uncovered. When this happens it is often possible to note the relief with which people take up the word and thus avoid stumbling about in discussion with gestures and rambling descriptions. It seems to me that it is one thing for a social scientist to do research in an organization, make observations, take notes, and then later write a paper producing his own concepts, definitions, and words; for they may never be used by the organization he has studied. It is another thing altogether for a crew of people with a problem and a social scientist working together to produce concepts and a vocabulary to aid discussion and to generalize a solution to a problem. The words and the ideas then live; they go into circulation very rapidly and become the normal currency of conversation. Visitors to our company include quite a number of social scientists, and it is interesting sometimes to note their reaction when they hear their own jargon evidenced by such words as role, social system, executive system, etc., being correctly used in ordinary discussion by simple people. It seems to me that we have here a two-way process of great potential value: social science helping people in industrial situations to solve problems and industrial people enriching the social sciences by putting their attempts to describe reality to the test of everyday use.

In this manner hundreds of managers, specialists, and other employees, plus representatives and others, have taken part in an analysis of the nature of organization in our company. Our consultant is constantly attempting to describe in objective terms the reality of the situation with which people are trying to deal. Individual managers or groups composed of a manager and his subordinates, or individual employees, or, sometimes, groups of representatives, frequently ask him to assist them with organizational problems by sitting in at the various types of meetings that they hold, which are part of the process of running the company. There is never any question of a manager asking our consultant to tackle somebody else's work or the organizational problems of others. The people who feel the problem are the only ones who can request this assistance. First, reports back are discussed, redrafted in the light of discussion, and rediscussed, and grow toward realism in this way. The concepts thus generated are put to the test of use by managers and others, and, if later they do not seem to fit well with experience, then more discussion takes place and new formulations emerge.

Thus it was that the issue of contraction during negotiation was resolved. The conditions under which managers now communicate with their extended commands and the need to do so is now formally established within the company. The ideas set forth in this paper form part of the content of teaching of The Glacier Institute of Management. There are still, I believe, many occasions when managers are faced with situations which could best be handled by the issue of contraction communications where such action is not, in fact, taken. Nevertheless, the company knows what is appropriate, and it has become a matter of training to ensure that the correct action is taken more frequently. It is now possible for the managing director to say to one of his immediate subordinates when trouble is brewing: "Have you contracted and made the issues clear?" If the answer is "No," then he can say: "Please get on and do it." Everybody knows in clear terms what that means, and this seems to me to be an advance.

I hope that the example of contraction which I have chosen demonstrates the operational utility of the sort of work we have been doing and shows that clarity about such an issue really does help managers to run a company and leads to notions which are usable also by others.

We would not have been able to argue out a solution to this particular problem unless those who took part in the discussions had not already been in possession of knowledge of a range of interlocking concepts about the whole field of organization. For example, we shared defined ideas about such things as executive systems; representative systems; legislative systems; appeal mechanisms; the rights and responsibilities of constituents and their relationship to representatives; the power position of representatives and the implications for the company of irresponsible use of that power; the sources of authority of managers and the interaction of that authority with the power position of shareholders, customers, representatives, etc. In addition, we all possessed a consistent knowledge of a range of defined concepts which gave us a precise meaning to attach to words such as manager, staff officer, specialist, appeal, policy instruction, task instruction, technical instruction, supervisor, etc. Thus, we had already grown concepts in terms of which we could discuss this or any other problem of organization with effectiveness because we had found, over the fifteen years of our work, that discussion, thinking, and organizational planning are likely to be sterile without defined meanings attached to the words which we use.

One of the results of working through organizational problems, of analysis, of research (I really do not know what to call it) is to produce a set of interlocking concepts which describe reality as we see it. The emergence of this body of knowledge set the scene for the setting up of our own managerial training institution so that the knowledge which managers are accountable for having, as part of their employment contract, can be taught and thus institutionalized through time.

We have opened this institute to managers from other companies, and the experience of those who are able and capable of digging sufficiently deeply into their own experience is adding support to the idea that this body of knowledge is relevant not only to our company, but to others also.

B WHAT CAN MANAGEMENT THEORY DO FOR THE PRACTICING MANAGER?

William F. Ballhaus

Who is the practicing manager?

Management is practiced at many levels in any working organization. The foreman is the first level in the shop, and the lead engineer is the first level in engineering. They are the first level of managers who are responsible for accomplishment of objectives through the work of others. In many cases, they may be required to do some of the shop or engineering work themselves. They are concerned with the output of their subordinates, although a large part of their day-to-day activities involves producing things rather than managing people. The basic management activities of planning, organizing, staffing, directing, and controlling are carried out at this level in an atmosphere where the time element is relatively short. Planning action may involve considerations of hours, days, weeks, or in some cases, months. Organizations may change daily, weekly, or monthly. Staff may change daily, weekly, or monthly, and control is provided through daily time cards, and weekly or monthly reports. Direction is usually given by face-to-face communication. The significant characteristics of management at this level are the brief time span of its activities; and the emphasis of these activities upon things rather than people.

If we consider the other end of the management spectrum, that of the president or other top management, we find that the top managers are almost always dealing with longer time elements and with people problems rather than thing problems. Planning, organizing, and staffing usually extend one, two, and even five and ten years into the future. Changes in plans, organization, or staffing may be made quarterly, but more often semiannually, or annually. Direction is usually given in relatively broad terms, many times over long distance telephone lines and at relatively infrequent intervals. Control is usually on the basis of weekly or monthly reports, and the management is judged on its long-term results. Top management finds that so-called "good decisions" made at the wrong time are no better than bad decisions made at the right time; that no decision is the worst condition; and that even a bad decision made early enough can be salvaged by corrective actions made soon enough to achieve good results. The timing of decisions is critical to management success.

All levels of management are involved with activities which can be separated into two categories, one specialized and the other generalized. The specialized activities have to do with each individual's specific professional, technical, or product functioning. The generalized activities are those which are common to all echelons in all professional, technical, or product areas, and these we will call management activity.

Management activity involves the basic operations of planning, organizing, staffing, directing, and controlling. We study these operations to develop basic management theory, and we do continuous research to improve our knowledge.

MANAGEMENT THEORY AND AERODYNAMICS

Management theory in many ways is like aerodynamic theory. Students and researchers for years have found phenomena which continually repeat themselves, so that laws of action are developed that form a body of theory which can be applied to most of the problems confronting the practitioner. In like manner, management research is like aerodynamic research. In aerodynamics, we can analyze, study, and calculate, and arrive at a general solution to a problem. As we go deeper into the subject, we find little intricacies of aerodynamic problems which may change the nature of the general solution. It is these intricacies which can cause difficulties in airplane design. In fact it is these intricacies which demand the use of wind tunnels.

The wind tunnel is a tool for studying the problems which extend beyond the fringes of knowledge embodied in aerodynamic theory. Wind tunnels are really useful, however, only to people who have a deep knowledge of basic aerodynamic theory. Such deep knowledge permits the simplification of problems, no matter how difficult, to render them solvable.

Management theory, developing as it has in recent years, has evolved general solutions to many of the problems which face managers every day. The large problems can usually be handled in some pattern which fits previously defined conditions and which will yield specific solutions under similar conditions.

There is no insurmountable problem in providing gross solutions to these large problems. The intricacies of the situation, however, can be the most difficult to overcome, because they are many times beyond the "fringes of knowledge" of management theory.

Perhaps we need management "wind tunnels" where we can study the effects of intricacies of management beyond the existing body of knowledge called management theory and research.

Attempts have been made to provide such "wind tunnels" for studying the intricacies of management. One is the use of management games simulating management situations, synthesizing solutions to problems, studying the effects of the solutions under an assumed environment, and critically examining the results and the effects of changes either in the solution or in the environment. Such an attempt is like the first wind tunnels where forces and moments were measured to find gross effects of changing airplane configuration and air speed. More modern techniques permit the solution of many detailed aerodynamic problems to very high accuracy. Perhaps more effort in developing management wind tunnels will yield more understanding of the details of complex management problems. Perhaps we should insist that our managers set aside time to learn from such techniques. The payoffs might be significant.

It is no doubt true in management as well as in aerodynamics that the best solution is usually the simplest. It is just as true that conditions may not permit the simplest solution; so you provide the best you can for the conditions that do exist. What is necessary is a deep understanding of the impact of conditions that exist upon the solutions proposed.

The modern surge of study, reflection, and teaching which has gone on in the management field has in the last two decades developed a tremendous body of knowledge, a tremendous flood of writings, and importantly, a large, specialized segment of our academic community.

What the Manager Cannot Learn from Management Theory

With all this, the practicing manager can certainly learn from the lessons which management theory and research have been developing. There are, however, things which we cannot learn from studies of management theory and research alone.

Uncompromising Honesty. Basic uncompromising honesty in all actions with customers, colleagues, competitors, and suppliers is something which I have never seen discussed in any management course or management writing. It is apparent that management and writers assume this policy exists. However, it is a not uncommon belief that it is more important to be clever than to be honest, and that it is good business to make a killing no matter what methods or procedures are used. In ancient times, business activity was looked down upon as "unnatural, . . . a mode by which men gain from one another."[1] Or "men . . . who have generally an interest to deceive and even to oppress the public. . . ."[2] And even today we see phrases like, "How to succeed in business without really trying," or "It's not what you know but who you know," implying that there is a shortcut to success provided you are ready to disregard high principles of behavior. Certainly we have seen such practices succeed—at least for a while. But they do not succeed, and they cannot succeed for very long. I say this not as a moralist but as a businessman and a manager.

[1] Aristotle, *Politics and Ethics.*
[2] Adam Smith, *Wealth of Nations.*

Strong Personal Integrity. Integrity may be a difficult term to understand, but its definition can be simplified if we tie it to honesty. Integrity is the willingness to use whatever capabilities and strength we have to ensure that action is taken on the basis of knowledge applied in an environment of basic, uncompromising honesty. Integrity will force you to set right what inadvertently was wrong. Integrity will force you to correct even the smallest mistake. Integrity will drive you to really solving the customer's problems rather than merely selling him your product. Such integrity must be presumed by most management theorists because I have never seen it mentioned in management writings or discussions.

Inherent Initiative. In discussions with people at many different levels of management, it is interesting to ask the question, "What is the most important single quality which an individual must have to succeed?" Some answers might be: good education, professional knowledge, good experience, ability. It is interesting that people with inherent initiative usually do what is necessary to provide themselves with the required education, professional knowledge, and pertinent experience to be able to handle the jobs at hand. Inherent initiative will provide the stimulus to develop the qualities and the energy necessary to overcome any lack of capability.

Professional or Specialized Knowledge. While such knowledge might not be necessary to a manager's success, certainly such professional and specialized knowledge as accounting, engineering, and law can add to the individual's understanding of complex management situations. As we discussed earlier, this is a collateral, specialized capability and is not in our category of management activity.

Ingredients for Organizational Success

Even with profound understanding of management theory and careful attention to latest developments from management research, it is possible for so-called well-organized, well-managed companies to falter, fail, or at best end up with mediocre results. What are some of the ingredients necessary to make a well-organized, well-staffed organization succeed? If we take a cross section of almost any company or organization, we see a certain percentage of highly educated people holding doctor's or master's degrees, a somewhat higher percentage of people holding bachelor's degrees in many different technologies, and an even higher percentage of people without college degrees, nonetheless some having outstanding capabilities. In some cases we even find large numbers of people who have not even finished high school.

In any modern, complex organization, it is essential that large numbers of people having various and diverse capabilities be organized so that maximum effectiveness of the group can be attained. Anyone who has studied management can evolve a number of different organizations each of which has the capability of performing successfully. Whether the organization be strong line with very little staff or strong staff with the line only as required for action, the type of organization alone will not cause either success or failure. Certainly if the principles of management theory are adhered to in developing the organization, the probability of success will be significantly higher than if such principles are violated or ignored.

Before any organization can effectively perform, one essential requirement is that clear objectives be given to that organization so that all management activity can be conducted in a direction leading to these clear objectives. Again, knowing where the target is and what the target is does not provide the ingredients necessary for success.

Powerful leadership is necessary to create the frame of mind and the drives and to show the path toward the objectives. Powerful leadership may many times run counter to the stream of general opinion. Yet, because of its power and strength and ability to withstand criticism and opposition, powerful leadership can take an organization successfully to its objectives through difficult times and against unfavorable odds. Many times the answers to the question, "Can it be done?" are "Perhaps," "We might," or "It's marginal." This is when powerful leadership steps in and provides inspiration which can pervade the entire organization.

Inspiration is the force which opens the eyes of the organization to see the clearly defined objectives. Once the organization is inspired not only to see the objectives but also to see a path toward the objectives, then it is possible for one of the most profound forces in management to act. That is the very contagious force of enthusiasm. Enthusiasm is a powerful force in business. As with any powerful force unless it is properly controlled and directed, its power can be used in a detrimental way as well as in a beneficial way. Enthusiasm in a man entering a new field can be deadly because the enthusiasm can blind him to the pitfalls which are obvious to more critical, less enthusiastic colleagues. Enthusiasm directed toward the right goal in the right path can be the difference between success or failure of a tough, complicated business.

Competition has proven to be a powerful force in external business activity. Even inside an organization, the force of competition when coupled with powerful incentives can be used to energize working organizations. Like any other powerful force, competition, too, can be detrimental as well as beneficial. Competition among suborganizations to the detriment of the whole has resulted in failures of some organizations. When properly controlled and directed, the same force has helped organizations to rise head and shoulders above their contemporaries. The difference between the course to success and to failure is actually a fine line between the extent of risk which provides growth, and the extent of conservation which causes stagnation. Under the microscope provided by management theory, the line can become wide enough for significant success with good measures of both risk and conservation.

Business management even today is thought of by some people as exploiters of the working class, as robbers of the governments, as cheaters of customers, as fleecers of investors. Early scientific management students like F. W. Taylor and Henri Fayol were some of the first to codify the simple laws of management theory and management responsibility. Considerable effort has been spent since their time to overcome the burdens of suspicion aroused in prior centuries by management's unstudied, usually misunderstood, approach to its responsibilities to its investors, its employees, its customers, and its community. Only when all managements realize the pervasive importance of their many-sided responsibilities can the burden be removed. As more and more people begin to understand that managements are responsible, and as management theory and research are improved and extended to sharpen management's action and assumption of its responsibilities, the burden will begin to ease. But the burden is still here. Proper management action can eventually remove the burden.

Management Theory Improves Management Action

Management theory, well understood, is a basis for improving the management action of all practicing managers. Knowing the functions of a manager, the concepts of authority, responsibility, and accountability, the principles of organization, the importance of proper staffing, the principles of direction, the essential nature of planning, and the underlying reasons for effective control are essential prerequisites for the modern practicing manager.

Being able to reflect all decisions against a background of knowledge of management theory is a powerful aid to a manager in today's complex business world. Knowing that managers in sheet metal shops have the same problems as managers of carpet installers, that managers of airlines have the same problems as managers of newspapers, gives any manager the strength and depth of perception necessary to make him a better manager than one who ignores the lessons to be learned. "He who ignores the errors of history is destined to live them again," is just as true in management as it is in battle.

That is not to say that the old saw that experience is the best teacher can still be applied blindly. Actually, a student of management knows that experience per se can be the worst teacher if experience in one situation is applied to another without carefully examining all the conditions prevailing in each situation to ascertain that they are precisely the same.

Being able to test alternatives in a deep and complete body of knowledge lends strength to the direction to be taken. When facts can substitute for opinion, they certainly can prevail. However, waiting until all the facts are in to decide alternative courses of action may make the decision too late for success.

To the practicing manager, management theory forms the skeleton on which he can build his own body of knowledge. Management research is the food with which he can feed this body. As in the human body where muscles provide the forces for action, so in the manager's body of knowledge, the actions are energized by the forces of leadership, enthusiasm, and competition. As in the human body, the brain and the nerves provide the sensitivity and precision of action, so in the manager's body of knowledge, the policies of honesty and integrity provide the sensitivity and acuity of true observation necessary to direct the body of knowledge down the proper road to real success. Management theory and research can be invaluable to the practicing manager if he is not lulled to sleep, but rather is awakened, by it.

C WHAT THE PRACTICING MANAGER EXPECTS FROM MANAGEMENT THEORY AND RESEARCH

E. D. Kemble

As part of a general discussion about how the manager views management theory and research, it has been suggested that there ought to be some clarification of "what the practicing manager *expects* from management theory and research." There is one difficulty for a manager in this particular approach to the discussion which is shared with the whole general approach to the subject. This is the matter of identifying *the* manager.

One of the varied assortment of pieces of knowledge that many managers share is that there are many kinds of work and an even greater variety of workers. This truism is part of the more general statement that there are many kinds of people, and that they have many personality patterns. While obvious, it is very emphatically so to managers who are trying to create orderly situations and who keep finding that their stereotype images of customers and workers continually evaporate in the hot glare of the reality of differences among people.

MANAGERIAL STEREOTYPES

Now if it can be accepted that managers are people, it is similarly going to be difficult to pinpoint a stereotype of *the* manager. Furthermore, many managers with similar titles have different responsibilities, which complicates the situation of the variety of titles that identify managerial work. In addition, as Professor Koontz has pointed out, many people believe that managing work is applicable to a variety of institutions so that it could involve attitudes and expectations within such different areas as business, government, and the church.

In such proliferation of possibilities, it may be possible to establish a general stereotype. However, such an approach would defeat the intent of conveying managerial attitude toward research and theory, because the essence of general managerial attitudes is to try to reach for something that is specific. So, in this spirit, this discussion will deal with a theory about a particular group of managers, and it will be in the sense of considering manager*s* rather than *the* manager.

The broad objective will be to consider managers *in business*. However, there is frequently a marked difference in attitudes between managers of businesses that are truly privately owned and those in businesses which are corporately "owned." So, where there are valid insights in this discussion, the test should most frequently be against the expectations of managers in corporations. On the other hand, the notion of a general framework of business is important because the assumption is one of an economic environment that includes business—hence profits —and which has sufficient wellsprings of initiative so that the term "competitive enterprise" is applicable.

Perhaps one further point should also be made about the nature of the managerial expectations that are brought to bear on management theory and research. This is that, among the managers who perform the managerial work for a corporation, there are probably three general attitudes that could be found.

One group could be expected to say, somewhat whimsically, that they could not care less about any subject than this one. So they probably have no expectation at all. This is one of the challenges for those who *are* interested—especially since the general attitude of such individuals is reinforced by their awareness of the "jungle" which Professor Koontz has outlined.

Another challenge comes from a second grouping of managers. These are individuals who are familiar with the laws and the predicable results of physics and chemistry which underlie much of modern industrial technology. So, from this background they expect that theory and research are going to establish rules for success. They expect that the risk can be taken out of managerial responsibilities for men who have competence in understanding the theory and the facts which are established by research. For men with such expectations, any lesser accomplishment may be derided as "unscientific" and to be disregarded.

The third grouping of managers according to expectations about research and theory may be the least numerous. Yet, in further narrowing down this part of a general discussion of "theory and research" to a typically managerial attitude, it is their viewpoint which will be expressed. There will be no immediate attempt at characterizing the individuals involved other than to state:

They are interested in management research and in the development of a theory of managing.

They realize that the "science" which is involved will share in common with the other social sciences some limitations on the sort of predictability which has been developed in the physical sciences.

The balance of this paper is partially a characterization of this third grouping of managers.

REALISM IN MANAGERIAL ATTITUDES

One of the significant attitudes of successful managers—and there are many such individuals in the group this paper deals with—is the intent to be realists. Sometimes they are referred to as "practical," but this has a tendency to synthesize their observations of situations and the action which they then initiate. In referring to them as "realists," the intent is to first focus attention on the way they look at the world.

One possible insight which emerges from the notion of managerial realism is the recognition of an analogy between such managerial attitudes and the basic attitudes of scientists. This might surprise both groups of people. Nevertheless, there is certainly a similarity between the objectivity of scientists and the realism of many managers. For both, the intent is to observe with a minimum of prejudice or bias so that there will be no confusion in understanding of the situation because of distortion in the way it is being perceived.

Of course, neither successful businessmen nor outstanding scientists expect to grasp the entirety of reality. From somewhat different backgrounds, there is common realization of the complexity of interactions which are involved. Nevertheless, there is an expectancy of a high degree of validity in observations of specific aspects of the total; and this includes considerable recognition of the limits of boundaries for observation.

This apparent kinship of outstanding scientists and successful businessmen is important for social scientists who are interested in managerial expectations of research and theory:

Because of it, managers expect that theory will be founded on the real world in which business exists; and they expect that theory will reflect observations about this real world that are distorted by neither idealism nor cynicism.

In addition, there is the expectation that research and theory will particularly deal with the modern world of industrialized societies rather than historic periods where present forms of technology, transportation, communication, and "democracy" were less significant.

The analogy between scientists and businessmen breaks down at the point of understanding the reasons for objectivity in observation. For the scientist, each step in the process of gaining understanding is primarily only for the purpose of having a valid basis for further understanding. For the manager in business, however, the next action after gaining understanding of a situation is to initiate activities by which a new situation is created that they believe to be an improvement.

Incidentally—and at the moment only incidentally—the action in which managers are so involved is of a different sequential nature than the interactions of nature which the physical scientist studies. With the latter, in the sense that there are "causes" and "effects," the cause precedes the effect. On the other hand, in initiating remedial action, managers first visualize some other situation which appears to be more desirable; and the more desirable future is, in effect, the cause of the action for attaining it—or something resembling it.

This somewhat subtle difference in viewpoint as to cause and effect is involved in a difference in attitude between scientists and managers toward the notion of "purpose." With the former, neglecting personal purposes, objectivity most frequently requires such a denial of purpose in natural phenomena that general denial of purpose sometimes becomes almost a fetish. For the businessman, however, remedial action is so much more preoccupying than continual observation that the requirement *for* purpose is almost a fetish.

Furthermore, the "desirable situation" which is the cause of remedial action is most frequently *chosen* from among several alternatives. These possible choices obviously are of differing subjective values. So, while managers' observations of situations in which they are interested have a high requirement for realism, it is subsequently necessary to put a value judgment on them for comparison with other possible situations which can be visualized as realistically feasible.

Now, in keeping with the intent of this paper that it be from the viewpoint of managerial attitudes, it might be stated that:

The purpose of the foregoing characterization of managerial attitudes is to point up that managers will expect research and theory to deal with purpose, with values, and with value judgments. Managers may even be expected to be impatient with research into their personal activities or into business organizations which exclude purpose and value from consideration.

RELATIONSHIP OF MANAGERIAL ATTITUDES TO GENERAL SOCIAL THEORY

Although managerial expectancies for research and theory concerning managerial work are affected by their preoccupation with action, the greatest need may be for more adequate understanding of the reality of environment in which business exists.

For highly placed managers of business with national or international operations, this environment is a vast complex of interactions. So, although it is true, as Professor Koontz has stated, "the theory must recognize that it is [but] a part of a larger universe of knowledge and theory," there is nevertheless a need for consistency with this "larger universe." However, the principal problem for managers—*and therefore a source of hope-*

ful expectation as to theory—is that their viewpoint of the larger reality does not coincide with the way it is perceived (or expressed) by many institutional leaders in nonbusiness arenas.

There is certainly a possibility—and perhaps a high probability—that the viewpoints are incorrect, both for managers in business and for others, many of whom are strident critics of business. Further, the responses of businessmen to their critics are so varied that their common viewpoint is not obviously discernible. Part of this variety is undoubtedly because of actual differences in viewpoint. However, a substantial part of the variation is also because of a feeling of a sort of political necessity for countering unprovable or irrelevant criticism with a posture which appears aggressive in order to avoid the political error of being on the defensive. It may even be that, to some extent, the business posture is merely an extension of the frequent advertising practice of "putting the best foot forward."

Perhaps more relevant to the needs of reconciliation of viewpoints between managers and representatives of the nonbusiness world is the desirability for its development to have significant participation by nonbusiness representatives—preferably from universities.[1]

This is partly because even valid viewpoints of businessmen may suffer from an apppearance of "special pleading." More importantly, however, is the fact that the social role of universities is to continually update human understanding and knowledge

[1] A somewhat querulous limitation may be needed with regard to this managerial expectation. It is perhaps a corollary to Professor Koontz's comments about proliferation of theory, since the limitation has to do with the proliferation of *books* already produced by academicians. It seems appropriate for academics to publish to *each other;* but the intent seems to be to publish for businessmen. For instance, at a recent meeting of "alumni" of one of the university programs for "executives," forty-six fairly recent books were displayed as of interest to the alumni. A casual questioning of faculty members disclosed the probable fact that *none* of them had read all the books. From the viewpoint of the role of the university, it would seem that scholars and social scientists would *first* evaluate and classify such material before recommending it to those who are supposed to practice what the books teach. In fact, a very lively managerial expectation with regard to managing theory is that it will be based on a science that establishes relationships among the subject matter in this proliferation of publishing.

so that successive generations have viewpoints which are appropriate to the historic period with which they interact.

What seems to be needed, then, is for the business viewpoint of reality to be captured by social scientists who are associated with the business schools and introduced to the other parts of universities for analysis and evaluation—and for appropriate introduction into new perspectives of society. Research and theory which have such a purpose will provide a means for managers to integrate their efforts with appropriate general expectations of other people.

It will be noted that this suggestion is a little different from those of business critics who believe that representatives of business should integrate their efforts with the viewpoints which are *now* being taught in the universities. It is a suggestion that the realism of successful men offers an opportunity for a contribution to the continuing role of the universities. It is a suggestion that some currently held viewpoints may not be so valid for current generations as they were for previous ones.

It is a suggestion that managerial attitudes toward research and theory include an expectation that they will be founded on progress in *general* social theory.

To Professor Koontz's point, referred to on page 151, this expectancy about general social theory probably relates to that part which is synthesized by managers from organization theory and economic theory. While the exact nature of the progress cannot be anticipated in this paper, it is the intention to roughly sketch out some managerial perspectives of reality that have a bearing on the matter. In view of the differing managerial responses to criticism which have already been mentioned, only some very elementary observations will be introduced—observations which may generally underlie the more complicated and differing managerial attitudes.

ORGANIZATION THEORY

Although business activities are generally a *combination* of organizational events and economic events, the underlying reality does partially lend itself to a description of this combination as if they were separable. On such a premise, it seems to managers whose position is represented by this paper that human life has a few organizing aspects that do not get adequate consideration in theories about human organization. These are important to managers, however, as they attempt to exercise their internal organizing responsibilities in a manner consistent with general social theory—and as they establish suitable relationships between their particular organization and those external to it— external organizations which are both business and "nonbusiness" in orientation.

Division of Labor

One of these aspects is especially obvious in industrialized societies. It is that:

All individuals are interdependent—mutually dependent—on many other individuals for their very existence, and for their mode of existence. Furthermore, this "mutual interdependency"—if a phrase of such redundancy is permissible—frequently exists among individuals who are unknown to each other, so that each individual has a personal responsibility for his personal contribution to others who cannot personally confront him.

It will be noted that this general proposition relates to division of labor, both internal and external to any organization of more than a few hundred individuals. Its significance is further meaningful in the light of a few corollaries:

This mutual interdependence and division of labor crosses national boundaries; and a significantly human aspect of it is that it exists between successive generations of people.

In this division of labor, there is increasing specialization of skills and knowledge required to make an individual contribution.

All contributions are "important"; but in various ways society establishes differing values and relationships of values for them—which have some relationships to: the effort involved in obtaining competence in contribution; the frequency with which the competence is available, whether due to natural aptitudes or to foresight in acquiring the competence; and the determination and relative abilities with which the competences are exercised.

For many reasons there are differences among individuals in the kind and degree of their acceptance of responsibility for personal contributions; and each individual is subject to change in his manner of acceptance.

This general proposition and its corollaries are not a unique viewpoint held by managers in business, of course. Their significance, rather, is in the degree to which they have emphasis for managers—as individuals whose contribution is a direct part of the continually ongoing industrialization which characterizes an industrialized society.

The particular significance to managers is in the complexity of the situation. They have found that it is probably impossible to have detailed understanding of all the interactions of even one business establishment. So, to them, it is obviously not practical to consider the entire social fabric as if it were possible to have complete understanding of an industry, of an economy, or of all the other institutional aspects—governmental, educational, recreational, spiritual, etc.

Optimistic Acceptance of Reality

There are, of course, many ways of facing such a viewpoint of social fabric—some of which include denying it. Most of these approaches are already represented on our university campuses, and need not be mentioned here. If the managerial viewpoint is to be "captured" and introduced in addition, however, it needs forceful presentation of an attitude of realistic acceptance of living with this kind of world. It is even more than this, because it is basically an optimistic acceptance.

It should be noted that "optimism" in the foregoing sense is not a matter of naïve hope that some*one* or some formula will emerge to point the way to social progress. Rather, it is a belief that things can be gained by venturing. However, this is not revolutionary venturing in which previously established foundations for additional progress are thrown overboard for bright new ideas. It is venturing by individuals and by individual organizations among many organizations—venturing which probes possibilities inherent in technological progress, and possibilities in the current of changing human values. In fact, the essence of optimistically accepting reality is that by means of a tremendous variety of "ventures," in all aspects of the social fabric, there is a high probability of uncovering the most feasible of the possible technologies and the most acceptable of the increments of change in social values.

In a sense, this viewpoint of reality is one of chaos, and for some people—especially those who do not have a sense of the overall ecology that binds all forms of life—this chaos is so frightening that they blindly thrash around in attempts to impose *their* sense of order on it. The managerial viewpoint of optimistic acceptance, however, is more nearly that of attempting to find patterns of order that do exist or that can exist within the limited part of the environment with which they are purposefully interacting. In this, they are guided by habitual attitudes resulting from the modern business climate.

Expectations and Commitments

A great deal of business activity is voluntarily limited and directed by contractual arrangements. Some of these are legally enforced and many more are at least legally enforceable. However, a surprising number of business commitments trace their continuity to mutual benefits which are available, rather than to the "dotted i's" and "crossed t's" of a contract. In effect, businessmen search out opportunities that exist in conscious or potential expectancies of other individuals who are accustomed to some degree of satisfaction of their expectations within a social fabric of division of labor. The integrity of commitment to such satisfaction is largely a matter of prudence as to the amount and type of commitments that are undertaken.

So it is in this frame of reference to business that managers arrive at a viewpoint for finding patterns of order in the social fabric. The interdependence of individuals is visualized as a network of commitments and expectations; and this viewpoint seems a means of having consistency between internal organization theory and the organization of society itself.

Competition and Power

One of the most significant of such insights is concerned with the matter of social power. It is obvious that within this network, which outlines the division of labor in society, the ability to satisfy expectations—the ability to withhold satisfaction—is a source of social power. In this sense, however, power is a secondary and derivative social phenomenon rather than a given fact of life.

It seems to managers, however, that too often power is treated as a first-order phenomenon, with derivable norms that are overly concerned with division of power or countervailing power. In fact, worry about power frequently is a fetish with many people.

On the other hand, managers whose viewpoints include the technology of modern industrialization are accustomed to thinking of power which is *developed* in the process of using. Power and use are thus inseparably linked, as power is controlled and directed *to* use. Furthermore, as is the case with many modern technologies, *massive* amounts of power are frequently required. So, while there is understandable concern about "illegitimate" use of power in large aggregates, it does not seem practical, to practicing managers, for normative prescription to rely so heavily on dividing power or reducing its effectiveness.

From the viewpoint of practicing managers, those notions about competition which are oriented to vying for power as a reward—and corollary notions of countervailing power to reduce the effectiveness of power—seem particularly irrelevant. This is not to deny that there are many individuals who seek power for its own sake; rather, the point is that emphasis on such a viewpoint distorts the understanding of more useful concepts of competition and of rewards.

Successful managers have found that this competition in doing is involved in the mysterious organization ingredient of good morale. Further, such morale is associated with socially valid value measurements of resultant contributions. From such viewpoints they believe comes understanding of competition and theories of power. So a managerial expectation of management theory and research is that they will contribute to progress in general social theory which will:

Provide a basis for consistency with understanding of internal good morale and a basis for understanding of the effective dynamism in the social community of which the organization is a part.

Leadership

Introduction of the matter of internal organizational morale into the subject of managerial expectancy as to management theory raises one further point for consideration. This is the matter of leadership. This is because effective leadership seems to be a necessary component of good morale; yet, there is an implicit expectation that management theory will also encompass the concepts of individual responsibility and initiative within an organization.

The problem with which managers are confronted is that leadership which is effective by their standards does not seem to fit the expectancies which many other people have of leadership roles. Sometimes managers are depicted as bosses; sometimes they are depicted as benevolent despots; sometimes they are depicted in terms of the necessity for them to be all-knowing and all-wise. In total and in many different guises, the role of leadership is established by differentiating it from something which might be considered as "followership."

Perhaps this popular habit of pairing leadership and followership is an outgrowth of tribal or feudal traditions. At least, as history is frequently taught, it seems to be a matter of leaders who were successful by varying combinations of such personality traits as great physical courage and high wisdom. Furthermore, followership traits are all too often considered in terms of such complete loyalty that it is almost a matter of complete dedication of the follower's personality and life to the course of action selected by a leader.

Managers who sense the expectation-commitment fabric of life, however, realize that in such a context for any individual, the business organization is only part of the network. This is true for both managers and nonmanagers in an organization; and in fact the relationship among all individuals of an organization is at least as much institutional as it is personal. And, while the ideal may be for each individual to commit his whole personality when he is accepting organizational responsibility, nevertheless each individual has other commitments also—to his family, to his community, and to his own ideals.

Furthermore, managers who sense the specialization of knowledge and experience which is so pervading in an industrialized society realize the folly of expecting any individual to be all-knowing and all-wise. Such an expectancy is irrelevant in any modern context for either managers or other individuals. Thus there are some matters on which managers will defer to other employees—including some other managers; and there are only some specific matters and some specific reasons for other individuals to defer to any given manager.

Managers therefore expect that management research and management theory will recognize modern needs and limitations, so that progress and morale will properly blend leadership, responsibility, and initiative for all individuals in an organization.

ECONOMIC THEORY

In separating the organizing events from the economic events which make up business activity, it appears that managers would expect managing theory to help bridge the gap between their own viewpoints and some generally expressed viewpoints about such matters as: the division of labor; attitude in facing up to current realities; the primacy of contribution relationships rather than power relationships in society; the utilitarian nature of competition; and the relationship of leadership to the social needs for individual responsibility and initiative.

If this seems to be a large order, then managerial expectations with regard to explanation of *economic* events may appear to be staggering. However, if there is to be a theory of managing which is directly applicable to business activities, there is a need for confronting the fact that most managers see but very little operational usefulness in what is generally understood as economic theory. Perhaps more importantly managers believe that many popularly stated characterizations of the nature of economic theory are closer to being caricatures. It seems to them that far too often such theory is not only a far-fetched abstraction from real life, but it also indicates that participation in business is demeaning for an individual who has the healthy combination of self-respect and also a concern for other individuals in society.

The Dismal Science

One such caricature of economic activities, which seems to capture the spirit of many of them, is the frequent recurrence of Carlyle's reference to the Malthusian notion of a "dismal science."

To businessmen there is something a little Olympian in a dismal attitude toward the realities of current scarcities, the necessity for making choices, and the wisdom of making effective use of resources. Certainly, in view of the tremendous technological progress which has been achieved since the time of the gloomy predictions of Malthus, there is reason for optimism about the possibilities of mankind's successful wrestling with adverse situations which are part—but only part—of the reality of human existence.

The nondismal viewpoint of economics which could be embraced by businessmen is one which merely accepts the realities of existence and considers *economic activity* to be:

The complexity of events by which individuals obtain possessions on whose subjective value they disagree, so that exchanges are effected to obtain greater mutual satisfactions.

A corollary to this concept of economics might be one which considered *economic growth* as:

The succession of events in this complexity, by which ever-increasing mutual satisfactions are obtainable.

The Wealth of Nations

Such a concept of economics and economic growth has much in common with general understanding of what might be termed "Adam Smith philosophy." In fact, many businessmen are on record as being strongly sympathetic with "Adam Smith economics." For the particular grouping of managers whose position is being represented, however, there is a feeling of a need for a disclaimer to the *context* of the *Wealth of Nations*.

There are two significant reasons for this uneasiness about an uncritical acceptance of Adam Smith. One of them is that in the almost two hundred years which have elapsed since the first publishing of the *Wealth of Nations,* there have been many changes in the substance and in the nature of the concepts of both "wealth" and "nations." The other reason is that Adam Smith was concerned with "political economy" at a time when the results of the United States experiment in democracy were almost inconceivable so that the possibility of complete ownership independence of "wealth" from the "State" or from a "monarch" had not had adequate exploration.

Of course, economic theory has had considerable development since the milepost established by Adam Smith. Very much of it, however, is still rooted in the original context; and the realism of modern managers calls for a fresh look at economic environments, rather than merely making corrections to historic stereotypes.

A theory of managing which adequately includes economic theory should do more than merely update the notion of land as a basic—and relatively scarce—resource. The notion of labor should have direct operational relationship to the use of educated minds, as well as to muscular brawn, so that something more than supplementary attention is paid to engineering, marketing, business information systems—and managing work itself. The notion of capital needs to directly include the dynamic—perhaps liquid—element of money which is involved in banking, in formally contracted credit arrangements, and in the network of commitments which are involved in such practices as charge accounts, checking accounts, and the placing of orders by telephone.

Perhaps the greatest expectation of explicitness in economic theory which managers expect of managing theory is in correction of the oversimplified stereotype of "models of a national economy." This is not merely because of the disparity between whatever is meant by the "economy" of a recent African nation and the "economy" of the United States. This should not be neglected, however, because very fuzzy business planning can result from not recognizing the differing degrees of oversimplification which are involved.

The great difficulty which is involved in the use of present models of national economics, however, lies in the resultant dialogue between proponents of the competitive enterprise system and the more strident critics of the progress which has been achieved under this system. An obvious and logical conclusion which can be reached from such mechanistic models is that "things would be better if someone just operated the mechanism." This natural conclusion, drawn from political economics, has had some degree of success in Russia; and there is no reason for not believing that—granted intelligent operation—initial success could not be obtained in those of the smaller and least complicated economies which can be found among the less industrialized nations of the world.

In this whole pattern of multinational complexity and continuity within individual industrialized nations—such as the United States—it can be seen that economic events are indeed an ecology, as Professor Boulding has stated. Economic theory for practical managers, therefore, must explicitly handle the limitations inherent in the notions of economic models for any political or geographical entity. In fact, economic theory will need to recognize more significantly the difficulty of establishing boundary lines between economic entities—just as ecologists recognize the unity of margins which are involved in such matters as adjoining land and sea ecologies.

Managers therefore expect that, to the extent which economic theory is a basis for judgment in venturing and risking, it should be explicitly consistent with the reality of human ecology. Particularly, they expect that economic theory will deal with the complexities of industrialized societies, including the accelerating rate of change in such societies because of technological developments.

Profits and Ownership

Managers are not only impatient with economic theory because of the appellation of "dismalness" and with obsolescence of the notion inherent in the concept of national economies, but they also believe there is an unnecessary gap between their experience as to profits and the explanations they read about this concept. Particularly this is so when the notion of profit is referred to in disparaging fashion.

Managers therefore expect that research and the development of a theory of management will include their own insights as to the nature and importance of profits in obtaining progress in the development of general social theory. Their insights arise from their fundamental viewpoint of economic activity and economic growth. In this respect, their attitude has a different utilitarian emphasis from the nonoptimistic viewpoint which starts with historic attitudes toward usury. It is also different from the communistic viewpoint of profit which is really an arbitrary tax that is imposed in order to have the wherewithal to support the government and its "plans." Further, this managerial attitude is different from the simple models of equilibrium diagrams by which many people think of resultant prices— which are an important part of the business concept of profit— as part of the byplay between *given* quantifications of supply and demand.

Managers think of profits in terms of the *complexity of events* which are involved; and they think of them in terms of relationships of values which are part of human interaction— including the currents of change which are involved in these relationships. They think of profits in terms of the differing values involved in possible *creative action.*

In such terms, business profits arise from complex and purposeful action in which there is a surplus of money resulting from the values of the *action* inputs and the price of the output. That is, this surplus of money is a value beyond the currently accepted values of the combinations of commodities and human competences which are *exchanged* in the process of "action inputs." As such, it is an accumulation of money capital. Since this is one of the requirements for the process of general economic growth, it is a matter of social value—in the sense of the "ever-increasing mutual satisfactions" which are associated with economic growth.

This, of course, is recognized by those who have thought through the place of profits in a competitive-enterprise system. Profits in this sense become personal motivations for the individuals involved in the action inputs. Since such personal motivations generate the resulting capital accumulation, there is thus a social motivation that there be a profit system.

As a fictional person, a corporation introduces an unusual element into that network of personal expectations and commitments which is economic activity. The complexity of events which is involved thus includes possession by a *thing*—not a person—in the whole process of exchanges for mutual satisfactions among people. Within the framework of this limbo of personal ownership, individuals can fulfill commitments to efficiency in the use of relatively scarce resources; they can apply invention and innovation to new products and services for eventual personal satisfactions; and profits that are expected to arise from these *personal* processes have no actual personal ownership at the time of occurrence.

So managers expect that progress in social theory which must go hand in hand with the development of management theory will establish a legitimacy for managing work, while the theory of managing itself lays the base for competency in managing, which is also a requirement of social legitimacy.

Economic Man, the Entrepreneur, and the Firm

Progress in economic theory which will contribute to progress in general social theory will need to disassociate corporate managing from the popularly understood economic stereotypes of "economic man," the "entrepreneur," and the "firm."

To begin with, this understanding of economic man is too much oriented to the stereotype of the "marketplace"—where final economic values—prices—are legitimately established for the outputs of corporations. However, there are *many* marketplaces which are involved in the corporate network by which an output is finally achieved. And the stereotype of the all-knowing economic man is an unreasonable expectation for *all* these marketplaces. Perhaps even more important, the judgments which are visualized at the marketplace are *short range* in character because the supposed requirement of "all-knowingness" is with regard to *current* facts about supply and demand. However, the corporate process is long range in character because it depends on judgments about *potential* demands, on judgments as to feasibility and timing of the work process in expanding technologies, and on judgments as to the values of work process outputs, relative to the pluralistic demands for a variety of mutual satisfactions which can be anticipated at the time of *delivery* of the outputs.

In recognition of the shortcomings of the stereotype of economic man, popularly understood economic theory uses the stereotype of the entrepreneur. Like economic man, he is all-knowing as to the marketplace for products and services, but his vision is long range as to potentials in a period of slowly changing values. So, with time on his side, he creates the enterprises by which potential demand can be satisfied.

The entrepreneurial stereotype is conceived to have some of the private ownership attributes of economic man. However, his relatively long-range risks sometimes require more personal capital than he possesses. Sometimes, on the other hand, he does not want to put all his eggs in one basket. So popularly understood economic theory sometimes substitutes "the firm" for economic man or for the entrepreneur in recognition of a small degree of plurality in ownership.

The firm is probably a prototype of the modern corporation. However, as a stereotype it is too unrealistic because the actions of a firm are still described as those of an *individual*—but now a *fictional* one. *It* thinks; *it* imagines; *it* takes risks; *it* reacts to economic and political forces; *it* can be motivated, rewarded, punished, or controlled. Actually, of course, real individuals have disappeared from what is supposedly *social* theory. Managers who deal with other employees—not "labor"—and who deal with *customers*—not "consumers"—realize that if they fall into the trap of thinking in terms of *this* economic model, they will be acting as if they were not human. *However,* they find that because this is popular economic understanding, they are *expected* to be like the model and they are frequently judged by its non-human criteria.

So managers expect that economic theory which will be valid and useful for management theory will directly relate to individual responsibilities and accountabilities in a corporation, rather than foreclosing them by resorting to anthropomorphization of a mechanistic model.

BASIC EXPECTATIONS OF MANAGERS

Several statements have now been made about the expectations that managers have with regard to management theory and research. Perhaps it needs to be recalled that these statements relate only to that group of corporation managers who are actually interested in these matters and who understand the intrinsic difference between the physical sciences which deal with what *is* and those particular life and social sciences which deal with the phenomena of beings—who are always in a state of becoming.

Acceptance of Theory Itself

It may be of more importance to recall the statement of belief that most managers probably aren't at all interested in management theory. To the extent that this is valid, it is an interesting situation for individuals who continually deal with the powerful social impacts that have resulted from the development of physical science *theory*. The question could well be raised as to why so many such people are distrustful of theoretical approaches to business.

For the group of managers who are represented in this paper, an additional facet of the situation is also interesting. This is that, among the individuals who have corporate business responsibility in the American economy, the proportion who are comparatively well educated is currently much higher than has been the case for the past several generations. From the viewpoint of the social division of labor, therefore, it would appear that there is a possibility of a relationship between such attitudes and the experiences which were gained within educational institutions. It may even be that managerial practices which are most criticized and are the source of public distrust of corporate managers are the result of attitudes developed because of educational experience.

Some managers therefore expect that management research will include a study of the relationship between current managerial attitudes and the current educational level of managers.

This is certainly a matter of research which would be most appropriately conducted by individuals in educational institutions. It is an additional reason for managerial expectation that universities will take a leading role in management research and

in theory development. However, there is an even more com-
pelling reason for this expectation by those managers who are
interested in theory. It is an outgrowth of their observation of
the explosive growth of knowledge which is available to mankind.

This growth in available knowledge is, of course, partly a
function of the tremendous research efforts which have been
associated with the twentieth century. Research in the physical
sciences is an outstanding example but by no means the only one.
Biology, medicine, psychology, archeology, and ecology are but
a few examples of individual areas where it is probably impossible for any single person to comprehend the factual knowledge which is now available.

The total of such knowledge is even more impossible to
grasp; but this is not even the end of the story because research
is not the only source of additionally available information.
Modern communication and transportation have brought about
the readiness with which all sorts of international and inter-
cultural information is available; and much of it is available with
a timeliness which creates opportunities for action involved in
human progess.

Such wealth of available knowledge is an embarrassment.
Where wisdom and competence in human action is needed, it is
frustrating not to put it to work. One approach to more widespread utility of knowledge, of course, has been the increasing
specialization of skills—conceptual skills—which are involved in
mankind's division of labor. This, however, creates a new challenge in organizational relationships, because of the need for
teamwork among individuals who have difficulty in understanding each other's work.

Increased emphasis on development and teaching of theory
by educational institutions is one of the possible means of facing
up to this organizational challenge. This should be theory about
observed relationships in observed facts and situations—in the
current tradition of the physical sciences. Of course, it should not
be mere speculation about relationships in which there is fuzzy
observation or fuzzy nomenclature which stimulates fuzzy observation. (For instance, to draw an example from the physical
sciences, there is a need to recognize the pitfalls in uncritical
usage of terms which may have traditional acceptance but have

not had the critical examination of such concepts as "sunrise" or "a straight line.")

If understanding and comprehension of many theories with but few supporting facts were to be available, it could be a basis for understanding the relationships between the theories themselves. Thus, a highly specialized worker in one area of conceptual skills could be intimately acquainted with known facts of his own specialty and could, at the same time, act in teamwork with individuals who had different specialties because of his theoretical comprehension of their activities. This is, of course, the present basis for teamwork among specialists in well-developed disciplines. It is an approach that is receiving some attention in the universities by creation of interdisciplinary faculty groupings. The roadblock to effective emphasis may be in the need for fresh theory. In view of the challenges involved in the current embarrassing wealth of knowledge, however, it might be unfortunate if lack of appreciation of theory itself were a roadblock to acceptance of theory.

Information Technology

There is also a development in modern technology which offers an approach to more widespread utility of available knowledge. This is the computer. Here is an instrument which has capacity for storing knowledge, and particularly for storing knowledge in terms of the logic inherent in theory. Further, it has potential capacity for assisting in the sorting out of relationships which are inherent in apparently random information, so that it is a useful tool in theory building. Finally, computers have an inherent potential for making relevant information readily available at the needed action points in an organization and thus improve the opportunity for both individual initiative and teamwork among individuals.

Managers who are interested in managing theory and research therefore expect that universities will validate this interest by developing and teaching theory; and they expect that managing theory will be directly adaptable to the use of computer techniques in the practice of managing.

Since the availability of computers figures so frequently in decision theory approaches to managing and organizing theory, it may be well to point out a managerial expectancy in this area—an expectancy with regard to their viewpoint of intrinsic differences between problem solving and decision making. This is particularly important because increasing use of computers in industry is adjusting the substance—though not the essential nature—of managerial responsibilities.

Managers understand problem solving in the meaning associated with their study of mathematics. It is a matter of having adequate information about a problem, formulating the problem, and then getting an *answer* which is "correct" in terms of the information and the logic of problem formulation. Traditionally, many managerial responsibilities have been based on having experience which provided insights into the formulation of problems which could be "solved." Beyond this, when adequate information was not available, managerial responsibility has been to make decisions among alternative possibilities which could be visualized, even though the information was not available to obtain a "correct" solution.

It is probably trite to introduce the fact that there are at least three factors involved in the combination of reasons for the necessity of making a managerial *decision,* rather than having the correct answer to a problem. One of them is involved in those situations where there actually is insufficient information which can be made available in order to properly set up a problem. Another reason for decision making is when it is impractical to have adequate information—perhaps because of the cost of obtaining it, or because the length of time required for obtaining it is greater than the time limits for initiating a course of action. The third reason is that the personal managerial experience which is involved may be too limited, so that the formulation of the problem from available information is not readily forthcoming. It is, of course, important to note that the necessity for dependence on the risks of decision making rather than having the security of problem solving is quite frequently some combination of these three factors.

These obvious truisms have been introduced because managers expect that the operations-research approach to business situations will reduce the frequency with which the factors involved are cogent in traditional managerial responsibilities. Furthermore, the advent and constant improvement of computers powerfully reinforces the inherent useful potential of operations research as a tool for enhancing the manageability situation. This is because of the massive potential of computer "memories"; because of their speed in sorting out and producing relevant information; and because of their speed in synthesizing simulations of a variety of courses of action which seem possible because there is an actual lack of adequate available information. So, the use of computers makes possible the introduction of actual problem solving in many areas which have heretofore required decisions. And, in much of the remaining decision-making area, the nature of the risks involved is made much more explicit than traditionally so—which permits more accurate follow-up and correction of decisions—as predicted, possible, or adverse situations actually develop.

It will be noted that these business advantages provided by the combination of operations research and computers apply to areas of managerial responsibility that have traditionally tended to preoccupy managerial attention in decision making. Furthermore, there are further potential reductions in such managerial preoccupation because the requirements for communication of both the exact decision and the nature of the decision to non-managers are considerably reduced.

If this were the end of the matter, the conclusion could be drawn that the pathway is emerging, by which there could be an expectation that new managerial theory would indicate reductions in managerial work requirements while improving organization effectiveness. However, such a conclusion would overlook the managerial responsibilities which have traditionally been slighted because of preoccupation with detailed decision making.

Actually, the application of information technology to the work of a business will make it possible for management theory to place emphasis on responsibilities which are frequently poorly handled at present. It may even force attention to critical needs which are inherent in the concept of a modern corporation.

One of the distinctly nonhuman aspects of the "fictitious person" (corporation) is that it has possible continuity of existence well beyond the life spans of people. To achieve this, however, it is necessary that its activities be directed by purpose and by ends which are adjusted so that they are consonant with the changing value systems of the generations of people who serve the corporation and are served by its outputs.

The operations research aspect of information technology requires that this purpose and these ends be explicit. This is so because they establish the *values* which are the criteria for the "correctness" of either problem solving or decision making. Yet these are matters which have frequently had uncritical acceptance and frequently have been ignored to a point that corporate work is frequently performed only for its own sake, or for the purpose of providing employment—even though it is meaningless.

There is, therefore, an expectation that management theory will deal with the requirements for explicitness in purpose and ends; and, from this expectation, emerges the paralleling one that management theory will deal with the matter of long-range planning in terms of the means for accomplishment that are caused by explicit purpose and ends.

THE MOST SIGNIFICANT EXPECTATION OF MANAGEMENT THEORY AND RESEARCH

It should be noted that the terms "ends" and "long-range planning" are relative in nature. When they relate to the work for which a factory foreman is accountable, they may frequently cover a matter of a few days and a handful of factory workers; at other times they relate to preparation for production of new models and the teamwork which is necessary for other factory activities. An engineering manager may be thinking in terms of several years of engineering work. And executives are necessarily thinking in terms of the entire business and the new ends which are to be served when current ones become obsolete.

Regardless of this aspect of relativity, adequate regard for the socially useful continuity of existence of the corporation is vital not only to those individuals who are currently involved in the network of expectations and commitments of which the corporation is a part. It is also vital to society. The emergence of the concept of the competitive-enterprise corporation in the industrialization of society has potentials of benefit and of hazard which are comparable to those involved in the emergence of atomic power; and it is the managers whom society must hold responsible for the adequateness of corporate activities.

Corporate managers require a competence—including attitudes—which laymen must accept on trust just as they must do so in many other vital areas of specialized divisions of labor. This trust is betrayed if the stereotype of managers is of individuals who are necessarily "wheelers" and "dealers." It is betrayed if the stereotype is one of short-range, expediency-motivated workmen. It is betrayed if the stereotype emerges from traditional notions of political economy rather than ecological economics which deals with spreading the benefits of industrialization throughout the world.

If the trust is betrayed, there is every indication that society will doom the concept of corporations in a competitive-enterprise system. There is the further probability that the marginal boundary between the welfare state and the authoritarian one will shift in the direction of the latter.

The most significant expectation of management theory and research, therefore, is that it will establish criteria for competence in corporate managing work which will attract to it men of high character to whom can be entrusted the accountability for needed corporate success.

D MANAGEMENT'S NEED FOR THEORY AND RESEARCH

Richard F. Neuschel

Theory is the constant but unseen companion of management. No manager can function long without it; yet few are aware that they use it. Fewer still can state what their theories are.

Much of the work of the manager is problem solving. There are many other things he does, of course. He trains his subordinates; he tries to inspire them with his personal example and leadership; he represents his organization to the various publics with which it must deal. But most managers feel—and they are probably right—that their major contribution to corporate welfare rests on the decisions they make. These decisions are arrived at by some process of problem solving. The process may be highly structured and visible or it may be unstructured and quite personal.

PROBLEM SOLVING AND THEORY

For the solution of most important business problems, four things are required: models, concepts, analytical process, and data. The first three are intimately associated with the theories of management.

The use of the word "models" is new, but the use of models

themselves is old. Whenever a man undertakes to solve a problem, he does so with some idea of the relationships involved. This idea of relationships constitutes a model. It may not be stated with elegance or expressed in nonverbal symbols, but for all that it is a model. When a businessman thinks of his organization as a distribution of tasks or an allocation of formal authority, he is thinking in terms of a model. When he thinks of pioneering research as a kind of investment with remote payback, he is thinking in terms of a model. When he speaks for or against decentralization, he implies a kind of decision-making model.

No manager can manage without a large number of *concepts*, which are essentially abstractions and generalizations he derives from the particulars of his experience. As with models, many managers employ concepts unconsciously; they use words like field sales management, planning, accountability, expense control, merchandising, product development, and so on. Each of these stands for a concept that embraces a great many individual events—memorandums, journal entries, discussions, and operating decisions. Without the generalizations and aggregations that are concepts, the manager would find himself hopelessly mired in detail, unable to talk about most of his important problems and severely handicapped in thinking about them.

When a manager is confronted with a problem, he needs not only some concepts and some ideas of relationships but also an *analytical process* with which to attack the problem. Suppose, for example, an executive has a problem in organization. He starts off with a view or views of organization, i.e., a kind of theoretical model. He has a number of concepts that enable him to generalize usefully about functions, positions, and relationships. In addition, he needs a way to diagnose the difficulty and to develop and evaluate alternative solutions. He needs, in short, a method of analysis.

Finally, the business problem solver needs data. He cannot arrive at a pricing decision without information or guesses about present prices, present volume, present costs, industry practices, government positions, and, perhaps more important, future developments in all these areas.

The past ten years have seen an enormous increase in the talent and effort directed toward the development of management theories, concepts, and analytical processes. Extensive research programs have been instituted in many universities, not only the graduate schools of business but in the social science and engineering faculties as well. A few large corporations have undertaken their own management research activities. The Federal government through the Department of Defense, the National Aeronautics and Space Administration, and the National Science Foundation in particular has provided substantial support for studies of administration.

The practitioner can judge the work of scholars and researchers only in terms of its immediate usefulness. He is unlikely to know about it until it reaches a point of application; and he is unlikely to have a background or vision that would enable him to evaluate the promise of research still in process. Perhaps it is not surprising, then, that many businessmen believe there is little of use to them in the outpouring of management theory and research.

There is one substantial exception to the generalization that recent advances in theory have had little effect on the practice of management. That exception is in the field of quantitative analysis. The scheduling of production and the management of inventories are undergoing a revolutionary change. In some companies, the results have been far-reaching and profound. The physical configuration of businesses has been altered. Traditional cost and profit relationships have been discarded and have been replaced, in some instances, with relationships that seem to run directly counter to common sense and experience.

But great as are the contributions of quantitative analysis, it is not at all clear that they are the result of new theory. It might be argued that the chief contributions of quantitative analysis, or operations research, lie in improved methods of analysis, more powerful computational devices. Many of the most successful applications of these new techniques are in fact based upon theories and concepts long ago advanced by economists. Of course, new theories have also been developed in the field (game theory, for example), but applications have been limited in number and significance.

But, although the manager may not, perhaps, be able to point to a long list of advances he can ascribe to theory, he cannot reject theory, for he has nowhere else to turn. Every manager and student of management is confronted by the inescapable fact that the number and complexity of problems far outpace the capacity of management to deal with them.

Of course, the problem-solving capacity of management will continue to grow. There will be vastly more data, not only about the internal operations of individual businesses but also about the practices of other businesses in similar situations. There will be more information, too, about the economic and social environment in which the business functions. Certainly there will be advances in analytical techniques developed for operations management to the problems of marketing, for example. Practitioners of management will advance new ideas, such as the concept of the world enterprise[1] proposed by Gilbert Clee in 1959. Managers may even contribute to theory; one would look here to the men who have responsibility for the management of technology in large industrial laboratories, in technologically oriented corporations, and in the science-based government operations.

But the practitioner can never long lose sight of the immediate problem or the tangible result. And he must, therefore, look to the scholar and researcher for the speculative inquiries that yield new concepts and theories. What the practitioner can do, which may be of some help, is to identify the problems for which his present resources seem to him most inadequate and on which he needs all the help he can get from the theoretician.

Among these especially difficult problems, I would list seven:

1. The selection of organizational alternatives
2. The reconciliation of authority and expertise
3. The motivation of executives
4. The development of executives
5. Complex allocation decisions
6. Management of major change
7. Formulation of corporate strategies

THE SELECTION OF ORGANIZATIONAL ALTERNATIVES

It is an interesting and informative exercise to take the organization chart of the corporation for 1962 and compare it

[1] Gilbert Clee and Alfred di Scipio, "Creating a World Enterprise," *Harvard Business Review*, November–December, 1959.

with the organization chart for a period ten or twelve years earlier. Or, for a fuller flavor of change, one can compare the company's telephone directories over some such period of time. The dominant impression in most corporations is that of the proliferation of highly specialized functions. As these simple comparisons are made for a number of corporations, the observer is struck by a second impression, which is one of the great variety of organizational arrangements.

The range of alternatives available to any management in developing its formal organizational structure grows constantly. An organization can be a holding company, a federation, or an operating company. It can be monolithic or decentralized. It can have a strong corporate staff or a decentralized staff. It can group individual activities in an almost endless variety of ways.

Decisions about structure are inescapable. The top management of the diversified company either has a corporate marketing function or it does not. It has a centralized data-processing function or that activity is distributed among the divisions. It sets up a central corporate planning group or decides that planning is an intrinsic part of the job of managing and requires no separate organizational provision. It establishes a corporate development group or decides that the function can adequately be handled by the R & D and marketing people. And so on.

Management has alternatives in abundance; what it does not have is any reliable basis for prediction. There is almost no way to compare the future of the corporation under alternative A with the future of the corporation under alternative B.

Contrast an organization problem with an inventory problem. In the latter case, the manager first determines the kind of problem with which he has to deal. He discovers the general nature of demand and supply and identifies any special restraints with which he must deal. Then he selects the appropriate model from the growing stock of inventory-decision models and generates the data he needs to feed into the model.

No counterpart of this process exists for most organization problems. The manager knows he has to deal with personalities and with functions, but he has no well-established set of rules under which to describe his problem. And even if he did, he has no models into which he can fit the problem. Instead, he has to approach each problem *de novo*. Using some theoretical framework he has probably never made explicit, employing concepts only loosely defined, and collecting a great deal of data which may or may not be relevant, he ends with the feeling that one alternative is somehow better than the other. Yet he has no confidence that another manager, in possession of much the same information, would have arrived at the same conclusion. On the contrary, confronted with the diversity of structure that he sees all about him, he knows there is a very strong probability that another man's answer would have been different from his own.

RECONCILIATION OF AUTHORITY AND EXPERTISE

The technical specialist began to present annoying complications for management during World War II and immediately thereafter. For a long time, some American industries—steel, petroleum, and aircraft—had depended heavily on men with scientific and technical backgrounds. But these men had constituted no serious problem in supervision and direction, for many of the executives themselves had come from the technical groups. Then two things happened. First, science and technology began to play a critical role in a great many industrial organizations that only a few years before may not have had a single Ph.D. on the payroll. And even in the traditionally technological organization, the scientific disciplines divided and subdivided so rapidly and scientific knowledge grew so enormously that the academic training and early work experience of the scientist-administrator no longer enabled him to direct the efforts of other scientists with full understanding.

These trends continue apace and show no signs of slackening. Unfortunately, management's ability to deal with the problems they cause seems not to be growing with anything like the same rapidity. There was a time not long ago when students of the problem would cite the university as an example of an organization in which institutional authority and individual expertise had been reconciled by the development of certain structural devices and day-to-day working relationships. But if one can believe the academics, the problem may now be at its most acute in our universities.

In the management of technology as in any other aspect of the work, managers do make do. They develop new methods of control; they experiment with new titles, functions, service organizations, and the like. But they stand in need here, as in the selection of organizational alternatives, of new theory and new concepts.

MOTIVATION OF EXECUTIVES

No one who has looked closely at even a small number of industrial corporations can fail to be impressed by the dependence of the entire enterprise on the vision and vitality of a relatively small group of highly placed managers. It is true that good fortune or brilliant strokes of strategy in the past will enable a company with indifferent management to prosper for a limited time and to survive much longer. And, conversely, it is true that drastic changes in the environment can damage a corporation, despite the counteractions of the most brilliant management. Nevertheless, most managers believe, and this is one of their most deeply held beliefs, that the future of a corporation will be determined within a very broad range by the excellence or inadequacy of its management group.

Over the long run, present managers can and will be replaced. And, of course, in crisis situations a replacement can occur almost overnight. But studies of executive succession show that most corporations are blessed, or stuck, with the managerial talent they now have, and the task of top management is to make the most of itself and its subordinates. And for this reason, effective motivation of executives becomes critical.

It is largely to this end—executive motivation—that the elaborate structure of executive compensation has been developed. The justification of stock option plans, pension plans, bonuses, high salaries, and special arrangements of every sort is that they somehow do more for the stockholder than they cost. And the accumulated experience and wisdom of almost everyone who has carefully studied the subject suggest that in the main this is so. Yet, "in the main" is about the highest degree of precision so far attained.

First of all, management needs some better understanding of what motivates executives. It is perfectly clear that money is not the whole answer. Almost anyone can run off a fairly long list of other considerations—the need for personal achievement, power, influence, status, and the like. But the theory of executive motivation is so undeveloped or poorly expressed that when an executive comes right down to it there are very few concrete things he can do to motivate his executive group. He is virtually reduced to promoting, firing, or changing compensation. Most of the research and the development of theory, if any, seems to have been directed toward blue-collar workers or the lower levels of industrial supervision. The literature is almost silent on the motivation of executives. And this despite the growing recognition that not only the health of individual corporations, but the prospect for the survival and development of national economies, rests more and more on the work of a relatively small cadre of professional managers.

DEVELOPMENT OF EXECUTIVES

In 1955, the Columbia University Press published a book entitled *What Makes an Executive?* The book resulted from a research symposium sponsored by the McKinsey Foundation for Management Research. Distinguished men in the social sciences, government, business, and the church explored the process by which a man becomes an effective executive. They answered the question "What makes an executive?" with a great many other questions.

In the seven years since, our knowledge seems to have advanced but little. Our needs, however, have multiplied. Somehow executives do get developed; but increasingly, it seems, they are developed in ways that are no longer appropriate for the responsibilities they must assume. The rising tempo of change alone would place the development of executives in the front rank of problems to which scholars and researchers should turn their attention.

RESOURCE ALLOCATION PROBLEMS

Although we can congratulate the management sciences for the light they have shed on certain kinds of problems, notably inventory and production control, we must at the same time acknowledge that many of the economic decisions of management become constantly more thorny. As an example, take the pricing problems that confront today's executive. The theoretical framework available to him shows little, if any, advance over the formulations of managerial economics now more than ten years old. Part of the problem is data. How many demand schedules exist? How many real-life price-volume curves can be drawn at all, to say nothing of drawing them with the elegant simplicity of the elementary economics text? And even if data were available for the simplest demand schedule, what data are available to evaluate the effect of price changes over time? The manager today is not only concerned with changes in the volume of the product being priced but—and sometimes even more—with the long-term effect of the price change on competition within his own industry, on the vertical integration of customers, or on the choice of alternative materials.

But, the difficulties of the pricing problem illustrate only one type of economic decision which needs a firmer basis in theory and method. Let me mention just two others to point up the immediacy of this need. The first of these involves the allocation of corporate resources in a worldwide enterprise. The other is the determination of the optimum investment in research and development.

THE MANAGEMENT OF MAJOR CHANGE

Fundamental change is almost a commonplace in contemporary corporate life. Such change takes place partly in the way of doing business and partly in the very businesses the company is in.

At the beginning of this paper, I advanced the view that most corporate executives would base their value to the corporation on the decisions they make. Many of their decisions are answers to the question, "How should the company change?"

Answering this question is only part of their role, for they must also see that the answers they provide are put into effect. This is the process of *managing* major change.

Let me refer to another Columbia University Press book, this time *Effecting Change in Large Organizations,* the result of a collaboration between Eli Ginzberg and Ewing W. Reilley. The book was published in 1957 and was the result of a careful review and assessment of research in the social sciences and business that bore on the management of corporate change. The book was a substantial step forward in organizing and systematizing a great deal of empirical evidence. Its conclusions have been demonstrably useful to many corporate executives since the book was published. But this book intentionally raised many questions, and the answers to these questions have been slow in forthcoming.

Ginzberg and Reilley observed that there was no science of change in business. They held that students and practitioners of management alike must look to the various social sciences for help. If significant advances bearing on this problem have been in some of the social sciences in recent years, most managers are probably unaware of them if they exist. And today, as five years ago, the manager approaching the task of effecting large-scale change is dependent chiefly on his intuition and his own experience.

FORMULATION OF CORPORATE STRATEGY

The last in this short list of problems in search of theory is the formulation of corporate strategy. Recent years have seen the emergence of corporate planning as a visible process. The papers prepared for a seminar at UCLA in September, 1962, attest to the development of processes by which programs and plans can be developed to attain institutional goals. The key to planning, of course, is the establishment of the goals. We are getting better and better at figuring out how to get where we want to go. Our problem is deciding where that is.

We do not even have a good vocabulary for corporate strategy. We do not even have an adequate system of classification of strategies. We have little in the way of data to tell us what strategies have been pursued in the past with what results. Much of our terminology, maybe even many of our ways of thinking about strategy, have roots in military science. But it is not at all clear that the lessons of military strategy are useful to today's corporate leaders.

Like so many other things in business, developing a strategy simply cannot be put off. The question is not whether a corporation has a strategy. It is simply a question of whether the strategy that it has is a good one. All the signs point toward more and more conscious preoccupation on the part of managers with the formulation of corporate strategy. There are few areas of management where fresh concepts and fresh theories can make a greater contribution or receive a warmer welcome.

This list of seven problems is by no means exhaustive; there may be other problems that are more deserving of attention today. Certainly there will be others in the future. But this list is sufficient, I believe, to demonstrate the dependence of the practitioner on the contributions of theory and the necessity for some viable partnership between the theorist and the practitioner. That partnership may not be a simple relationship in which the practitioner works directly with the theorist. In my view that will probably not be the case. What is required here, as in other fields of advancing knowledge, is the development of intermediaries who can make the unacknowledged theory of the practitioner explicit, make known the needs of the practitioner to the theorist, and interpret the advances of the theorist to the practitioner. What we may look for, therefore, and strive to foster could well be this kind of tripartite collaboration in the solution of the major problems of management.

V THE ROLE OF THE UNIVERSITY IN MANAGEMENT THEORY AND RESEARCH

Because universities are perhaps the most important social institutions for expanding the horizon of knowledge and for disseminating this knowledge, the symposium understandably turned to the role of the university in management theory and research. One of the great needs of any time, particularly as sophistication in knowledge grows, is compression of knowledge and efficient transmission of it. This is a particularly urgent problem with the scientific understanding that underlies the arts. Because creativity in human affairs is the task of the arts and creativity may be expected to rise with knowledge of underlying sciences, it is important that universities play a major role in the major fields of art, such as management.

It is particularly urgent that this role be undertaken by the universities because the practitioner has neither the time nor the energy to absorb all of the new discoveries in knowledge, read all the papers describing new knowledge, and still keep up with his practice. It is urgent also because universities have a responsibility of transmitting culture, including available new knowledge, and providing students with tools and understanding of science which underlies creative practice.

It is the role of the universities not only to develop new knowledge, but to distill the known and to transmit it efficiently in a limited period of time. There is probably no greater challenge than to compress knowledge, both old and new, and to transmit it to those who practice the creative activities of the arts. Since managing—the creation of an environment where people operating in groups may effectively and efficiently pursue roles desired by such groups—is regarded as one of the most creative of all arts, the place of the university in management theory and research is vital for improvement of practice.

In order to bring the role of the universities into focus, those who arranged the symposium asked for brief papers from three prominent individuals, all of whom have had or are having significant experience as deans of major schools of business administration. While Prof. G. L. Bach is no longer dean of the Graduate School of Business Administration at the Carnegie Institute of Technology, he acted as dean during the most formative years of this outstanding school. Moreover, Dr. Allen Wallis, now President of the University of Rochester, was for some time dean of the Graduate School of Business at the University of Chicago during one of its most interesting periods of development. Dr. Neil H. Jacoby, Dean of the Graduate School of Business Administration, University of California, Los Angeles, has received worldwide acclaim for his pioneering development of the curriculum at that school, employing management theory as an integrating force in the entire business school program.

A UNIVERSITIES, BUSINESS SCHOOLS, AND BUSINESS

G. L. Bach

A major purpose of this seminar is "to synthesize various approaches into a valid general theory of management, useful in guiding research and improving managerial practices." I doubt that attempts to arrive at *a,* or *the,* general theory of management are the most useful road to progress. But it is certainly essential to have a clear picture of what our goals are if one is to discuss intelligently the role of the university in management theory and research. Let me, therefore, state an alternative, but closely related, approach to the problem as a basis for considering what the university, and the business school in particular, can most usefully do to advance both understanding and practice in the area generally termed "management."

I suggest that the business school, working with related parts of the university, has three main tasks to perform, and that the first of these three provides a framework for such synthesis as is useful.

1. *Teaching focused on helping young men develop a foundation for management and on helping present managers do their jobs better.* (I shall explain below what I mean by management and what this implies.)

2. *Research focused on developing basic analytical concepts,*

working hypotheses, and models; on achieving more thorough under-standing of prevailing business and managerial behavior in all its aspects; and on developing normative aids and guides to managerial behavior.

3. *Doctoral level teaching to train the teachers and researchers of tomorrow.*

The key to the entire role of the business school and of the university in the business world, I believe, is clear recognition of the central place of "managerial decision making," or "managerial behavior," in both teaching and research programs. I mean by managerial behavior the entire three-part process of: (1) deciding what decisions ought to be made, i.e., what problems need managerial decisions; (2) making decisions (operating decisions, plans, or policies) concerning those problems; and (3) getting the decisions implemented effectively. Exclusive emphasis on the second stage of this process—actually reaching a decision after the problem has been isolated and defined, without concern for getting the decision carried out—is clearly an overnarrow view of the managerial function, and is an equally overnarrow focus for education aimed at developing men for management.[1]

Focus on managerial behavior, so defined, in business school teaching and research rests on some underlying presumptions that need to be briefly mentioned, so the case will be clear. The first is the pervasiveness and rapidity of change in the business world. To be useful, management training must look to the future, not to the present, and to the long future. We are now teaching students who will be active businessmen in the year 2000, and most of whom will not reach positions of major leadership until 1980 or 1990. No one can know what 1980 will be like, and what the role of business management will be then. We can only be sure that the business world, like the rest of the kaleidoscopic world, will change greatly in the next quarter-century. Given the certainty of change and the uncertainty as to its direc-

---

[1] I have elsewhere termed this whole process "managerial decision-making"—in "Managerial Decision-making as an Organizing Concept," in Frank C. Pierson (ed.), *The Education of American Businessmen* (McGraw-Hill Book Company, Inc., New York, 1959). The argument here closely parallels that article, which was directed primarily toward the teaching side of business schools.

tion and outcome, the argument is strong that we must place central importance in university training—for business as elsewhere—on students' thought processes and not on the particularized subject matter and operating practices of the present.

Second, over the quarter-century ahead management will almost certainly become more analytical, more rational. The role of "hunch" and even of "informed judgment" will become smaller as the years go by. There will be an increase in the clarification of variables that need to be considered in making decisions, an increase in the use of carefully obtained quantitative information concerning these variables, and an increase in rigorous analysis weighing and combining the variables involved. We all know that in some vague, intuitive way this is what we must be doing now when we make decisions. The change, therefore, is likely to be one of clarifying and of bringing to the surface the variables and implicit models our minds must be using now, and of persistently improving the logic of these models.

Third, it seems likely that management will continue to move toward a more "professional" status. The need for effective administration per se has been widely emphasized, as business grows in size and complexity, as greater need for conscious planning and control develops, and as growing difficulties of communication are faced. Management must make decisions, but even more of its time and energy must go into getting decisions (plans and policies) carried out effectively. The status of the manager is likely to become increasingly that of a coordinator of diverse interests and "pulls" in a modern firm and in modern society. This argument stresses the need for thorough understanding of the organizational and administrative processes, for it is through these that decisions must largely be made and implemented. Human behavior is at the center of managerial decisions and their implementation.

Fourth, it seems likely that the social responsibility of the corporation will receive ever more attention and stress, that it will loom larger in the day-to-day life of most business firms than it does now. Explicit focus on "the public good" as a legitimate and important goal of business behavior will continue to grow. Business is likely to be judged increasingly by the community on the way it participates as a good citizen, as well as by the older criteria of production and prices. This argument reinforces and adds emphasis to the need for the manager of tomorrow to understand, and be sensitive to, the entire political, social, and economic environment.

To behave effectively as a manager, the individual thus must develop his abilities to think, to adjust, and to learn independently in a world of rapid change after leaving the campus. He must become an effective problem solver in the broad sense outlined above, prepared to make and implement decisions on unknown problems with unknown, yet to be developed, analytical tools. If this argument is correct, it says much about the role of the university in teaching both the managers of tomorrow and those of today who need to improve their performance, and about what we must know to do an effective teaching job. It emphasizes, rather than the teaching of today's best prevailing business practice, development of capacities like the following:

1. Orderly, rational, problem-solving ability
2. Understanding and repeated use of basic analytical concepts
3. Ability to learn from experience and to grow in understanding in a changing world
4. Ability to deal effectively with others, both in person and through written communication
5. Understanding of the role of business in the entire environment and of sensitivity to the processes of social change

THE RESPONSIBILITIES OF THE UNIVERSITY AND THE BUSINESS SCHOOL

If the above analysis is correct, it tells us much not only about the kind of teaching business schools should do, but also about the kind of research they should engage in and the kinds of teachers and researchers they should be helping to develop for tomorrow. It suggests that the focus in all these responsibilities should be the development of a professional man—an effective problem solver in the broadest sense—well equipped with fundamental tools and with the ability to continue to learn and to adapt. It suggests that this, rather than the development of a synthesized "general theory of management," is the way our teaching and research should be focused.

More specifically, what does this argument imply for university administrations, for business school deans, and for business school faculties?

RESEARCH

The traditional role of the university has been to search for truth, and to impart truth. If we look at business schools, is this changed? Not fundamentally, I think, but we must add a third role—to teach the skills of a professional man—of managerial behavior—which is related to but something different from the traditional goal of teaching the "truth." I think the argument above has strong implications for both the kind of research on managerial behavior which is proper in the university and its relation to teaching programs.

The search for truth deserves a far more important role in the business schools than it has held in the past. The parallel of the other major professions—medicine, law, and engineering—is illuminating. Over the past half-century, the leading medical schools have undergone a major revolution. On the one hand, they emphasize strongly the development of "medical practitioners"—doctors who are imaginative, flexible problem solvers, very much like the managerial problem solvers I have described above. But equally important, the best medical schools have increasingly built in, and have become closely affiliated with, researchers in the underlying basic sciences—for example, biochemistry and biophysics. In alleviating the ills of mankind, the results of research in the basic sciences have probably vastly exceeded all the good done by all the individual medical practitioners in the history of mankind. Indeed, it is likely that the "wonder drugs" alone, over the last quarter-century, have saved more lives than the skills of all doctors in the history of mankind. DDT alone, through its use in public health measures in the "underdeveloped" countries over the past two decades, may even deserve the same accolade. This is not to minimize the importance of the individual practitioner of medicine. It does say that his ability to prevent and cure disease depends very largely on research, not on medicine per se, not carried on by medical doctors per se, but on the underlying sciences, and on work carried on by men trained in these underlying sciences and disciplines.

In engineering, the picture is pretty much the same. Engineering is rapidly becoming in essence applied science, and the best schools see the job of teaching engineering as largely the job of developing thorough understanding of the underlying science and skill in its application to engineering problems. In parallel, "engineering" research has increasingly stressed the underlying sciences and their application.

But in the law, with medicine the oldest of the professions, the picture is significantly different. Stress in the leading universities is still on the training of legal practitioners, and legal research has long been concentrated on the finer points of the law. Only in some instances, and in recent years, has a parallel development begun in the law schools, looking back, for example, into the explanation of human behavior and the relation of such behavior to legal processes. The reasons for this are easy to see. Most important, basic research in the social sciences themselves, which must underlie more basic understanding of the role of law and its relation to human behavior, is very new. Until such research becomes more feasible and its results larger, the shift of legal research toward applied science is likely to be slow. Perhaps it is not mistaken to suggest, also, that the enormously rapid growth of our understanding in medicine and in engineering, compared with that in the law, may be attributable to precisely this difference in their relation to, and reliance on, fundamental research in underlying sciences.

I believe the lesson is a valid one for the business schools. It suggests a large allocation of resources to basic research, in the business schools and in collaboration with the underlying disciplines—most obviously economics, the behavioral sciences, mathematics, and modern quantitative methods (especially statistics). It also says much, in my judgment, about the wisdom of focusing research along three major lines.

First, more research is desperately needed in the underlying disciplines themselves to provide the analytical concepts, working hypotheses, and models needed to give better guidance to our understanding of, and skill in, managerial behavior. All the underlying "tool" areas mentioned above (with the exception of mathematics) are relatively new. In the history of human knowledge, economic analysis has long dealt with public policy issues, but until recently has given little attention to managerial problem solving. The behavioral sciences are only beginning to come of age, and few of the leading practitioners have given careful attention to the problems of making working tools of the field useful for managerial purposes. Statistics has undergone a major revolution in the past few decades as it has mushroomed. Mathematics itself is moving forward rapidly, and mathematicians have recently begun to display some interest in developing concepts especially useful for handling the problems of the behavioral and social sciences and management science. Basic research, involving cooperation between business school faculty members and men from the other disciplines involved, needs to be encouraged in every practicable way.

Such fundamental research is often "impractical," with little obvious direct usefulness. For example, fundamental research is now under way in human learning and problem-solving processes themselves, using large electronic computers to simulate the human mind. The prime objective is to understand how the human mind must work, say, in learning formal mathematics or in learning how to play chess well, as examples of human problem solving. My argument is that such research is entirely appropriate in the business schools, or for business schools to cooperate in with men from the underlying disciplines. A comparable example arises in the area of statistical decision theory, much of which now seems highly abstract and distant from business problems. Still another example is fundamental research in psychology on the meaning and processes of "influence" in human behavior. Far removed as such research may be from operating use today, it may well prove to be the most important being done in the entire business area, far more so than studies of operating business practices faced in the real-world factory or store.

Should the business schools leave such research to the other disciplines? I believe the answer is a clear no. If they do, the lag in relevance to business problems may be great. Most behavioral scientists, economists, mathematicians, statisticians, and so on, have little direct interest in management problems—indeed, they are often not aware of what the problems are. Closer involvement of such outside experts in the business area can help bring their powerful talents to bear on business problems. Traditionally trained business school faculty members alone can seldom carry out such fundamental research in the "analytical tool" areas, because their training has not provided the foundations for it. But researchers from the other disciplines and business school faculty members can combine their talents in building up more fundamental and directly useful tools for the management of tomorrow. Most important, imaginative researchers can be lured into business school faculties. Happily, as a few of the leading business school doctoral programs begin to produce Ph.D.s trained for such research, at least a few individuals are becoming available who combine such talents within one person.

Second, more thorough understanding of prevailing business and managerial behavior in all its aspects is needed—not merely at the level of particular case studies but looking toward useful generalizations. Such generalizations are few indeed in the current state of knowledge. The textbooks abound with contradictions. Accurate and useful generalizations will come only slowly and with careful observation and research, well-planned and oriented toward the development of such generalizations, if indeed the regularities exist to be found.

Of course, research of this kind is not new to the business schools. I argue, however, that we need a much stronger focus on the search for generalizations, and much greater concern for careful research methodology than has characterized most business school research. Mere description of business institutions or practices may be useful, but it is unlikely to lead toward a more general understanding unless it is done with painstaking care to obtain and preserve objective data and with forethought as to how the description may fit into later attempts at generalization. Case collection to obtain teaching material is thus unlikely to contribute substantially to constructing a larger body of discipline-tested knowledge of business behavior, because it is seldom planned to fit into broader research objectives and because the research for teachable material almost invariably colors and biases what the collector sees and writes up in the case. This observation, of course, is in no way intended to detract from the importance of case-collection activities in obtaining teaching materials and in helping to educate faculty members who have had limited contact with business operations.

Third, we badly need more fundamental research on the development of normative aids and guides to managerial behavior in the functional fields and, indeed, in all areas of management. This is what I call "applied" research, generally involving application of fundamental concepts and approaches from the underlying disciplines to managerial problems. For example, modern research utilizing economic and mathematical-statistical concepts in applications to problems of production scheduling and inventory control has produced formal decision rules which clearly surpass accumulated know-how in the handling of these problems. Capital budgeting and the analysis of consumer behavior are other examples where similar progress has been made. I see little likelihood that such applied research will soon produce results to replace informed business judgment in most areas. But there is every reason to suppose it can increasingly aid such judgments and, especially in many of the middle-management areas, effectively replace current rules-of-thumb in traditional operating practices which have not been carefully analyzed. The development of computers and the rapidly expanding area of systems analysis may well prove the most significant development in this entire range.

TEACHING

If the argument at the beginning of this paper is accepted, the implications for teaching in the managerial area are clear and strong. As a professional school, the business school needs to reorient its teaching approaches and programs to help students to become effective professional men—effective practitioners of managerial behavior. I have tried to emphasize what seemed to me the most important qualities on which teaching must focus on pages 189 to 190. Others might come up with different lists, but the central focus of developing the potential manager's own ability to recognize problems, to make decisions on them, and to get the decisions carried out effectively must surely be the core of any such list. The past decade has seen the beginnings of a real revolution in business education, especially at the graduate level, in the directions I am arguing. But, the reorientation has only begun if one looks at the nation as a whole.

The main focus of discussion here is on research and its implications. In these terms, our teaching programs badly need to give more attention to finding the relevant basic and applied research from the three areas outlined above, and to build it promptly and usefully into our teaching activities. Fundamentally, a university is a subversive institution—devoted to searching out the truth and teaching it, however uncomfortable the results may be. And here they may indeed be uncomfortable—both for the teachers who will have to unlearn a great deal of what they have been teaching, and for managers in the field whose basic presumptions and clichés may be challenged on every side. But the university that fails to play its role, however uncomfortable the implications, fails to make its basic contribution to the long-run improvement of the lot of mankind.

Developing effective managerial behavior in an explosively changing world is not a problem for students in the universities alone. Men at every level of business face it. In engineering today, it is commonly said that the engineer ten years out of school who has not made a major effort to keep up with the changing state of science and technology in his field is largely obsolete, and indeed may have a negative value since he blocks introduction of needed change. In twenty years, he is useless for most important engineering tasks. Clearly this is not yet true in management. But only a decade or two hence, it may be truer than most people dream today.

Already, every forward-looking firm recognizes this need to keep its managerial pool alert and growing. One way is to accept the fact of rapid obsolescence for many potential managers, and to slough them off when they become useless, counting on the continued acquisition of younger men to maintain vitality and up-to-date contact with the rapidly moving state of managerial technology. But this solution is rejected by most. Some firms have already faced up to the necessity for positive efforts to keep potential managers continuously adaptive and learning. I believe universities, through their business schools, face one of their greatest challenges in this connection—that of restructuring their educational focus to take into account managerial education as a life-long process, tied to the increasingly rapid movement of research.

This is hardly a novel idea. We have many executive programs and a vast amount of afternoon and evening part-time educational activity. But in most cases these are peripheral to the main intellectual life of the university and of the business school involved. Even in the best executive programs, I believe we have fallen short of our best achievements in our regular graduate programs in making available effectively to present managers the flavor and results of major developments in basic and applied research. The problem is to make the research *usefully* available, not merely available. The problem is a new one for us in business education, and it is not surprising that we have not conquered it—for it is very difficult. But conquer it we must if we are to play our most useful role in the rapidly changing business world.

THE CLIMATE OF THE UNIVERSITY AND OF THE BUSINESS SCHOOL

What I am proposing is a revolution in the business schools. The ideas in the revolution are far less shocking than they were a mere decade ago, and a few of the leading graduate schools have accepted them, in principle if not yet entirely in practice. My argument on research, its role in the university, and its relation to teaching programs at all levels would require for its implementation a major change in the climate toward business education and toward research related to management on nearly every campus in the country. Every administrator knows that effecting significant change in the mores, goals, and patterns of organizations is not easy. Universities are among the most traditional of all organizations. Effecting major change in the universities is thus even more difficult than in most other organizations. Nevertheless, I believe it is the major responsibility of university administrators, including especially business school deans, to establish a new climate, a new set of mores, a new set of goals, and a new set of patterns on their campuses in the directions outlined above.

It is important to emphasize that this argument does not imply a monolithic structure of research, or an attempt to fit all research into any particular narrow mold. On the contrary, history suggests there is no one "best" method of research. Increases in human knowledge and understanding have come through many channels and will undoubtedly continue to do so. The wise business school deans and university administrators who want to encourage research along the lines indicated above will do well to recognize that individual research talents and tastes vary widely, and that much freedom is properly left to the individual research man. Especially this is true of those few truly imaginative research pioneers on whom we probably must count for the really big ideas and advances in the field.

Having emphasized this point, I hasten, however, to urge increased awareness of the necessity for team and interdisciplinary research focused on particular problem areas. The fact is that very few individuals as yet have the arsenal of knowledge and technique from the various disciplines to deal effectively by themselves with the central problems faced in understanding and improving managerial behavior. For example, the fundamental and exciting work in systems analysis clearly calls for the abilities of mathematicians, electrical engineers, computer experts, social psychologists, and business administrators to deal with the important business problems where its promise is so great. Some parts of the job can best be done by individuals in the various disciplines working alone, but other parts must be done by teams of research workers, with the solution of a particular problem as the organizing focus for their common efforts.

On the other hand, I have grave doubts about the usefulness of "interdisciplinary" research which merely involves saying we must get research workers in various disciplines to talk more to one another. This is an excellent objective, but it just doesn't seem to work. What has been more successful, though by no means uniformly so, is the suggested device, so common in the physical sciences and engineering, of pulling together teams of diverse backgrounds to solve reasonably well-stated problems.

The universities which make the greatest contribution over the decades ahead, I suspect, will be those which most effectively manage to bring about this kind of research on their campuses.

FACULTY

About ten years ago, I argued—then with a lonely voice—that the related disciplines, especially the behavioral sciences, mathematics, and statistics, would have to provide a vital and essential source of business school faculty members if the business schools were to make real headway toward the kind of teaching and research I have outlined above. In preparing this paper, I tried to assess how much progress has been made in this direction.

On the one hand, the results are impressive. In the dozen leading business schools of the nation, one now finds a substantial group of behavioral scientists, statisticians, and mathematicians, a far larger proportion of the total faculty than a decade ago. In the small group of schools with highest prestige doctoral programs, this is even more strikingly true. Not surprisingly, the impact of new faculty members from the behavioral sciences, mathematics, and statistics appears to have been strongest at the research level and next strongest at the doctoral training level, with their impact on M.B.A. and undergraduate programs far less clear except in a few cases.

If we look into industry, the results are less clear. Casual observation suggests that computers and mathematics have become respectable in much of American industry, and that there is by now an appreciable, though small, range of managerial problems in whose solution they are actively being used. Certainly the industrial demand for Ph.D.s from the business schools trained with this interdisciplinary type of tool kit suggests that industry has accepted the contributions of the basic disciplines and their application in at least some areas.

Interestingly, in the area which managers almost uniformly acknowledge as their greatest problem—a better understanding of human behavior and of ways to get human beings and organizations to behave as managers want them to—industrial acceptance has apparently been less. While psychologists and sociologists are found in many large corporations, most of their work is devoted to fairly routine jobs, such as personnel testing. Although I would like to report the contrary, I could find comparatively few instances of direct impact of the behavioral sciences on managerial behavior at the middle and upper levels.

But perhaps this assessment is wrong. Perhaps there is indeed a higher degree of sophistication on such matters, a better understanding, beginning to pervade through American business as a result of the research and teaching of the leading business schools, which does utilize much more of the behavioral sciences than was true a decade ago. It is well recognized that managers are anxious to use the latest developments in the physical sciences and engineering, but that they boggle badly when the new developments bear on their own individual roles and the way they do their jobs. I suspect, therefore, that we must wait for a gradual infiltration of both understanding and personal skill from the behavioral sciences as younger men, increasingly trained and sophisticated through the business schools and the universities, move up into managerial positions. But on this, two closing comments:

First, how to help operating managers make the most effective use of recent developments in the behavioral sciences seems to me one of the major challenges faced by the business schools. Group dynamics, counseling, and other techniques have been developed in considerable part through university contacts. They have become fads in too many instances, I fear. I suggest that the major job remains to be done here, and that real progress can be made if we put our heads and energies to it.

Second, although I have been an outspoken advocate of the behavioral sciences, mathematics, economics, and statistics as essential disciplines for the advance of business research and education, it seems to me the time has come to point a finger the other way. The representatives of those disciplines haven't been as helpful as I had hoped. A decade or two ago, the whole idea of cooperation between the underlying disciplines and the business schools was novel. It was proper to emphasize the need for patience, and for understanding of the wariness and distrust of teachers and researchers in the underlying disciplines when they were approached by the business schools. And much of this same patience and understanding is still essential. But much of the novelty has worn off, at least at some of the leading universities. Working on business problems has been proved to be fruitful and respectable by more than a few leading figures. It seems reasonable to hope now that the disciplines may spend a little less of their time looking disdainfully at such "practical" uses of their concepts and results as the business schools want, and a little more in showing they can meet the tough problems of making their research relevant. The main responsibility for pulling in and applying such research will rest on the business schools for a long time to come. But insofar as universities value pioneering professional education and research in their business schools, they could well give more attention to the interesting lessons to be found in their medical and engineering schools, and to establishing the type of cross-school climate that has underlain the rapid professional advances in those areas.

B THE UNIVERSITY AND DEVELOPMENT OF MANAGEMENT KNOWLEDGE

W. Allen Wallis

There are four aspects of the university's role in developing knowledge about management through the medium of a business school.

The first of these is to bring together a competent group of people to work in the field.

The second is to provide these people with the facilities, resources, and incentives necessary to do the work in the area of management.

The third is to disseminate the research findings of faculty and students through publication to the profession and, ultimately, to practitioners.

The fourth, and in many ways the most important, is to generate a continuous supply of researchers in the general area of management.

My topic is the first of these aspects, getting together a competent group of people. There must be coverage of the various fields and disciplines and adequate depth. It is no longer enough to have accountants and marketing experts and representatives of the other traditional business subjects, essential as these are.

To these must be added people who are competent in the sciences and in disciplines that underlie the business fields—the behavioral sciences, economics, quantitative methods, and law.

There must also be effective interaction among these people, because a school is more than a collection of qualified individuals. Joint courses and research projects may produce this interaction and sense of common purpose, as may meetings like this one held on a small local scale. Coffee rooms may help, too. However it is produced, intellectual interaction is crucial to the development of knowledge about management.

Two implications can be drawn from this view of the group. One is that the internal organization of the business school should be relatively open and unstructured; it should not be organized into departments or divisions in terms of subject matter. Thought, in other words, should not be forcibly channeled, and graduate students and members of the faculty should be encouraged to cross lines and trespass in other disciplines than their own.

Decisions about staffing and curriculum, which are properly the concern of a specific field, can be made by special committees appointed to represent the discipline. The advantages of evaluation by peers, which are so important to the strength of the university, can be obtained without departmental organization. The experience of many schools of business bears this point out.

The second implication is that the business school must be closely tied to the whole university, because it must draw heavily on so many different fields. The following quotation from Warren Weaver states this responsibility very well:[1]

Suppose that all the thinkers in whatever field be thought of as digging down through layers of ignorance, each going deeper and deeper in his penetration of the previously unknown. By the word "thinkers," I did not imply pure mental activity. These persons will combine research, using whatever tools with all methods of analysis, always being stimulated by curiosity and imagination, always inspired by the creative urge, always finding beauty in the revelation of new

[1] From an unpublished paper entitled "Private Universities and the New Unity of Learning," given on May 3, 1961, at a dinner sponsored by the Board of Trustees, University of Chicago, in honor of George Wells Beadle.

order in old confusion, always sustained by faith in the order of nature and the discoverability of knowledge.

As these persons dig deeper and deeper, each in his own ditch, so to speak, each finds it necessary to develop knowledge, verbal and mental, which is special to his task. This makes it more and more difficult for the thinker in one ditch to communicate effectively with the thinker in another ditch, even one nearby, and as the ditches become deeper and deeper, it becomes progressively harder for one thinker to shout up out of his deep crevice with the hope that the sounds will reach other thinkers, each of them equally deep in his own private crevice. Each thinker sadly remarks "I am becoming more and more isolated. What seems so important and lovely to me is gradually being considered by others as more and more remote, more and more special," but it is possible that as these individual thinkers dig down deeper and deeper, they come to fissures running out in various directions and then a tunnel opens up which connects so effectively with some other ditch or with several that he begins to hear the remarks of other thinkers and it is conceivable that a thinker ultimately finds himself penetrating down into some large subterranean open space, some really mammoth cave with chambers radiating out in all directions and at this moment he finds himself again in free communication with all his fellows. He finds that at a deep enough level they are not isolated, they are not working at disconnected topics, but rather are all back together discussing common interests. Each, to be sure, brings it in spite of his special experience but he brings it to bear on a common task.

It seems at least to me clear that something like this is occurring in the whole present world of scholarship.

It seems to me clear that something like that is certainly happening in the narrower field of advanced scholarship in the field of business, that the major problem of administration in a business school today is to adapt to that process so as to facilitate rather than impede it.

C THE ROLE OF THE UNIVERSITY IN MANAGEMENT RESEARCH

Neil H. Jacoby

I take it as self-evident that the role of the university in management research is, or should be, essentially the same as its role in relation to any other field of knowledge, be it astrophysics, space medicine, or linguistics. That role is to provide appropriate resources of funds, personnel, and facilities, and to facilitate fruitful scholarship by proper organization and administrative procedures. But what is the appropriate amount of resources the university should devote to research in management? Specifically, how can productive scholarship be fostered in this discipline?

No doubt my responses to these questions are colored by my own experience, which is that of a dean of an established school of business administration in a large, state-supported university. Fortunately, my colleagues in this panel discussion have been executives of schools of management with other characteristics and in other environments, and will be able to correct my biases.

THE PRESENT STATE OF MANAGEMENT RESEARCH

Perhaps it will be helpful, first of all, to agree upon some primary features of the field of management research, in which there has been a rising tempo of activity in recent years. Surely the truth of the following four propositions will not be questioned:

First, the theory of management (or administration) is a synthetic discipline, drawing heavily upon older organized fields of knowledge, such as economics, accounting, politics, psychology, and sociology, as well as logic, mathematics, and statistics, for concepts and methodologies. Conceptually, it is a body of correlated and consistent principles for guiding management action. Research is necessary to establish these principles precisely and to define their interrelationships. Because management pervades human society, from the national state down to the PTA for P.S. Number 5, and the demand for management grows more than proportionately to population, the task of evolving a theory of management is both infinitely complex and vastly important.

Second, the field of management theory is now in the midst of an intellectual revolution. New logical, mathematical, statistical, and computational tools are being applied to a widening range of organizational planning, controlling, and decision-making problems, along with new concepts and analytical methods from the behavioral sciences.

Third, the potential yield to society of investment in management research is comparatively very high. Larger allocations of resources to this activity would therefore add to the social welfare. While this assertion is incapable of rigorous proof, there is much evidence to support it. Thus Stein and Denison recently estimated that merely narrowing the gap between the average level of business techniques and the best known level would per se add $\frac{1}{10}$ of 1 per cent a year ($550 million) to the growth of GNP in the United States.[1] If this is the right order of magnitude, think what billions might be added to annual GNP as a result of *improving* the best current management policies and practices through research.

I realize that efforts to justify academic research on economic grounds are anathema to those who believe in "pure" research solely for knowledge's sake. One is reminded of the two professors walking across the campus together. One said to the other:

[1] Herbert Stein and Edward F. Denison in *Goals for Americans,* Report of the President's Commission on National Goals, Prentice-Hall, Inc., Englewood Cliffs, N.J., 1960, p. 189.

"Are you doing basic research or do you have something in mind?" In actuality, does not all research have some useful end in view at some time in the future, with an ultimate payoff susceptible to economic evaluation? The only meaningful distinction that can be drawn is the prospective time of payoff—between projects promising a quick reward and those whose practical values are problematical and lie far in the future. Let us not forget that the basic astronomical researches of Tycho Brahe and Kepler were initiated by the Royal Navies of Denmark and Britain in a straightforward search for better methods of navigation. The U.S. Office of Naval Research has also supported rather fundamental investigations in management science without any obvious short-term payoffs, although its interests certainly are not academic. So I make no apology for applying an economic test to the value of what we are doing.

Fourth, the enlargement and refinement of management theory through research is currently limited not so much by the availability of funds as by an acute shortage of highly qualified research personnel. Good researchers in management theory are scarce because the field requires men equipped with the modern intellectual tools of analysis who *also* have a sufficiently profound knowledge of business institutions and processes to be able to assess the validity and relevance of models and data. A good number of researchers have one or the other type of talent; but few possess both. One evidence of this shortage is the high starting salaries offered well-prepared business operations researchers in industry. Halbricht and Company of Chicago, a broker in such talent, regularly circularizes dozens of highly paid openings.

These, then, are the primary imperatives governing the progress of university research in management science: a synthetic discipline, undergoing an intellectual revolution, having a high social return, and yet beset with shortages of qualified research personnel.

FOSTERING RESEARCH IN MANAGEMENT SCIENCE WITHIN THE BUSINESS SCHOOL

Let us approach the problems faced by the university administrator who aims to elevate the quantity and improve the quality of research in management, particularly research using the newer intellectual tools and approaches. For convenience, I shall refer to this as research in "management science," in contradistinction to research of the traditional types such as case studies, surveys of practices and ideas, and speculative work of a judgmental, intuitive, or historical type, which I shall refer to as a "management institutionalism." Both kinds of investigative activities are worthy of support. But emphasis now should be placed on management sciences. What obstacles must be overcome? What devices can be utilized?

In established business schools one obstacle to progress has been the lethargy—if not downright antipathy—of part of the faculty within respect to management science. Many of those committed to older research methods feel threatened by the new ones. Usually being senior in age and rank, they wield power in faculties. Apart from their sly references to behavioral scientists as "happiness boys" or to mathematically oriented scholars as "slide-rule kids," they are often in a position to block faculty appointments or curriculum changes which would integrate new research and instructional materials into existing courses and research activities.

In this situation the optimal available strategy of the dean is separation rather than integration! He has a better chance of succeeding if he obtains new funds to establish separate and new courses, curricula, and research units devoted to the new approaches and methods. Later, as they prove themselves by attracting disproportionately large numbers of the better students, it is feasible to begin integrating them into older curricula and research organizations. Of course, the dean of a newly established school of management is able to skip this intermediate stage, which requires a number of years to complete. It will help if an established business school is growing, because new activities are more easily accommodated by an environment that does not require rapid displacement of the old. The law of industrial economics that a growing market helps to reduce concentration and economic power also has its application in the academic marketplace. Happily, the strong postwar growth of management education in the United States has enabled many established business schools to take advantage of this law.

The problem of overcoming obstacles to the progress of research in management science in an established school is basically the problem of introducing technological changes into any human organization. By rights, an economist should defer to the behavioral scientists who have grappled with this problem. However, I make bold to suggest some administrative techniques which have been found effective.

First, the administrator should establish in his own school, and encourage his mathematically backward faculty members to attend (in his own or other schools), special courses for faculty members in modern business mathematics. The Ford Foundation has sponsored excellent courses on several campuses, and we have run our own "faculty bonehead math" course on this campus. One should not entertain highly ambitious expectations about such enterprises. Even a solid year of intensive study cannot make a management scientist of a faculty member whose highest previous mathematical training was courses in elementary calculus and statistics taken fifteen or twenty years ago. The value of these courses lies in the cultivation of ability to read modern professional literature and to discern opportunities for applying quantitative methods to the faculty member's own field. These are not inconsequential gains.

Second, the administrator should arrange to establish a series of seminars for the business school faculty, successively dealing with modern methods of analysis and their application to specific business problems. Therein, the institutionalists can be exposed to the applications of such tools as dynamic programming or Bayesian analysis, some of their mysteries penetrated, and their practical utility demonstrated.

Third, the administrator should strive to set up a number of research teams on various topics. Each team should be composed of institutionalists with intimate knowledge of the substantitive facts and processes pertinent to the subject plus management scientists possessing the quantitive tools that are necessary to construct models and test hypotheses regarding it. The experience of working in a research team will soon enable each member to appreciate the value of the others' talents and the way in which it fructifies his own efforts. Gradually, a melding of interest and methodologies can occur, which will ultimately find expression in a more unified research program and curriculum.

ENLISTING OTHER DEPARTMENTS OF THE UNIVERSITY IN MANAGEMENT RESEARCH

The devices just described can help to accelerate the pace of research in management science within an established school of business administration. But the business school is only a minor part of the university; and we are also concerned with enlarging the role of the university.

For many years I have believed that the theory of management provides the primary integrating force within the business school and, even more importantly, that it forms the appropriate subject for binding the research and teaching programs of the business school to those of many other departments of the university. I gave voice to this view in a 1956 paper before the American Economic Association, which produced mixed reactions among my fellow economists, many of whom then considered business administration as being merely a province within the domain of economics.[2]

Being a synthetic discipline, management theory necessarily has intellectual ties to many departments of knowledge. This important fact provides the business school faculty with golden opportunities to work with colleagues throughout the campus on problems of mutual interest. Even more pertinent to the present subject, it offers a method of breaking the bottleneck to progress in management science, enlisting in our research ranks scholars from mathematics, statistics, engineering, economics, political science, psychology, anthropology, sociology, and history.

When we have exhausted the possibilities of strengthening our research activities by "retooling" men trained in business administration, we can further enhance our capabilities by bringing in scholars from other disciplines who share our intellectual problems. The political theorist and public administration expert necessarily have a deep concern with management theory. So do

---

[2] See "Economics in the Curricula of Schools of Business," *American Economic Review*, vol. 56, pp. 551ff., May, 1956.

the sociologist and social anthropologist; so does the specialist in individual and social psychology; so does the engineer interested in the workings of human "systems" and their relation to machines; so does the microeconomist involved in optimization processes within the firm; so does the macroeconomist seeking to link business behavior with overall economic performance; and many logicians, mathematicians, and statisticians find that the data and problems of management to which the business school has ready access provide attractive opportunities for the application of their methods and the testing of their ideas.

Despite its obvious mutual benefits, active cooperation between the faculties of the business school and those of other departments of the university is not easily brought about. Developed professional business schools are relative newcomers on many campuses, and are commonly viewed by the old-line departments (often along with other professional schools) as being not quite "respectable" academically. Too often, let us concede, there has been some cause for this attitude, arising from the relatively superficial level of much of the research carried on in the business schools.

Apart from this factor, the organizational structures and administrative procedures of many universities have been comparatively inflexible and slow to adapt to changes in the progress of science, including management science. Rigid departmental boundary lines have so separated faculties and students as to impede the evolution of new academic organization better fitted to deal with the great tasks of the times. Able graduate students with wide interdisciplinary interests may find that they can obtain only limited credit, if any, for work taken in other than their major department. These are the principal reasons why management research does not benefit from active and enthusiastic campuswide support in most American universities.

It is up to the dean and faculty of the business school to initiate efforts to gain the interest and cooperation of the faculties of other relevant departments in management research. I believe that a number of devices can be helpful in this regard.

First, joint appointments of outstanding scholars can serve to link the business faculty to that of other departments, in cases where the intellectual interests of a senior man clearly cross departmental boundary lines. At UCLA we have had joint appointments with the departments of engineering, psychology, mathematics, and economics, and we are seeking them with sociology-anthropology. Sitting in two faculties, each joint appointee becomes a *de facto* representative of one to the other group, an interpreter of its aims and policies, a referrer of exceptional graduate students, and a generator of ideas for interdisciplinary research and teaching enterprise. Some of our best doctoral students, now serving in the business administration faculties of UCLA and other universities, have been the protégés of these joint appointees.

Second, the business school can initiate interdisciplinary seminars on generic topics within the field of management theory, attractive to researchers from many departments. For example, Prof. Jacob Marschak has operated an interdisciplinary colloquium on mathematics in the behavioral sciences on this campus, which has drawn participants from all the departments mentioned previously plus biomedicine, anatomy, psychiatry, education, linguistics, and a number of other organizations including RAND Corporation. Emphasis has been upon methodologies and concepts rather than substantive problems. To take another local example, an interdisciplinary seminar on comparative enterprise studies has been launched under the leadership of Prof. Frederic Myers of the business administration faculty, in which graduate students and faculty members from history, political science, economics, and other units concerned with foreign areas are engaged along with those from the Graduate School of Business Administration. Out of this undertaking it is expected that numerous doctoral research programs will emanate, some in the general field of management theory and policy.

Third, the business school can undertake to organize research institutes and centers which offer funds, computing facilities, and other research assistance to scholars *in any department* whose projects fall within the general area of management. Again drawing upon experience at UCLA, two such enterprises have been established within the Graduate School of Business Administration within recent years, primarily with the extramural financial assistance of foundations and business corporations. They are the Western Data Processing Center and the Western Management

Science Institute. WDPC conducts a research program of its own on computer methodologies; but it is primarily a laboratory offering computer services to faculties at UCLA and seventy Western universities and colleges, with emphasis on research projects in the area of management, but with no limits on subject matter within the time available. So far, the majority of projects using WDPC's facilities have been those of faculty members in departments other than business administration. WMSI was established in 1959 to encourage and facilitate research in management science at UCLA and other institutions of higher learning in the Western United States. Like WDPC, it is governed by a faculty committee representing many disciplines. Its active staff members and research grantees come from mathematics, engineering, psychology, economics, and other departments as well as business administration. Both WDPC and WMSI have greatly enlarged the academic constituency of management science on the UCLA campus.

I have cited these illustrations of research cooperation between the faculties of the business school and of other departments at UCLA only because I know them best, and not because we have attained an ideal situation on this campus. On the contrary, we have only begun to realize the potentialities that inhere in cooperative efforts. Through these devices, we in the business school have, at least, succeeded in convincing many colleagues around the campus that we are concerned with fundamental intellectual problems worthy of their own attention. No doubt members of this seminar are able to cite other and better illustrations on their own campuses.

Of course, what is needed above all on the university campus is an intellectual atmosphere and an administrative milieu which is conducive to new combinations of resources. There must be a willingness to experiment with new organizational plans. The relentless forward thrust of scientific knowledge has, by this time, impressed even conservative academic minds with this imperative. On the many campuses which contain such recent academic units as centers of African studies, institutes of planetary physics, and department of space medicine and radiation biology, surely it is reasonable to expect an attitude of receptivity to interdisciplinary organizations dealing with management theory and research.

FUNDS FOR MANAGEMENT RESEARCH

I shall give short shrift to the matter of enlarging financial support of research in management science, because of a conviction that money is not a serious impediment to progress in this field. Today any academic organization with qualified personnel and good researchable ideas can get the funds it needs without intolerable delay. Federal governmental agencies like the National Science Foundation, the research arms of the Department of Defense, and National Institutes of Health support much research on various aspects of management. The Ford Foundation has given a powerful impetus to scientifically oriented research in management, and other large philanthropic foundations like Carnegie and Rockefeller have begun to provide support to work in this field, along with a host of smaller ones. Some large business corporations have been willing to support fairly fundamental studies.

Apart from such extramural sources of support, most university budgets provide a limited amount of fluid research funds to support the researches of faculty members. Fluid funds fulfill a vital role in the financing of research. They provide a means of filling the interstices between large organized projects, of meeting the needs of the "lone wolf" type of scholar with an idea he wants to pursue by himself, but who has not attained sufficient eminence to get "public financing" on his own, or of quickly taking advantage of new research opportunities. Universities need far more of such fluid funds than they possess, and more of these funds should be devoted to research in management. It is to be hoped that public appreciation of the truly important values of improving management through research will soon result in supporting it on the scale that agricultural technology has long enjoyed. After all, it is absurd for American society today to spend more on research on peanuts than on urban affairs, which I am reliably informed is a fact. It is time that an overall assessment were made of the costs and prospective social returns from research in various fields. I am confident that the field of management would receive additional support as a result of any such inquiry.

D RESEARCH AND BUSINESS SCHOOLS: A DISCUSSION

Mr. Brown: I see this as part of the theme Professor Koontz started. I was very impressed when I heard Dean Jacoby say that after all research has an economic end in view. That is a true statement, I think. I would not have dared to say such a thing in this country because I think the ordinary view is that pure research has no economic end in view. I think it has.

I wonder whether the research that is done in the schools of business would not be better related to the real problems which exist in industry if more attention were given to the idea that all research has an economic end in view.

Soon after the war our Department of Scientific and Industrial Research, which does an enormous volume of research in Britain, sent out its young men to industry to ask the question: "Why do not you fellows use more of the valuable research that we do in the Department?" From many people the answer came back: "Because you do not do research on the problems that trouble us; you do research on problems which you assume to be important to us but which are often not so." I am worried that your business schools may have been misled over this matter of research. Our company was extremely fortunate because government money was forthcoming for research into what made a business tick and the institute that received this money asked us to work with them on a collaborative basis. A team from the Tavistock Institute lived with us for three years on the job.

When the three years were up, the leader of that research team joined us in a consulting capacity and has been with us for the last twelve years. The thing that has struck me throughout this research was that not only did this research worker and his team join us with a large range of quite unreal notions about our business and our problems, but it was soon demonstrated that we ourselves possessed a whole range of stereotyped and unreal notions of how we ran our business. Our descriptions of our methods, our organization, and our work were highly inaccurate. This situation was disclosed through the close association which grew up between the research team and hundreds of people in our company who allowed this sociologist to get insight into what they were really doing. The information which they gained, fed back to us in the form of generalized reports, disclosed to us that our perceptions about our own company were extremely faulty.

If this degree of unrealism on the part of managers who work for years inside a business can exist, then I wonder how far the perceptions of those who do research in the business schools about industrial problems are accurate? I know they visit firms as consultants and they often spend months at a time in business; but is it enough? I have often wondered whether there was a possibility for members of a university to become attached, with the agreement of people who work in firms, not for a few months but for years so that over this period there was a continual feedback of perception from inside the plant to those who were thinking about industrial and managerial problems inside a university.

Dean Jacoby: Please recall that I did not say that research should be undertaken only for economic ends. What I said is that it was possible to assign economic values to practically every kind of research activity that is undertaken. This may not be the motivating factor, of course, for the researcher.

Mr. Brown: As I have apparently misquoted Dean Jacoby, I will have to take the onus of supporting the point I made. Some time ago I had a discussion with a senior member of a very large American organization. This organization has many research laboratories and this executive was talking about their super "pure" research science laboratory where eminent scientists worked on "pure" research. I said that I did not believe that it was "pure" research.

The reply was: "I do not understand you. There are no bounds to the lines of research which those who work in this laboratory can follow, for their job is to acquire knowledge." I said: "Suppose one of these scientists, after spending some years working very hard, puts in a report on work he has done to add a new flavor to chewing gum?" He said: "Well, there are limits of course."

Having put one foot in, I may as well jump in with both feet and suggest to you that there is no such thing as "pure" research, even in a university. Research always costs money and involves the use of somebody's time and, this being so, somebody in authority wants to know, at some time or other, the usefulness of the way in which time or money is being spent. If that authority comes to the opinion that the work that is being done is related neither to the needs of the university nor to the needs of society itself, then I question whether that research will continue to receive approval. Is that not the experience of many people in this room? Has anybody here ever done completely untrammeled research in the sense that no approval from any other person or body is required and no criteria external to that person exists as to whether it should go ahead?

Professor McGuire: May I offer a definition of basic research? Basic research is research you see the reason for, but your boss does not.

Professor Wagner: Inevitably when academic scholars and business executives are convened, the question arises as to whether the researchers are providing solutions to real business problems.

In particular, businessmen frequently accuse academicians by saying, "Your theories do not take into account all the relevant complexities of real business situations." What are these complexities? Surely managing a factory, a marketing department, a finance department, etc., is a serious responsibility. But quite often the difficulties foremost in an executive's mind are of a transient nature, in that they involve volatile factors such as the individual personalities of the personnel that happen to be affected at some moment in time. In contrast, many of the truly fundamental factors that ought to underlie a rational decision process are given secondary consideration by executives. I suspect one reason for the latter phenomenon is that these factors, while immediately being recognized as highly significant to an efficient operation, are too difficult to analyze by conventional managerial methods. Such problems are universal in nature and are the proper province for study by business research scholars. I think these scholars are justified in saying to businessmen, "Your present methods of problem solving do not take into account all the fundamental relationships which govern the operation of your firm." In other words, businessmen themselves may be unrealistic about their solutions to real problems.

Mr. Osborn: In the Federal government, we support a very significant amount of research in management. This came to my mind rather vividly when Dean Jacoby said, "If you've got a good project and a good man, the money will come rather easily," and having some knowledge of the United States budget, I can understand that. You should also recognize that top management in government comes generally from the business world or the academic world. We operate schools in the government—many in management and others covering a wide spectrum of subjects. In many cases, your people teach in these schools, and in addition we send our people to your schools, so there is extensive interchange. Last, but not least, we are not afraid to innovate. In an agency like the National Aeronautics and Space Administration, innovation has to be the way of life.

It is clear to me that the same processes or the same influences that are bringing about better management in industry are also at work in government. I have come to the conclusion that the public image of the public servant is wrong, that the government is much better managed than most people are aware. I won't say that it's all good. In government, we are doing some very brilliant things and some not so brilliant, but the general level of operation is surprisingly high to most outside people who come and look. We have in government a mixture, of course, which also characterizes private industry and the academic world. I am personally biased, to be sure; but I would not hesitate to defend our own management operations against practices in industry and on the campus.

We have both big organizations and programs and little ones. I suppose we are more characterized by the large than the small. We have the biggest material handling company in the world. This is the United States Post Office. There is nothing that compares with it. It is full of opportunities for improved management and research, and that agency is making a valiant effort to realize them.

We have a very large union organization which might be of interest to those of you who are concerned with union problems.

We have the third largest life insurance company in the United States, and if anyone cares to debate the question of increased productivity, particularly the way the Veterans' Administration is handling life insurance policies, I would be glad to take you on.

What I am trying to say is this: The Federal government is a very large organization. To a considerable extent, we are faced with the same kind of management problems that have been discussed here at this conference. We are intensely interested in improving the management of the government, and we are aware that research is desirable to solve some of the problems in government just as it is in industry. We are conducting or sponsoring some research ourselves, particularly in the fields of work design, measurement, and decision making. However, it is manifest that it would help us if we could take advantage of the work that some of you are doing. To this end, we would be glad to exchange experiences and findings with you and to discuss progress in management research. If some of you in this room are particularly interested in conducting research in a governmental environment, we would be happy to discuss this with you, although I am sure that you can appreciate the fact that the circumstances under which we live have a tendency to limit such activity.

I am firmly convinced that during the last ten years we have seen the beginning of a complete revolution in the field of management. The things that I learned when I went to business school—I'm not going to say how long ago—these things have changed and are changing more rapidly every day.

We are trying to bring about this revolution in government just as you are doing in industry. Mr. Neuschel listed seven problem areas earlier. We are interested in research that may be undertaken in any of the areas he named.

In addition to the seven areas that were mentioned, I would like to mention one or two more. I don't quite know just how to describe this adequately, but one is the problem of underutilization. You people have talked about motivations and morale, but I am more concerned with productivity. If people produce, this is what we are interested in, and I am not sure there is always a direct relationship between morale and getting things done.

A friend of mine happened to have an opportunity to examine the results of a massive work-sampling effort in one of our large government agencies. There was a significant proportion of the time that people were not producing at their primary jobs. Some were not even at their primary workplace. Now, I hasten to add that I was so disturbed by this that I went to another friend of mine in one of your very prominent management consulting firms and talked to him about it. He said, "You are lucky. Our experience in industry shows that you are ahead of us. There's 10 per cent more time unused in industry than the figure you have given us." So I relaxed somewhat, but knowledge that we are all in the same boat does not solve the problem. I am interested in this problem, the President is interested in it, and the heads of government agencies and Congress are interested in it. We are working hard to find ways to do something about it and certainly more effective ways than the traditional ones.

In regard to the question of decision theory, I am interested in the decision process for several reasons: We operate more than 10 per cent of all the computers there are in the United States. I am not saying this to brag. I am just saying this as a fact. We have them. But I am saying with pride that we started this whole business. The first digital computer for business-type applications was developed to handle a government problem, and I wonder if the men who were responsible had an inkling of what they started.

Here is what I am worried about in decision making. I believe that the government has done quite well in using automatic data-processing equipment in the administrative and routine functions, e.g., payrolls, supply managing, and so on, and we have some rather outstanding examples of this. We are now getting more and more concerned with the use of this equipment to produce useful information for management and to assist it in problem analysis and decision making in nonroutine situations. This is the present thrust of our efforts. When you talk about data systems, most people immediately think of hardware. A salesman comes around, shows you the machine, and works up the proper forms, and there you are. Of course, we have gotten beyond this stage and are now teaching that before we even consider hardware, we must consider the system in which the machine is to be used. We are doing this quite well in most instances.

Beyond the data system itself, there is a lot of thought going into what data are actually required by the manager. We are not going to progress in this field properly until we can get some real answers on the question of what kinds of decisions managers at different levels and of different operations are called upon to make. When we get somewhere with that, we can start determining the kind of information we need to get those decisions properly made. We can then start designing systems to produce this information, and then we can get the hardware to do it. I have enough confidence in the people making this equipment that once we know what we need, they will produce the machines that will supply it for us.

The advances being made outside of government are tremendous. In government, the problems we are faced with, the activities we are called upon to manage, are growing in size, complexity, and importance, and affect us all. We must push the pace of change in management improvement if we are even to maintain the present gap between technological developments and management ability. I think we have pretty good management in the government, but we need to advance, and we will do our best to take advantage of the work that you people are doing whenever it is applicable.

Professor Haire: I cannot resist the temptation to tell the deans what research to do. There is one thing about the kind of research that I wanted to mention. Because there has been so much emphasis on behavioral science and the allied disciplines and even though I am a behavioral scientist, I feel very strongly the need for an emphasis on developmental research something midway between basic research and applied research.

I would not, if I were dean of a business school, urge my social scientists to do any more basic research. I do not mean that it should not be done, but a lot of people are going to do it without our urging them. I certainly would not urge them to do the applied fire fighting, pebble picking, kind of thing because nothing is going to grow out of that, but I think the thing we do not have is any meaningful applications from behavioral research at the basic level to practice.

A great many of us have either exhorted managers to do better, using social science concepts, or, in a kind of superior fashion, pointed out to other people that their theories were inadequate because they did not take into account the complexities that we knew about. When anyone says, "Yes, but how do we do better?" we grandly say, "Ah, but that's your business. That's not our business to do." It is just this: "How do we do better?" That, we don't know much about.

Professor Bach: There are two questions. I think I can answer both briefly. The first is that Professor Haire means by developmental research what I meant when I was talking about getting busy and building bridges and making things relevant from the behavioral sciences to management.

Second, there is a distinction between descriptive and normative propositions. We need to be a little clearer here. I was not describing; I was making a normative proposition of how deans ought to behave if, in fact, this is their set of goals. The answer is they do not so behave in most cases although in some cases they do.

I was making, I thought, a very simple and elementary managerial proposition that if deans or presidents are managers and if they say this kind of research is the most important kind or is a very important kind, it is then important for them to set up a reward system that will reward this even though by and large the academic structure does not reward it now. I do not think there is any secret about what the standard rewards are in the academic game. They are money and promotion, by and large, and such things as allocation of time.

If a dean says, "This is very important, it ought to be done," he had better face up to some consequences. If he can do it in his own shop, fine. If he cannot, he should see the president. You know, you manage people upward as well as downward; so I just say: face up to the consequences of good management.

E WHAT SHOULD THE UNIVERSITY BUSINESS SCHOOLS DO? A DISCUSSION

Professor Koontz: As I hear this presentation and others, I get the idea that if we study mathematical approaches or behavioral science approaches, this is going to give us the answer to business school education, to the problems of management, and to managerial motivation. Now, is this really enough? Don't we get a great deal of motivation of people by such basic approaches as defining a person's task, assigning his duties, delegating authority, exacting responsibility, and even from good control? In other words, are people not motivated by the setting up of an environment where they can perform—by a manager establishing those environmental factors where men can do a job?

I do not underestimate the importance of mathematics or behavioral sciences, but I get the impression we sometimes forget that some of the environmental factors are even more important. I am interested in Wilfred Brown's company and the Tavistock Institute type of research; and I believe, if I understand it correctly, that Brown came to such conclusions as this. When the deans and others here say that if we would just do this, this will solve our problems, are they just emphasizing it to make sure that we do do it or do they really think that this will solve our problems?

I wonder, too, as for Dean Jacoby's remarks about mathematics, whether or not everybody needs to be a highly proficient mathematician in order to understand the conceptualization of, say, an operational research type of problem. I doubt it. I think it is entirely possible to conceptualize a problem and then turn it over to a Ph.D. in mathematics to work out the intricacies of the model. I gather that even so competent a mathematician as Professor Schlaifer has done this in his attack on many decision theory problems.

President Wallis: I certainly never said now or on any other occasion that if we will just do this, it will solve all our problems; and I never heard Professor Bach say anything like that in all the time I have known him, and I have never heard Dean Jacoby say anything like that.

Professor Bach: I would suppose that no respectable dean of a business school would say we ought to stop business education until we get lots more research done so we know better what to teach. Some of the things Professor Koontz says sound awfully plausible about environmental factors, and I guess I agree with him. I'm not quite sure whether they are right or wrong, but for the time being we have got to teach people how to behave and we do the best we can. This is what I mean by managerial behavior. We teach them to be orderly problem solvers—we teach them a lot of things—but that is not to say for one moment that we need to be satisfied with this, that we are not kind of uncomfortable about it.

We ought to get on with the research job of being much surer about many of the propositions that we are making. This is Professor Roethlisberger's point, if I understood him, that we desperately need propositions that we feel comfortable about, that we feel reasonably sure about, even though in some sense they are not scientifically valid in the same sense that, say, one might find in the field of physics.

Professor Koontz: I agree with that.

Professor Dale: I'd like to support Professor Koontz, if I may. I think the deans must, after all, be quite a bit concerned with the acceptance of their products by industry quite apart from the improvement in the laboratory research which they are already doing very well and will continue to improve.

It would seem to me in the first place that the research goals of some of the people here represented are somewhat different from those of the industrialists who hire the people. They are, I fear, to some extent concerned with peer approval. In business one is not necessarily concerned with that; in fact, the most successful men do not have peer approval. These men may be disliked even, because they are causing a lot of trouble by being much more successful than others. In fact, by not conducting himself in terms of peer approval in business, a manager is often likely to make a more substantial contribution to the profit goal.

Also, I would like to ask: If some of the people here say that the only thing that counts is what is publicly tested, then doesn't business also have a public test (which I grant you may be less satisfactory sometimes than yours)? The financial statements over a period of years, especially on a comparative basis—the best and the worst—are a test of sorts.

The second point that I would like to question is this: It seems to me there was somewhat of a tendency—maybe I have been oversensitive on this—to think that all or most of the contributions, the real contributions, in management research came from the professors and not from the practitioners. To examine this allegation perhaps we have a better analogy than medicine, namely, the field of economics. Are there not some very outstanding men of experience who have made some outstanding theoretical contributions? For example, Von Thunen was a famous German farmer who developed the theory of marginal productivity and the theory of location without ever having any university connection at all. John Stuart Mill spent all his life in the India office. I remember John Maynard Keynes, under whom I studied, told me that some of his developments in the theory of interest actually came from his experience in the India office and as a member of the British Treasury over many years. He always emphasized this playback between experience and the academic and spoke very highly frequently not only of the hypotheses of businessmen but also of the fact that they do test them out.

Now, you can say it's not properly tested. But you must go beyond the solitary managerial mouse (or group of mice) in the laboratory. Someone like Donaldson Brown has. He independently developed marginal pricing analysis, standard volume analysis, gross national product analysis, multiple break-even analysis, much before academics were ever thinking, much less testing.

These were tested in the sense that General Motors was copied by Ford, and General Electric, and other companies. I grant you it may not have been done as scientifically and in as well controlled a way as you would wish. But when you consider that Professor Roethlisberger had to take many years to come up with his very interesting conclusions with a great deal of financial support and a great many associates, you realize that a hypothesis is not easily tested successfully, I would say, even in the academic world. Therefore, I think you should not be quite as impatient as some of you are with the businessmen. They appear to be more patient with you.

In political science, too, if you take that analogy, some of the great theoreticians have been great practitioners like Machiavelli or Harold Laski, whatever you may think about their philosophies.

My third point is to question to some extent the universality by which some of you think a management student is accepted in business. Now, mind you, you can argue it is no concern to us how he is accepted. I recall that the authors of recent investigations into business education found that the business school product, intellectually speaking, was slightly above that of home economics and physical education. Business schools claim to have made tremendous progress, but I do think this has to be proved. As far as I can see it, the business school student—and I have been teaching for twenty years myself—certainly adds quite a bit, but it may be no more than a marginal addition that he makes.

A man's knowledge of management is only a relatively small part of what he is judged by in a business enterprise. That is no criticism of the schools or the business enterprise, but we have to accept a stubborn fact here that there are many other things that the business school student has to learn to become a successful practicing manager. Some of it he can learn from the analysis of best experience. He sometimes gets the wrong impression that if he has been so highly educated by such outstanding scientists as are represented here that he doesn't have to add much more because he has the intellectual apparatus. This gives a sense of false pride and assurance to these students—as well as an inability to carry out successfully the tasks assigned to them.

What he has got to know also is what he is managing. Hence I would finally like to propose to the group the following: Let us compare for the moment the performance of the so-called new managers with that of the old managers. I have not come here to say let's go back to Alfred Sloan and educate lots of Sloans. This is, of course, not possible. That's why I am in consonance with this group in its attempt to develop a new type of manager, and I agree that many adaptations have to be made, particularly toward the scientific field. But if we look at the performance of the old colorful managers with their encyclopedic knowledge—mind you, they did go to M.I.T. after all—Pierre and Irénée du Pont and Alfred Sloan—they were scientists and some of them rather good scientists. They did have, it seems to me, a grand intellectual equipment which enabled them to develop some of these techniques as well as the theories or hypotheses that some of you think are so inadequate, without, however, explaining specifically why. Maybe they are not the best possible, but they are perhaps the best that it has been possible to develop so far.

I would like to say in conclusion that I admire much of what the behavioralists and mathematicians have done. It's excellent work, but please let us consider that, when we sell this as our educational product, it is only obviously a part of what is needed. Another part still has to arise from experience or by analysis of experience gained by some of the older faculty members in these business schools, who have, I think, made a real contribution. What I am pleading for is perhaps a better sense of balance between the old and the new.

Mr. Brown: I listened to a lecture a little over a year ago by Professor Jones of Aberdeen University. He is professor of moral philosophy. I did ask him why he continued to call it that, and he said if he did not continue to call his department moral philosophy, somebody else might choose to set up such a department, and he thought that wouldn't be a very good thing for the university. Anyhow this was, I thought, a brilliant lecture. He went through a good deal of the history of scientific endeavor and what he opened my eyes to—and you are probably much more familiar with that than I am—was the fact that a very large proportion of the real contributions to the science—the study of our physical world—had been made by people who had very practical and immediate ends in view. I can't remember all the people he recited—dozens of them, one after the other. I remember just two. He referred to Newton as being an officer of the Royal Ordnance Factories who was concerned about the study of the flight of cannon balls, and I also remember a reference to James Watt, who was rejected by Glasgow University as a young man. As I say, there were many others.

Now, Jones also drew attention to the fact that in a great society theorizing was the work of free men and very intelligent free men, but experimentation was the work of slaves. And if, broadly speaking, the data did not fit the theory, they discarded the theory rather than the reverse. At times I feel like a Greek slave in an assembly like this; because, frankly, gentlemen, I have not been able to follow much of what's been said in the discussions.

Professor Goetz: I have two things in mind. First, I think there is a great deal of interplay between the field and the faculty and that almost all—this may be an overstatement—but a great many professors in schools of business do do a great deal of consulting work with businesses in problems chosen by the businesses. A great many of our schools of business now have executive development programs where students who are saturated with business problems come to us for as much as twelve months at a time; so there is a great deal of this interplay, and I am not prepared at all to buy Professor Dale's plea that the businesses do not want our products. It seems to me they are snatching them from us at prices that threaten our whole junior staff. I suspect that businesses are buying our products and perhaps buying them with more enthusiasm than is warranted.

Dr. Shubik: The thing I found a little disturbing in Professor Dale's discussion was that he used the phrase "when you sell your product." Now, as far as I am concerned, there is a great question as to whom the business school is meant to be selling its product, whom we have to justify ourselves to, and what the particular rules of the game are. I don't particularly think that it is the job of the current business school to be patted on the head by every president of industry around today. For that matter, I even think it's not necessary that this should be the eventual goal. Consequently, when this question as to what the burning problems of industry are and what the right things business schools should be looking at are, I think that it is very healthy and very meaningful to have heavy interaction between the schools and the people running business. But I think it is absolutely foolish to expect that the value system and the goals and the selection of things to work on in the business schools should be strictly derived from what Mr. duPont or anybody else happens to have to say about it.

Dean Jacoby: I would like to offer a comment on one of Professor Dale's earlier several dozen excellent ideas. I interpreted him to mean that there was a tendency to disregard the value of analyzing business experience, the facts about business, and I certainly would not myself want to deemphasize that. In fact, it appears to me that the business schools have not yet developed an analogy to the medical schools' clinical research.

Now, this is purely empirical. This is not conducting experiments under controlled environments, but, let's say, finding that somebody breaks out in purple spots at midnight and analyzing a hundred cases. They associate with this temperature, blood pressure, body inputs and outputs, and various other factors; and they discover in the end that this was caused by drinking a glass of cointreau at 6:00 P.M. so they have a valuable, a useful result. This is the empirical approach.

I think you will agree that, while we have collected a certain number of cases, so-called business policy cases, we have not subjected them to the careful painstaking analysis that the medical practitioner with his clinical research has exercised. Therefore, I believe that one kind of activity, research activity, that the business school should be concerned with is this clinical research.

Professor Simon: I'd like to add my voice to that of Professor Koontz for balance, if we are to advance knowledge in the field of business as we all hope. Perhaps the conclusions I would draw from this view of balance, however, would be a little different from those Professor Koontz would draw.

Historically, and until the very recent past, business school faculties have consisted largely of people closely acquainted with the practice of business. The things that we have taught in the classroom, until very recent times, have been primarily descriptive of current or not too long obsolescent practice in the field of business. It is clear that if this field is to arrive at the same kind of status as a field of application of knowledge that engineering is reaching, and that medicine is reaching, we are going to have to balance such description with another kind of activity, the kind of activity that we have been talking about.

I think it cannot be a matter of serious worry or concern that all members of business school faculties be overeducated in mathematics or even be educated at all in mathematics or in any other particular subject that we mention. The number of business schools in this country today which have on their faculties any sizable number of people who are capable of contributing to the very important work going forward on the quantitative side or on the behavioral science side of research is still miniscule, and the important job of balancing that still remains to be done is the job that I thought I heard our three deans describing a little earlier. It is the job of bringing more of our business school faculties and more men on these faculties into this activity of pushing forward the frontiers of knowledge, not in an academic, or ivory tower, way. I don't see these new faculties being particularly more remote from the business scene than people who are interested in the description of institutions, nor do I see the great gulf that has been described between, on the one hand, studies of behavior and what was called the environment of behavior. Most of the environment of human behavior is the behavior of human beings, and part of what we are talking about is certainly not only research on the behavior of the foremen but also research on the behavior of the customers, and research on the collective behavior of human beings in those particular institutions we call organizations.

It is this enterprise, it seems to me, that we are talking about. If we are to succeed in the enterprise and push it forward at the pace that is needed to work with business and government in the revolution that's taking place, we are going to have to push this balance on the side of the fundamental disciplines much farther than it has been pushed. And we are going to have to do it rapidly.

Professor Albers: I would like to say two things. One is the assumption that we make that business education ends with a bachelor's degree or something like that. It continues in the business organization itself, and this is simply an aspect of education. In other words, after three or four years in the business firm, executives come back to Harvard and/or other institutions.

Also we are talking about the basic areas. Should we simply eliminate the business school altogether and have a college of liberal arts in which we train business leaders? We are talking about the business school, and yet we virtually eliminate the business school. Why do we bother with this? What is there unique about the business school?

Professor Bach: Wait a minute. Somebody ought to say something in response to you.

I didn't think I was saying we ought to eliminate the business school at all. On the contrary, it seems to me that the business school has a function of focusing on the development of what I was calling managerial behavior. It is in a real sense a professional school in the sense of being a problem-solving-oriented organization. In that sense, its function is indeed to pull together, to make useful in a managerial problem-solving way the contributions of all these things we have been talking about. Just having sociologists and psychologists cluttered around the university does not meet the goals of a business school.

VI MANAGEMENT THEORY AND RESEARCH: SOME CONCLUSIONS

Harold Koontz

The approach of this seminar was somewhat influenced by my concern that the development of management theory and research was going off in many directions, with confusion, inter-school rivalries, and wasted research efforts. Having expressed distress at the development of what seemed the husky beginnings of a "management theory jungle," and having had the rare privilege of chairing a meeting on this basic subject with outstanding scholars and practitioners in the field, it is natural that my conclusions should be materially influenced by how I perceived order developing from these meetings.

It is true that I feel a sense of urgency about the field of management theory and research. There seems to be no field where practice needs more the underpinnings of research and theory and where the payoff in terms of group productivity could be greater. I have seen the traditionalists, or universalists—often called the classicists—fending off the newer approaches of human relations and mathematics. I have noted behavioralists apparently feeling that they encompassed the entire field of management when they studied interpersonal relations. I have found many mathematicians who seemed to see management as a series of mathematical equations. Others have appeared to "discover" management systems without realizing that any assemblage of connected objects or relationships is a system. Still others have tended to look at management through the keyhole of decision making which had seemed to me only to be a part of the total managerial job.

In the middle of all this, I found the perceptive and intelligent manager wondering what all this meant, whether any or all of the findings and theory applied to him, whether he would be old-fashioned if he defined and structured tasks and delegated authority, whether he should even use the term "authority," whether his job would disappear and he would be made obsolete by mathematical programming, or whether his role as manager should be primarily one of a congenial superchairman of a permissively oriented group of sensitivity-trained prima donnas.

It appeared that there must be some way to use the contributions of many underlying disciplines, as well as the distilled clinical experience of managers themselves, toward the development of a discipline of management. It likewise seemed that a management discipline, while drawing on other disciplines, would surely have an independent and separable core of theory. While the development of a reliable discipline might be decades or centuries away, it was believed that a useful start had been made and could now be accelerated by drawing together the thinking of a representative group of scholars and practitioners in the field.

In drawing conclusions, one should consider the seminar objectives. One goal was to get those studying the field of management to understand and appreciate, with or without agreeing, what each is trying to do. Another goal was to get a better perspective on how the various approaches to the study of management might fit. And a third objective was to recognize the extent to which the differences were more apparent than real, and based upon such matters as semantics, concepts, and approaches, rather than on essentials. It was hoped in these ways to get a better idea of what is meant by management as a field of knowledge, to clarify some of the language of management, to see how the various approaches and tools might be integrated, and to carve out the beginnings of a useful general theory of management.

MANAGEMENT THEORY: "JUNGLE" OR ORDERLY ROWS OF TREES?

Some difference of opinion existed as to whether the present development of management theory represented a jungle, with confusion and entanglements of language and findings, or whether it represented a system of orderly rows of trees. Professor Simon made persuasively the point that there must be division of labor in any elaborate undertaking and that this is eminently true even in such "mature" sciences as physics. He found this particularly true in the field of management where some scholars make their contribution through analysis of events, others through controlled experiments, others through use of theoretical approaches, others by employing the tools of mathematics, and still others through concentrating on substantive or functional matters. Among the latter are those who study human relationships, leadership, decision making, and the functional process of managing.

As Professor Simon appropriately pointed out, scholars with these various approaches should think of themselves as cooperating participants in the same enterprise, not as representatives of competing and contradictory approaches or schools. Moreover, these various approaches and approachers must expect synthesis of their work only when theory is relevant to empirical observation and observation relevant to theory.

I suspect that no one would argue the desirability of Professor Simon's well-made point. But it still leaves open several questions. Are there semantic differences, or differences that grow

out of academic preparation, which make it difficult for people
to understand each other or even misunderstand? Are these differences important to those who study, as well as those who
practice, management? Can we, or must we, wait for research
and theory to grow in different ways and along different paths,
or should we make at least an embryonic start toward a useful
theory now? Can there be considerable integration of knowledge
now? What implications does this have for management teaching,
research, and practice?

Evidence of Differences. Throughout the seminar there was
substantial evidence of differences. Many of them stemmed from
semantics. Some seemed to arise from the definition of the body
of knowledge being discussed. Some unquestionably came from
the disciplinary background of various scholars. Undoubtedly
these differences were related. For example, those with a psychological background or interest tended to see organization as a
system of human relationships. Those with a management practice
orientation tended to see it as a formally structured system of
task assignments and authority delegations. Likewise, those with
an economics or mathematics background tended to see the manager's job as one of decision making; when pressed on the point,
they readily agreed that this concept included not only the matter
of rational choice between alternatives, but the study and analysis
of action and thought preceding such choice as well as the entire
process of decision implementation. Seen in this light, of course,
decision making is as broad as the role perceived by those who
approach the study of management as a process involving planning (in which function decision making is normally placed),
organizing, staffing, directing, and controlling.

Semantic Differences. Semantic confusion was evident
throughout the discussions. The discussion of what is meant by
decision making, the different understandings of managerial
behavior—in some cases to denote the entire role and performance of the manager and in others to denote merely *his* appreciation of the sociopsychological attitudes of his subordinates
—and the differences in using the word "management" itself,
are specific evidences of this. Other evidence was the difficulty of
the scholarly practitioners present, particularly in the group discussions, to comprehend easily the meaning of many terms used

by the academics. In fact, one head of a major company who has done and supervised meaningful research in management in his company for a number of years made the strong statement that much of what had been said by many members present was almost incomprehensible to him because he did not know how they were defining their terms.

As Professor Tannenbaum emphasized in his summary of the small group discussions, the participants in the seminars had real difficulty in understanding each other. The recorders for these meetings reported that terminological difficulties extended between scholars in the various schools or approaches, between scientists and scientists, and between academicians and practitioners.

This has seemed to be the major problem. Professor Jackson aptly put it in this way: "The problem in the semantic jungle is not that people use words in different ways but they don't bother to define the way they are using them." As Wilfred Brown pointed out, the science of electricity only developed to where it is when people in the field proceeded from simple definitions of erg and dyne and joule to more complex definitions of such things as volt, amp, and ohm, and from there to far more complex concepts. Without definitions clearly stated and understood, the science of electricity could not have arrived where it is.

In other words, the problem facing those who would build up a meaningful theory of management and who would be able to communicate the findings provided by the widespread division of labor now being undertaken is indeed partially semantic. This does not mean that management scholars should not develop a special vocabulary, if necessary, to sharpen concepts in management theory and science and make them more sophisticated, although even here there is some question of how much special jargon is necessary. But what is important is that terms are defined and understood. It would be ideal if the definition of common terms such as "organization," "management," "decision making," "manager," "planning," and "leading" could be made sharp and clear; indeed it is my opinion that this ideal should be more aggressively sought. But even if the ideal cannot be attained, *at the very least,* scholars and researchers have an obligation to define their terms and to recognize that they may be using a given word in a different way than someone else. Surely this much of the jungle can be removed.

Differences in Definition of Management as a Body of Knowledge. As has already been noted, there were differences in the definition of management as a body of knowledge. But these differences were often more apparent than real. Virtually all discussions, when they proceeded far enough, did seem to come down to the fact that managing is actually the task of establishing an environment where people can perform effectively in a formalized group, that is, in a group where tasks are fairly specific and clear (although not necessarily spelled out in such detail or specialized so much as to overlook the motivation involved in job enlargement). Some persons saw this entire process as decision making, others as a management process, and still others as the area of managerial behavior; but it worked out that all were talking essentially about the same job.

What did come forth in bold relief in the seminar was that the different "approaches" to management were not really different "schools" of management, but rather a kind of intellectual division of labor in studying the problem of managing. In other words, the human behavior approach is really a means of studying a portion of the managerial environment—an important one that was admittedly long overlooked. Likewise, operations research and other primarily mathematically oriented approaches, and even normative decision theory, were regarded as means of *contributing* to the study and practice of management, rather than a separate "science" of management. Indeed, this general realization may have been one of the most significant contributions of the seminar to the understanding of those present.

Synthesis versus Intellectual Free Enterprise. One of the most striking phenomena of the seminar was the widespread belief of the academic representatives that an attempt to synthesize findings and approaches might rob the scholar and researcher of some of his right to be, as one put it, "an intellectual free enterpriser." There seemed to be a fear that any attempt to develop a general theory of management now, or at least approach it in even a crude preliminary way, might stifle originality of intellectual approach. There was also the feeling that scholars should content themselves with "taking small bites," researching special areas, embarking on new ideas and approaches, and testing new hypotheses, while not worrying about putting this together in something approaching a general theory of management.

The patience of the academics in approaching the development of theory cautiously and piecemeal was in sharp contrast to the desires of those in the practice of management. Practitioners universally saw the need for immediate synthesis of research and theory, even though crude, so that it could be used to improve understanding and the practice of management.

These two striking differences are understandable. The researcher likes to deal with small pieces of a problem. They are more manageable, they can be more easily tested, the research can be more impregnable to criticism from academic colleagues, and often better research grants can be obtained from the various foundations. Moreover, many of the researchers in the field of management have come from disciplines other than management —economics, sociology, psychology, mathematics, and others— and they feel more comfortable in dealing with a bite-sized piece of research in their specialized field.

Likewise, one can understand the desire of practitioners. By their very role managers are results-oriented. They know that these results are difficult to get. They are aware that managing is a complex task. They realize also that, in these days of super-competitive rivalry for resources and results, they will be judged by comparison with others. Managers, therefore, are understandably anxious, particularly if they are alert and perceptive, to use *now* what scientific underpinnings are available for their job.

Unquestionably these diverse interests and needs must be and can be reconciled. Those responsible for practice cannot wait until research and theoretical exploration have made the theory sure and mature. There is enough that can be accomplished by using the theory now available, even though some of it is perhaps little more than hypotheses. But some of it has been perceptively distilled from experience, and some has been reasonably well (even though often somewhat crudely) derived from careful investigation and verification. At least some theory and knowledge can be made available to managers in an intelligible and synthesized form. And while doing this, those who would go on their free unsynthesized way can do so, contributing by bits and pieces to the science of management.

TOWARD A USEFUL MANAGEMENT THEORY

At various points in the seminar and, indeed, often in the discussion of management, the question was raised as to why anyone should worry about a theory of management. Some questions took the form of: What are the objectives of a theory, or what, after all is a theory? Even granting that these questions can be answered, the major query still exists: Is there a chance to develop now, or create the beginnings of, a useful theory of management?

The Nature of Theory. Theory is essentially a body of propositions, or principles (in mathematics, "theorems"), which are offered to explain phenomena and, by doing so, give a clear and systematic view of a subject. It is perfectly true that such principles tend to be interrelated because they are offered as explanations of the same subject matter area. It is true, likewise, that such principles are usually regarded as truths of a fundamental nature, basic to the understanding of a subject, and having a predictive value. In other words, even though a statement of a relationship—a proposition—may not be a law in the usual sense, it must be capable of reasonable proof which will explain the relationship in a set of facts wherever the same subject matter is encountered or the same phenomena exist. Theory and principles are simply an expression of belief in the fundamental rationality of nature, a belief that phenomena have a cause and by careful study, analysis, testing, and verification the scientist can observe the system underlying observed facts.

A theory is thus a way of organizing knowledge and experience. As Prof. Fritz Roethlisberger pointed out in his paper, scientific investigation begins and ends with theory. The scientist must develop a conceptual scheme as the result of his analysis of what happens in a subject matter area, establish hypotheses, and then investigate the validity of these hypotheses in the light of reality. As a result, many of the propositions of an original theory, or conceptual scheme, are changed, so that the theory which the scientist later develops is usually different from that with which he starts. This has so concerned many persons, such as Professor Roethlisberger, that they prefer to call the original approach a conceptual scheme rather than a theory.

This care in making clear that a theory is not "final" is admirable and accurate. Certainly, where the conceptual scheme includes classifications and propositions that have really met no tests for validity and are little more than intelligent guesses of what a person believes relationships to be, it is probably best that such untried classifications and hypotheses should not be dignified with the term "theory." On the other hand, if one did not refer to explanations of phenomena as theory until they were absolutely and incontrovertibly proved, one might ask the question whether there would be very much theory in any of the social or biological sciences, or, for that matter, in much of the physical sciences. The study of the history of any science has shown that there have been many time-honored principles which have been wholly or partly disproved as the result of later investigation and knowledge. In fact, it is often said that all principles are essentially hypotheses for further study and verification.

Thus, it still seems useful to regard a theory as a body of interrelated principles which give a systematic view of a subject area. If so regarded, and particularly if the principles have plausibility and usefulness for predicting causal relationships, the very fact that such propositions are not proved beyond a shadow of doubt seems to make them proper tools of the art. As Barnard pointed out some years ago:

It is the function of the arts to accomplish concrete ends, effect results, produce situations, that would not come about without the deliberate efforts to secure them. . . . The function of the sciences, on the other hand, is to explain the phenomena, the events, the situations, of the past. Their aim is not to produce specific events, effects, or situations but explanations which we call knowledge. It has not been the aim of science to be a system of technology; and it could not be such a system.[1]

[1] Chester I. Barnard, *The Functions of the Executive,* Harvard University Press, Cambridge, Mass., 1938, pp. 290–291.

Likewise, there is merit in the aim of theory to furnish a scheme of principles by which knowledge can be properly classified and summarized in a distilled form.

If one looks at theory in this way, he sees its usefulness in organizing the body of knowledge we call management. Likewise, we should recognize that managing is an art, like surgery, engineering, accounting, or baseball. But it is an art which should be vastly approved if there can be developed some scientific knowledge to underlie the practice. Yet it is an art, like other arts, which involves the *design* of workable techniques made on the basis of knowledge, but with the necessities for compromise in the light of realities, conflicts, and uncertainties in mind. Moreover, in management, as elsewhere, there would appear to be nothing unusual in regarding all propositions, or principles, as challenging hypotheses for further study.

Normative and Descriptive Theory. Several discussions in the seminar emphasized the usefulness of distinguishing between normative and descriptive theory. Descriptive theory involves the description of relationships in a situation. It merely states that when A occurs in a given environment, B will follow. It has no intent of saying what "ought" to be done in the light of seeking a given goal. Normative theory, on the other hand, implies a goal, and attempts to express a causal relationship by which it can be reached. Thus, as Professor Schlaifer emphasized in connection with decision theory, the system of propositions which comprise normative decision theory (in the narrow sense) proceed under the assumption that the decision maker is attempting to select the best rational choice from among alternatives.

Although it is well to recognize whether a theory is descriptive or normative, the distinction is primarily one on emphasis on desired ends or goals. It is with this in mind that Professor Simon likened normative theory to a theory of engineering or medicine, and descriptive to a theory of physics or psychology. While this simile is helpful in understanding the difference, one should not thereby confuse normative *theory* with the *art* of engineering or medicine.

The Need for Theory. Doubts were expressed by some members of the seminar as to whether it was wise, or even necessary, to develop a theory of management at the present time. But, for the majority, there seemed to be no real doubt that theories relating to managing *should* be developed in time. There seemed to be a tacit recognition of Talcott Parsons' statement which places the need for theory in the correct perspective:

It is scarcely too much to say that the most important index of a science is the state of its systematic theory. This includes the kinds and degrees of logical integration of the different elements which make it up, and the ways in which it is actually used in empirical research.[2]

At the same time, as Professor Tannenbaum pointed out in his summary of group meetings, there seemed to be a lack of appreciation of the nature and purpose of management theory. As he said,

We continually kept wondering about the nature of management theory. What are we striving for here? What do we really want to achieve by a theory of management or by a science of management? Perhaps if we could be more clear on our objectives, the answers to these and many other related questions would fall more readily into place.[3]

As was indicated by the attitudes and impatience of the practicing managers present, this apparent lack of concern or lack of a sense of urgency by the academics was a difficult thing to comprehend. As Richard Neuschel indicated so forcefully, not only is useful and applicable management theory in such short supply, but the practicing manager cannot reject theory because "he really has nowhere else to turn." The manager, like the artist in any field, knows that he can improve his art by knowledge of science. And this means knowledge and appreciation of theory.

It has been my primary objective, in doing what I can to see that some theory of management—albeit crude and often inadequately verified—is developed, to make available a systematic body of knowledge that can be used to improve the art of management. Certainly no one can believe that such guidance for those responsible for establishing an environment for effective enterprise performance is not sorely needed.

The first objective of management theory, then, should be to

[2] *Essays in Sociological Theory, Pure and Applied,* The Free Press of Glencoe, New York, 1949, p. 17.

[3] See pp. 91–92.

help improve the practice of management. To do this does not require a very sophisticated theory. Despite the general excellence of management in the United States, it is my opinion, based on hundreds of clinical situations, that many of the errors of managers, even some of the more intelligent managers, rest on the level of "cloud one" science or theory. For example, it is still true that many of the problems of management in practice rest upon such simple matters as understanding (and performing) delegation of authority by results expected, understanding the importance of clarifying delegations and line and staff relationships, establishing and communicating clear and meaningful goals and planning premises, designing control techniques carefully related to plans, and understanding and applying a concept of efficiency to the entire enterprise rather than to overspecialized parts and jobs.

There are many areas within the scope of management where knowledge is available, where systematic theory is developed, and where it can be communicated. Moreover, as the behavioralists come forward with such useful findings as the importance of job enlargement, as the mathematicians emphasize the importance of system relationships and their application to management, as sociologically oriented researchers come up with findings as to the impact of culture on groups, and as many other research results are fed into knowledge, there becomes increasingly evident a need for a mechanism to relate these new vistas of knowledge to the practicing manager's job.

It is exactly this relating of discoveries in various fields to the task of managing that a general theory of management can serve. The practicing manager is understandably confused and often misled by being fed findings in a specialized field. For example, the disillusionment in many quarters over "human relations," "management by mathematics," and "group dynamics," to mention only a few, happened largely because findings in these areas were presented, perhaps unwittingly, as panaceas and were grasped too indiscriminately by the frustrated manager facing his many immensely complex problems. If their new discoveries had been presented as contributions to *a portion* of the manager's job and not allowed to be seen out of perspective, their new insights might have resulted in a more effective total quality and operation of management. Thus, a conceptual scheme, or a general theory, of management can be useful in hanging new theory and discoveries in an orderly way on the tree of managerial knowledge where their true import can be comprehended, and their usefulness in practice optimized. For example, instead of the manager of a decade ago feeling that he was outmoded unless he operated as a permissive chairman of a committee of self-expressing employees so that he could practice awareness of people, he might instead have realized that the important discoveries of human motivations and cultural impacts would only modify his organization, staffing, and directing practices, rather than supplant his major task of managing.

A similar objective of a theory of management is to give an eclectic "home" to the orientation and findings of those specialized researchers and scholars who do not pretend to study the total managerial job. Thus, if somehow those interested in the field of management could agree upon such basic things as terminology and concept and what the field of management is, it would be possible to draw upon the pertinent findings of all the so-called "schools" of management and place the contributions of the increasing number of investigators and scholars of management into a meaningful and useful framework of management understanding.

Still another goal of a general scheme or theory of management would be to pinpoint areas in this field which need special research and understanding. By so doing, the available research efforts and talents would be better oriented and, therefore, more productive.

Likewise, a general theory of management would be helpful in training of managers. As it often is now, many managers properly ask the question as to how they can train and develop managers when no one knows what management is! A conceptual framework of the manager's task, whether based on the functions of managers, as I have found it useful to do, or on some other approach, can be used as a method by which content and meaning is given to the managerial job. It can act as a kind of pilot's "checklist" by which the manager's task can be spelled out, through which the best discoveries and knowledge of management can be transmitted, and by means of which management as a scientifically based art can be taught. With the fact that the science of management is moving very fast, and there is as great a danger of managerial obsolescence by practitioners in this field as in any other, the training needs for management theory are certainly great.

With such objectives as those outlined above, certainly no one can deny the urgency and importance of getting on with the task of developing at least the outlines of a useful theory of management. As a matter of fact, in this day when discoveries of knowledge are piling up mountainously in every area of scientific endeavor, there is immediate need for the distillation and compression of knowledge. No practitioner can be expected to read every report or essay which might include information useful to him in improving his practice. Indeed, even those whose task it is to keep abreast of their field of learning—the academics—find it difficult to do this. But certainly if the compression and transmission of knowledge is to take place at all, and the degree to which it will, depends on the effort and division of labor of those scholars who would undertake this task. But this, in turn, cannot be well done without an outline of a general theory of management.

Bridging the Gap—an Eclectic Approach. The answer to bridging the gap between the variety of approaches and approachers to the area of management study and the needs of management practice seems to lie in a combination of a conceptual scheme of management with an eclectic summation of pertinent knowledge from underlying disciplines. Note that this does not make of management a purely eclectic science but rather one with a central discipline of its own, buttressed and expanded by drawing from many other disciplines.

I believe that it can be made to operate this way: One can first define management as the establishment of an environment in which people can effectively perform in a formalized group for the attainment of group goals. Second, one can say that it is the task of the manager to do those things which establish such an environment for performance. The third step in developing the conceptual framework is to divide the activities that managers do (as *managers*, and not as salesmen, financiers, engineers, etc.) into a number of functions. I have found it useful to speak of these functions as planning (the choosing of goals, policies, procedures, and programs from among available alternatives), organizing (the grouping of things to be done and the establishment of necessary authority relationships to assure results and coordination of effort), staffing (the appraisal, selection, and training of people—the manning of the organization), direction (the guidance, overseeing, and leading of people), and control (the measurement and correction of activities to make sure that plans are being accomplished). Within the scope of these functions as briefly outlined, it is my opinion that any of the so-called schools, or approaches, to management can be fitted in. Moreover, I have found that this framework is intelligible to the perceptive practitioners, many of whom see their jobs pretty much in this context.

Such a framework is at the same time eclectic and operational. It is eclectic in that the underlying disciplines and the new discoveries of knowledge in the field of management can be classified and understood in the context of the total managerial job. It is operational in that it works in an environment of reality; it places compressed and classified knowledge in the framework of practice where the practitioner can understand the contributions made. For example, the use of systematic mathematical approaches involved in operations research clearly falls within the function of planning and even more particularly in the subfunction of decision making—rational choice. The contributions of psychology can be placed in the area of organization, if it has to do with task definition (e.g., job enlargement), or staffing if it has to do with building into the job itself inducements to perform, or direction if it has to do with leadership. Likewise, the feedback principles of cybernetics are useful to understanding the design of management control techniques and approaches.

If this is true, as I believe it to be, then it is a major responsibility of those who look upon management as an operational process, such as the management process school, or the universalists, or others with similar broad approaches, to be aware of the contributions of the other schools of management thought and the various disciplines underlying management. And to be more than aware. In addition, these scholars, whose task it must be to bridge the gap, must discriminately select those items of new knowledge which have meaning in the understanding of management and place them in their proper niche and perspective.

The Problem of Intellectual Free Enterprise. One of the interesting fears expressed in the seminar when the quest for a general theory of management was discussed was that this would introduce rigidity into management research and practice. As one scholar put it, any attempt to synthesize the area of management would tend to destroy free enterprise in matters of the intellect. As another scholar implied, instead of worrying about becoming intellectual collectivists, we should glory in our diversity.

These are understandable concerns. But, as I see it, they are not realistic fears. In the first place, by recognizing the existence of a generally accepted area of management and agreeing on some basic management terminology, there is no need to be concerned that this will stifle individual research, creativity, or ideas. All it would do is to make it easier for people to communicate meaningfully. Certainly none of these scholars who are so worried about freedom of thought and diversity of opinion and approach would claim that holding a conference and communicating in a common language, say, English, stifles freedom to think differently. Even William Whyte, who pleads so strongly for more nonconformity in his classic *The Organization Man*, would hardly feel that we are incorrigible conformists because we use the same language when we speak to each other.

There is no implication in the development of a framework of management theory understandable to all that *ideas* or *knowledge* will be stultified or placed in ironclad containers. Certainly, at present, I cannot see any development which is of primary concern and use to the manager which cannot be placed in the kind of framework I have outlined. Nor do I see how any new discoveries need be limited. If they are, then this is proof that the original conceptual scheme was inadequate and should be changed. This is not to say that *all* knowledge can be placed in this framework, at least without reaching far beyond the peripheries of the concept of management, any more than all knowledge can be embraced within the area of what is generally known as psychology or physics. As I emphasized in my earlier article, one of the criteria by which theory should develop is to carve out an area of knowledge that is "manageable" and to recognize that not all knowledge can be, or should be, incorporated into the framework of any field.

RESEARCH, TEACHING, AND THE BUSINESS SCHOOL

The role of the university in our society is to search for truth, to make it meaningful, and to communicate it to other members of society. Its role is, therefore, really one of developing the orderly knowledge of science, to compress it, and to translate it to those who can use it. Since the seminar was primarily concerned with business management (even though the fundamental aspects of all papers and discussions apply to nonbusiness enterprises as well) and most of the participants came from business schools, the academic concerns of the conference dealt primarily with the role and responsibility of business schools. Despite this focus, the problems of management research and teaching are as applicable to schools of public administration and other schools of management as to business.

Management Research: Pure or Applied? In all fields of science and inquiry, a common question is whether research should be aimed toward the solution of some particular problem on which an answer is desired, usually for economic ends, or whether it should be "pure" or "basic" in that it has no end in view other than the expansion of knowledge. This question often came to the surface in the deliberations of the seminar.

Because of the seminar's orientation to improvement of practice, much of the focus of the seminar was on applied research. There were those, such as Wilfred Brown, who felt that virtually all research usually must, and should, be applied research in the sense that it should have the solution of some need in view. There were others, such as Prof. Mason Haire, who felt that there would be enough pure research done in any event, particularly in the behavioral sciences, without any urging, and that what is needed now is more developmental research so that the findings in behavioral science could be adapted to practice. There were other participants, such as Dean Neil H. Jacoby, who expressed the opinion that most research could be measured in ultimate economic terms, but that, while it is possible to do so, this might not be the motivating factor for the researcher. Yet, there was considerable belief that much of the significant discoveries of knowledge had come when the researcher had no practical needs in view.

Be that as it may, there existed among the participants a strong concern for useful research. Likewise, there was disclosed a considerable feeling that much of the university research being done in the area of management was not often enough on the problems which have been of primary concern to managers. And it was quite clear that the volume of useful research being done on management was far below the needs of managers.

Among the more applied aspects of research on which need was felt is the development of normative guides for managerial operation. Both persons in academic environments and those from management practice expressed strong interest in having available research which would give rise to techniques for the solving of pressing managerial problems.

There is much to be said for more attention to developmental, or applied, research, but not to the exclusion of discovering new areas of knowledge; although it is probably true that as much or more new knowledge has come from applied as from pure research. Many are the researchers who, in attempting to get an answer for a specific urgent problem, made new breakthroughs in knowledge while doing so. Moreover, in a few cases, such as the discovery of penicillin, major contributions to knowledge have been made, almost accidentally, while looking for some other more immediate answer.

There is even more to be said for developmental or applied research in management. There is no doubt that practicing managers are not using the basic knowledge now available for management. There is no doubt, also, that many managerial inventions of great use, such as variable budgeting or the celebrated PERT (Program Evaluation and Review Technique), were designed out of simple principles and knowledge. If more researchers would spend their time and efforts in studying managers' problems and in designing methods or techniques to deal with them, using for the purpose little if anything more than the existing knowledge in and around management, the quality of management practice could be vastly improved. Also, it just might be that more research funds would be made available for management research when those in practice see what applied research can do for them.

Research and the Underlying Disciplines. Dean G. L. Bach made an interesting point that not only should management-oriented research continue in the disciplines underlying management, but more attention should be given by researchers in these disciplines, to provide the analytical concepts, working hypotheses, and models by which they could become more useful and applicable to management. He felt that many of these underlying sciences, such as the behavioral sciences, are relatively new and need more research impetus, and many need more specific orientation toward managerial problems.

Dean Bach and others also made the point that research in underlying disciplines should be done in the business schools. This is particularly true with applied research in order to assure a close involvement of the researchers with management problems. It is also true with pure research in these fields, where the researchers may both benefit from direct exposure to business and management problems and also stimulate the more practical-minded researchers in the business schools to more rigorous and detached research approaches.

This is an interesting point with considerable ramification for the traditional departmentation of universities. As a matter of fact, there are many disciplines which underlie management theory and practice. The most usually mentioned are economics, mathematics, psychology, sociology, social psychology, and statistics. But it would not take too much of a stretch of imagination to regard many other disciplines as having pertinence for management, such as history, medicine, mechanics, and others. If it were agreed that the business school should have these underlying disciplines provided for in their research and teaching staffs, particularly if such research or teaching were not rather directly related to the business or management problems of the school, the question might be raised as to building up duplicate empires within a university and destroying the departmental framework of the university.

On the other hand, there is much to be said for the view that destruction of time-honored academic organization is far less important than gaining a more effective program of research and teaching in an important area of knowledge. It would seem that, even if there were only a remote connection between the underlying discipline and the objectives and interests of the business school, the harboring of such research and teaching under the business school roof is a defensible and desirable practice. But it does place on those faculty members of such underlying disciplines an obligation often not realized in practice, to aim their research and teaching toward the problems of management and business with which the business school is typically charged.

The Need for Clinical Research. One of the important needs of management theory and research, one clearly recognized by Dean Neil H. Jacoby during the conference, is the requirement of meaningful beginnings in clinical research. Management is, unfortunately, an area of activity amenable to laboratory methods only to a limited extent. Certain problems can be examined under fairly adequate laboratory conditions and an increasing array of problems are being found subject to mathematical simulation. But these are likely to be rather limited ones, such as logistics planning or the determination of certain psychological factors affecting behavior. Most management problems exist in an extraordinarily complex environment in which it is extremely difficult, if not impossible, to isolate variables and where the laboratory or the computer cannot simulate reality.

That this problem of research is not new is evident from the difficulties encountered in many aspects of medicine, and even in some of the more complex problems of engineering. In these cases, and certainly as an important way of gathering knowledge, it has been found useful to employ the clinical method. In this, the researcher studies actual phenomena, notes variables, may try changing one or more of them through treatment or otherwise, and then notes results. By carefully observing individual situations and the variables involved, by painstakingly building up records of observations, and by analyzing these data to see if there is meaningful correlation between variables, the researcher may find new knowledge that is meaningful to science and practice.

Unquestionably, this approach would be fruitful in the field of management and it is a source of concern that it has been so little used. If those many case studies that have been carefully researched had been clinically analyzed, the results might have been impressive. If those management researchers and consultants who have studied countless actual situations, seen "treatment" prescribed and observed results, had made clinical records, the contribution to management knowledge would have been very great. I know from my own experience that I have carefully observed hundreds, if not thousands, of meaningful cases of management practice (or malpractice) and treatment. I feel reasonably sure of the results of these instances and have observed certain causal relationships often enough to feel that principles do exist that have a rational and predictive value. But I do not have the clinical data to prove it. Perhaps one of the most important contributions to management research would be to furnish adequate secretarial and clerical assistance to researchers who have opportunities to observe or participate in a large number of management cases!

Expanding the Management Research Effort. As important as management theory and practice are, it is generally realized that the level and magnitude of management research has been far from satisfactory. Much of this is due to the youthfulness of this field of inquiry. Much is due to the immaturity of the underlying disciplines. Much is due, of course, to the tremendous complexity of the manager's job and the environment in which he must operate. Much is due to the factors which comprise the "management theory jungle" to which I have called attention. And much is due to the fact that the level of financial support for research in all social sciences, including management, has been abysmally low, with estimates running to somewhat less than 2 per cent of the total amount spent for all kinds of research in the United States.

Adolescence is a state cured by time. There are signs that the youthfulness of management science is being cured by faster aging arising from general awareness of the critical importance of management in all kinds of enterprises. There are also encouraging signs in the rapidly growing programs of doctoral work in our major universities through which it is believed an increasing amount of research is being done and as the result of which a much larger number of researchers are being trained. It may be also that, as the quality of research and researchers improve, financial limitations will tend to disappear. It is perfectly true that many foundations, government agencies, business enterprises, and others who support research are likely to support it more freely if the chances for value received from an investment look promising.

The Goals of Management Teaching. The most explicit statement of teaching goals in the field of management was set forth by Dean G. L. Bach in his paper.[4] Outlining what he thought to be the qualities believed to be required by any manager as he meets the changes and increased sophistication of the future, he comes essentially to the conclusion that the goal of teaching should be to develop orderly and effective problem solvers, who can become effective professionals in the field of management, and who can think, adjust, and learn independently, in a world of rapid change.

The reader can note that these goals, in their essentials, could be applied to any area where an individual will be responsible for acting in a future, now unknown, but certainly subject to change. This is not surprising, for these qualities, which it is hoped the teaching process may help develop, are similar to those needed in law, medicine, engineering, and many other fields. They recognize the basic truth that those who would take responsible action in a society must be able to detect—even forecast—change, must be able to think clearly in the new and unaccustomed environment of change, must be able to conceptualize problem areas, clarify goals, solve problems on the basis of discriminatory selection of strategic factors, continue to learn, and be willing to act professionally in the final making and implementation of decisions.

This approach to stating teaching goals avoids the trap of the often-made grand statement that the goal of teaching management today is specifically and accurately to prepare the student for the managership of a quarter-century hence. While this pious hope sounds good, it overlooks the question of possibility, since the exact state of a knowledge so far in the future is one of those will-o'-the-wisps that no one has been privileged to see. How

4 See p. 192.

many scientists of today were specifically trained twenty-five years ago for their scientific discipline of today?

What can be done, of course, is to plant an attitude of looking forward rather than back, a willingness to learn, an ability to think conceptually and analytically, an understanding of the cultural environment in which human action takes place, and the grounds for thinking through and following wise value judgments in managerial conduct.

Certainly all these apply to the needs of the manager of the future, as well as to the scholar of management. Certainly without such qualities and abilities, a person in and around managership will find himself as obsolete a quarter-century hence as the physicist of today who attempts to solve problems on the basis of the state of his art of 1939.

But are there not other things toward which the teaching of management should strive? It seems to me that this teaching should plant an awareness of the nature of management and a careful understanding of its environment in business, government, education, and other enterprises. If management involves establishing an environment for performance, as I believe it does, then certainly *all* the significant environmental factors of managing should be examined and care should be taken that they are seen and appreciated in a balanced context. Management teaching should also give guidance on what factors a person should consider in reaching value judgments. Moreover, it seems desirable to teach the basics of the available technical tools useful to management, such as psychological evaluation and mathematics.

But there is some question as to whether teaching can do all the things desirable to meet the major goals of orderly problem solving in an environment of change and still develop the often-desired level of competency in psychology, mathematics, and sociology. I wonder sometimes, with the new pressure for teaching advanced mathematics, for example, if there is not often overpreoccupation with technique at the danger of losing some of the more primary values of seeing real managerial problems as a conceptual whole. A high order of mathematical gymnastics is not a substitute of knowing why, in what situation, whether, and when, to use this valuable tool of analysis.

The point is also made that students in a business school (as well as those from other university areas) must have some competence which is salable to their employer. This is a need not to be cast aside with the usual bromide that employers want broadly trained men who can think. As university placement officers have long found, they want this—and more. They want also a young man who can *do,* who cannot only think but think intelligently about *something,* who not only has broad perspective but who can also soon contribute to the company's profits, who cannot only tell the forest from the trees, but, as Marion Harper has said, "also distinguish between the leaves and chlorophyll while still not losing sight of the forest."[5] Certainly, these salable qualities do not in themselves interfere with the more lofty requirements mentioned above.

The Role of the Business School in Management Teaching and Research. There is no question but that the business schools of the nation have been seriously on the defensive, particularly because of the accusations of the now-celebrated Ford Foundation and Carnegie Foundation reports on them.[6] While these reports made some searing criticisms of American business schools, some of which were justified and others based on innuendo and hearsay, they overlooked many of the programs already installed in many major business schools to broaden the base and increase the stature of American business education. But their impact on the administrators and many of the faculty of business schools has approached that of panic accompanied by a strong desire to gain respectability and academic peer approval. Certainly, this seminar on management theory and research seemed to reflect this trend.

One of the impressions gained from this seminar, as well as from the widespread turmoil in business school curricula, is that the business schools are searching for a *raison d'être.* At one moment they seem to be trending toward a professional school of management in all its phases, with little more than a passing

[5] "A New Profession to Aid Management," *Journal of Marketing,* vol. 25, no. 3, January, 1961, p. 3.

[6] Robert A. Gordon and James E. Howell, *Higher Education for Business,* Columbia University Press, New York, 1959, and Frank Pierson *et al., The Education of American Businessmen,* McGraw-Hill Book Company, Inc., New York, 1959. The former is the Ford report, the latter the Carnegie report.

glance at business. At another moment they appear to be trending toward schools of applied mathematics, statistics, psychology, and sociology. At another moment they seem to be wanting to become a liberal arts college with heavy stresses on the humanities and the sciences, and minor attention to business. Some proof of these trends is found in the papers of the three administrators who dealt with the role of the business school. All appeared to stress underlying disciplines, particularly mathematics and psychology. There was a strong feeling that the "old" business school faculties were somehow unintelligently resisting the new to protect the old. Few references were made to *business* aspects of management research and teaching.

It must be recognized that the apparently heavy stress on liberalizing curricula and training in underlying disciplines is a natural reaction to criticism. But it is also due to the fact that business schools and, for that matter, engineering and medical schools, have long overlooked the usefulness for learning and research of the broad course curriculum and the study of underlying disciplines. At the same time, there is reason to fear that, in the process of reform, the real values of the business school will be overlooked, that in the process of introducing new techniques and approaches to studying management, the basic nature and needs of managing will be forgotten.

In the first place, since when has the business institution and the manager ceased to be an important and integral part of our social culture? I would define a liberal education as one that widens the student's cultural horizon, teaches the meaning of his cultural environment, gives him an ability to understand the nature of problems in his culture, and makes available a set of tools and values to deal responsibly with them. Merely because a course is one in Greek, Italian painting, chemistry, history of Rome, or kinetic theory of matter doesn't make it more liberalizing than courses in management theory, money and banking, accounting, business law, or principles of insurance. The real question is whether the subject, as taught, is liberalizing. When asked in this light, a high percentage of courses of the modern business school meet the requirements of a liberal education, a percentage which is probably as high as most in more-respected "liberal arts" areas of education.

In the second place, one may well ask whether there is so much emphasis on introducing and supporting underlying disciplines that the role of these disciplines in the solution of managerial and business phenomena is being overlooked. Comments are often made to the effect that some business schools are tending to become colleges of applied psychology, advanced data processing, mathematical model making, or social behavior of the human race. Granted that these are extreme concerns and I have not found them really justified, one does sometimes get the fleeting impression that the manager of the future is thought to be a mathematics wizard who acts as a democratic chairman of a group of computers and nonconforming individualists whose personal happiness is his prime concern. However, it is my impression that an increasing number of specialists in the underlying disciplines are beginning to see their obligation to contribute research and teaching toward understanding and solving the problems of management in general and of business management in particular.

It is hoped that this latter trend will continue. It is even more hoped that, in concentrating on the underlying, and often peripheral, problems of business management, those responsible for program will not forget that there is an entire core of discipline and technique largely indigenous to the area of management. These include such matters as formal organization structure, management appraisal and training, the delegation of authority, and many others. There is obviously much more to establishing an environment for performance in formally organized groups—the task of the manager—than to understanding the rationality of choice, the reasons why people behave as they do, and the kinds of things that make people and computers tick.

Yet one of the major problems confronting the business school is whether its central orientation—its intellectual and disciplinary core—should be management. There has been a strong trend in that direction. But does this central discipline belong in a business school or a school of management? Does it belong any more in a school of business than in a school of public or hospital administration or in a curriculum on engineering or educational administration? Or is the real central core of a business school the study of business with management as one of the major elements of importance in the study of business? If so, do we include in the concept of "business" large labor unions, government enterprises such as airports and the post office, universities, and other enterprises that have economic problems of optimizing the use of scarce resources and employ many of the tools and techniques of the typical private business?

In view of the pervasive effect of management in many disciplines and professions, it may be difficult to consider changing the central core and focus of the business school to that of a management school. But with what is happening in the world of science and practice, this might be a more meaningful approach to research and teaching. It is certainly a core to which could be logically attached many of the newer fields of learning and professional practice other than the rapidly developing professionalization of managing itself. Included in such related fields which are fast gaining specialized, and to some extent professional, status are programming, data processing and information system design, long-range planning, work sampling, and analysis of organizational behavior. Included also could be such already professionalized areas as accountancy, industrial psychology, and industrial engineering.

Perhaps the basic role of the business school has really changed and it should be reexamined in this light.

MANAGEMENT THEORY AND RESEARCH: SOME CONCLUSIONS

In reviewing the state of management theory and research, partly as the result of the conference and partly in reflection on the positions represented by the scholars and practitioners present, I come to some rather general conclusions. These understandably have to do with the status and probable development of the theory of management itself, with the extent to which it can contribute to improvement of the practice of management, and the outlook for future research in the field.

The Status of Management Theory. I still cannot escape the feeling that the area of management theory is somewhat a jungle of confusing semantics, varying concepts of the field of management, unwillingness and inability to understand, and failure to appreciate the usefulness and nature of a working conceptual scheme, or theory. On the other hand, even though it does exist, the jungle does not now appear nearly as matted, entwined, and overgrown as it seemed several years ago.

At least for those who participated in the conference, and I believe for many who were not represented, there is a better appreciation of the interests and areas of those who are working in and around the field. Many more scholars and practitioners are aware that a study of human behavior or motivations or a study of mathematical applications to business problem solving does not represent the entire field of management. Also, there has seemed to be an increasing appreciation that many of the approaches are not really "schools" of thought but rather scientists with different specialties and training probing different aspects of the total management job.

Likewise, even though managerial terms are still being used in different ways and semantics differences exist, there is greater awareness that words *are* being used differently. It is hoped that this awareness may lead to greater zest and care in defining many simple managerial words of common use (such as "organization," decision making," and "human behavior") in terms that the hearer can comprehend clearly. This simple step, on which much still needs to be done, seems to be a requirement for communication as well as for the development of any science.

There exists also a rising awareness that a discipline of management is emerging. There are considerable doubts as to what it is. Some see it as a synthetic science made up of bits and pieces of other disciplines. Some see it as a behavioral science in which the subject of study is the behavior of people and their managers in a group setting. Some see it, as I do, as an independently identifiable discipline dealing with the specific process of managing, but drawing, as many other disciplines do, on the findings and theories of related and underlying branches of knowledge.

Thus a science of management would be eclectic in part, but would also have an important and separately identifiable core. As I have mentioned before, I have found it useful to develop this core around the functions of the manager—planning, organizing, staffing, directing, and controlling. As a rallying point for explaining the nature of management and for placing new knowledge bearing on management in the perspective of the total managerial job, and as a means of making the knowledge of management, as crude and unsatisfactory as it is, available and understandable to the practitioner, I have found this framework useful. Perhaps there are better conceptual schemes on which to hang that which is known about management, but one thing is certain. The knowledge and research efforts and results cannot be made useful unless fitted into some conceptual framework.

The Need for Theory to Contribute to Improvement of Practice. There is a real sense of urgency that a useful theory be developed. Those responsible for managing have one of the greatest of all social responsibilities—to make it possible for those who report to them to perform effectively. Obviously, to the extent that management theory can help in putting some scientific foundation under the art of managing, and thereby improve the practice, the social contribution is great. Practitioners who understand the importance of improving performance are anxious for the assistance that organized knowledge can give them. And despite progress that has been made, as Richard Neuschel said in the conference, "In this whole area we are really shooting at a moving target and our real progress must be measured not so much by how far we have come in relation to our own past capability but where we stand today in relation to the growing need for greater management excellence on a great many different fronts."[7]

The Challenges of Research. Certainly to develop an adequate theory, far more meaningful research must be undertaken than has been the case to date. It is true that there has been much distillation of experience by many able practitioners who have reflected on their long life of managing and observing the results of management approaches and techniques. There has also been considerable research in specific areas of management, such as human behavior in formal organizations, mathematical techniques of decision making, systems approaches to planning and control, information systems, and many other areas of managing. There have likewise been many meaningful attempts to develop conceptual schemes of management and to identify principles of management.

[7] See p. 102.

But the major research task is only beginning. While more conceptual research is needed, perhaps the greatest needs are for empirical research which will lead to adequate testing of many hypotheses of management. Some of this can be done under simulated conditions and perhaps even under fairly well-controlled laboratory-type conditions. Some of it can be accomplished by utilizing the tools of mathematical logic and some by applying the findings already available in the various underlying disciplines.

Perhaps one of the most promising untapped sources of research is the clinical technique so widely employed in medicine. But this requires not only clinicians and facilities to do research, but also clinics. The clinic of management is the business or other kind of enterprise. Those who are in the actual practice of management, whether in an enterprise or in a consulting firm, would do well to open their doors and files to responsible researchers who could get valuable clinical information with the same degree of confidentialness that medical information is obtained and recorded. This is one major way, among many, that those in management could help along the cause of the field of knowledge so important to them.

Also, what is needed is for more academicians more actively and aggressively to enter the field of management research. While it is true that far too few resources are committed to all kinds of research in the social sciences, one can never be sure whether research efforts are limited by funds until more meaningful research projects are presented to those foundations, universities, and enterprises who might support the research. What is needed, furthermore, is for many more business, government, and other enterprises to sponsor research projects in the field of management. If more effective managing of an enterprise and its parts is a key to greater effectiveness and efficiency, as it surely is, perhaps some of the willingness to sponsor technical and marketing research could carry over to sponsoring more management research.

I believe that the challenges of theory and research will increasingly be met. The growing awareness of the importance and shortcomings of the field is an important indicator. The urgency of keeping ahead of this "moving target" can hardly be overlooked. The expanding interest of practicing managers and university faculty in this field is a startling phenomenon of the past two decades. With these developments we are moving toward the beginnings of a general theory of management.

Toward a Useful Theory. The papers and discussions of the seminar proved that there exists a need for progress to be made toward a useful theory of management. The variety of approaches to the study of management, the varying interests and underlying disciplines of the leading scholars in the field, the wealth of knowledge now developing, the fast pace of change and sophistication in management, and, above all, the social needs for translating knowledge into practice are some of the major factors which convince me. Moreover, I believe it is possible to develop the beginnings, at least, of a useful theory of management: not a "final" verified theory with all the elements, or principles, discovered, proved, and codified, but a conceptual framework that defines and classifies the field, a framework in which those credible bits of knowledge that have been distilled from experience and research can be placed with some order and where new ideas and findings can be seen in the perspective of the total job of managing.

Certainly this kind of start can be made. Neither its basic frame nor its semantics will be accepted by all. But it can be accepted by many and perhaps, over time, some of the words and concepts may have widely accepted meaning. There are signs that the practicing manager is ready. There were signs in the seminar that, at least, the variety of scholars present began to be able to talk to each other and to comprehend the varied terms and approaches of those represented.

If the seminar represented a fair cross section, as I believe it did, there is hope that some movement toward a useful general theory can be made. At least it can be recognized that the different approaches are often trying to explain different things. The next step in such a matter is for those concerned with management to come closer to a conceptual scheme which can act as a road map more accurately to see what these different things are.

NAME INDEX

Ackoff, Russell L., 9n.
Albers, H. H., 233
American Economic Association, 212
American Institute of Management, 26
American Management Association, 105, 122
Appley, Lawrence A., 26n.
Argyris, Chris, 13, 31, 32n.
Arnoff, E. Leonard, 9n.

Baake, E. W., 35, 36
Bach, G. L., 113, 119, 188–203, 227, 234, 253, 256
Ballhaus, William, 121, 141–149
Barksdale, H. M., 39
Barnard, Chester I., 2, 7, 35n., 243n.
Bendix, R. K., 24
Blackett, P. M. S., 29n.
Boulding, Kenneth E., 165
Bradley, A. E., 39
Bridgeman, P. W., 29n.
British Institute of Management, 105, 122
Brown, Alvin, 2, 12, 109
Brown, Donaldson, 39, 228
Brown, Wilfred, 100, 101, 105, 113–117, 121–140, 217–219, 226, 230, 231, 239, 251

Carr, E. H., 20
Chamberlain, Neil W., 26
Churchman, C. West, 9n.
Clee, Gilbert, 179
Court, A., 39

Dale, Ernest, 5, 20–40, 28n., 29n., 38n., 39n., 90, 94, 108, 109, 227–232

Davis, Keith, 94, 119
Davis, R. C., 108, 109, 111, 116
Dennison, Edward F., 208
Dickson, W. J., 34
Dodd, Alvin, 30
Donner, F. C., 39
Dubin, Robert, 6n., 106, 112–114, 117, 118
du Brul, S., 39
Dunlop, John T., 26n.
du Pont, Irénée, 230
du Pont, Pierre, 230
du Pont de Nemours Company, 22, 39
Durant, W. C., 22

Eubank, E. E., 20n.

Fayol, Henri, 2, 3, 12, 29, 30, 108–111, 147
Fisher, Lloyd N., 24
Follett, Mary Parker, 33n.
Ford Motor Company, 229
Fox, William M., 106
Freud, Sigmund, 34
Frost, Robert, 12

Gantt, H. L., 33n., 109
General Electric, 229
General Motors Corporation, 22, 38–40, 229
Gilbreth, Lillian, 33n., 111
Ginsberg, Eli, 185
Glacier Institute of Management, 139
Goetz, Billy E., 231
Graicunas, V. A., 30
Gulick, L., 28, 109

Haire, Mason, 224, 251
Hall, E. K., 33n.
Hamilton, Sir Ian, 13, 30
Harbison, Frederick, 25n., 26n.
Harper, Marion, 258
Henriques, Robert, 31n.
Housman, A. E., 22
Hoxie, R. F., 33n.

Jackson, James R., 104, 105, 239
Jacoby, Neil H., 101, 188, 207–218, 220, 226, 227, 232, 251, 254
Jacques, Elliott, 34n.

Kemble, Edward D., 101, 102, 121, 150–175
Kerr, Clark, 26n.
Keynes, John Maynard, 228
Koontz, Harold, 217, 226, 227, 232, 235–265

Laski, Harold, 229
Le Breton, Preston P., 119
Lewin, Kurt, 34
Likert, Rensis, 35, 40
Luce, R. Duncan, 8n.
Lynd, R. S., 28n.

McCloskey, Joseph F., 9n.
McGuire, C. B., 219
McKinsey Foundation, 183
Malcom, Norman, 24n.
Manili, M., 22n.
March, James G., 110
Marschak, Jacob, 114–116, 214
Marshall, Alfred, 27
Martindell, Jackson, 27
Massarik, Fred, 6n.
Mayo, Elton, 24n., 25, 34
Meloy, Charles, 39n.
Mill, J. S., 35, 228
Miller, David W., 8n., 9n., 106, 107
Mooney, James D., 2, 12, 29, 39, 108, 109
Myers, Charles A., 25n., 26n.
Myers, Frederic, 214

Neuschel, Richard F., 102, 103, 121, 176–187, 221, 245, 263
Newman, W. H., 3n.

O'Donnell, Cyril, 3n.
Osborn, Elliot, 26n.
Osborn, Gordon, 220–225

Parkhurst, George L., 118
Parsons, Talcott, 22, 245
Poincaré, Henri, 33
Popper, Karl, 25n.

Raifa, Howard, 8n.
Rand, 80
Raskob, John T., 40
Reiley, A. C., 29, 109
Reiley, Ewing W., 185
Robertson, Sir Dennis, 20
Roethlisberger, Fritz, 34, 41, 77, 80, 97, 99, 100, 117, 118, 229, 242
Roman Catholic Church, 26
Roos, C. F., 39

Samuel, Marcus, 30, 31
Samuel, Samuel, 30, 31
Schlaifer, Robert, 68, 77, 97–99, 115, 116, 227, 244
Scott, Walter Dill, 111
Sheldon, Oliver, 2
Shell Oil Company, 30
Shils, E., 22n.
Shubik, Martin, 231, 232
Simon, Herbert A., 7, 8n., 77–85, 91, 93, 96, 98–116, 232, 233, 237
Sloan, Alfred P., 22, 39, 230
Sofer, Cyril, 34n.
Standard Oil Company of New Jersey, 25n.
Starr, Martin K., 8n., 9n.
Stein, Herbert, 208
Summer, Charles E., Jr., 3n.
Systems Development Corporation, 80

Tannenbaum, Robert, 6n., 87–96, 117, 239, 245

Tavistock Institute, 34*n*., 134*n*., 217, 226

Taylor, F. W., 3, 25, 108–111, 147

Tolstoy, Col. Ilia A., 20*n*.

Trefethen, Florence N., 9*n*.

Urwick, Lyndall F., 2, 3*n*., 13, 29, 108

Valentine, R. G., 33*n*.

von Szeliski, Victor, 39

von Thunen, 229

Wagner, Harvey M., 118, 219, 220

Wallis, Allen, 188, 204–206, 227

Weschler, Irving R., 6*n*.

Western Data Processing Center, 214, 215

Western Management Science Institute, 214, 215

Westinghouse Electric Corporation, 31–33

Whyte, William, 250

Wilson, C. E., 39

Wittgenstein, Ludwig, 20*n*., 24

SUBJECT INDEX

Aerodynamic theory and management theory, 142–144
Authority, 32, 114–115, 123
  reconciliation with expertise, 181, 182

Basic research, 218, 219
Business schools, business acceptance of graduates, 229–231
  enlisting aid of other departments, 212–214
  and faculty, 201, 202
  fostering research in management science in, 209–212
  main tasks, 189–190
  and mathematical learning, 226, 227
  relative to practice, 228–234
  and research, 193–197, 207
  responsibilities, 192, 193, 204, 205
  role of, in management research and teaching, 251–261
  and teaching, 197–199

Carnegie Institute of Technology, systems major at, 83
Change, management of major, 184, 185
Comparative analysis, 32
Conceptual schemes, 48, 59
Contraction, concept of, 122–134
  example of, 134–140

Decision making, analysis of, 71–73, 113–119
Decision theory, and management theory, 68–76
  as basis of management theory, 112–119

Decision theory, need for training in application of, 73, 74
  normative, 68, 69
  and probabilities, 71–73
Decision theory school, 8, 9
Descriptive propositions, 59–61
Descriptive theory, 98–100
Development of executive, 183, 184

Economic theory and management theory, 162–168
Empirical school of management, 5
Expertise, reconciliation with authority, 181, 182

Facts, selection of, 37
Faculty and business schools, 201, 202
Formal and informal organizations, 46–48
Fostering research in management science in business schools, 209–212
Functional approach to management, 20–40
Functions of management, 4

Human attitudes and risks, 74
Human behavior school of management, 6, 33–36, 41–67
Human relations, 33–36
  shortcomings of theories in, 35
  training, 54–58

Investigation, confusion between external and internal factors, 61–63
  problems, of explanation, 64
  of verification, 64

Leaders, informal, 53
Leadership, 52, 56, 146, 161

Major change, management of, 184, 185
Management, approaches to theory, 2
  as art, 2
  as body of knowledge, 240
  business school education for, 94, 95
  criteria of theory of, 17
  decision theory school of, 8, 9
  defined, 14, 15
  development, 183, 184
  different views of, 11
  empirical school of, 5
  as field of knowledge, 14, 15, 18, 19
  functional approach to, 20–40
  functions of, 4
  human behavior school of, 6, 28, 33–36, 41–67
  management science approach to, 28
  mathematical school of, 9
  operational approach to, 29–33, 39
  problems of semantics, 92, 93
  process school of, 3
  as science, 89
  social system school of, 7
  systems approach to, 77
  as theory, 2, 98–101
  values and ethics, 94
  (See also Major change; Management theory)
Management process school, 3
  fundamental beliefs of, 3
Management research, contribution of practice, 228–231
  and economic ends, 217–219
  expanding research effort, 255
  funds for, 216
  need for applied research, 224
  need for clinical research, 254–255
  need for interdisciplinary research, 200, 214, 215

Management research, opportunities for, in government agencies, 220–223
  and practicing manager, 120
  present state of, 207–209
  pure or applied, 251
  role of university in, 207–216
  and underlying disciplines, 253
Management science, 36–40
  progress of, 79–83
Management teaching goals, 256, 257
Management theory, a priori assumption, 12
  and aerodynamic theory, 142–144
  clinical approach, 108–111
  decision theory as basis of, 76, 112–119
  as division of labor, 78, 79
  eclectic approach, 248–250
  and economic theory, 162–168
  importance, for practice, 176–179
    in research and teaching, 169–171
  inadequacy of traditional principles, 52
  jungle, 1n., 10, 11, 14, 15, 236–238
  misunderstanding of principles, 12, 14
  nature of, 97–101, 242–244
  need for, 101–103, 244–248
  needs for practice, 91, 263
  objectives of, 245–248
  operational principles, 29
  organization theory as unrelated principles, 80
  and practicing manager, 120, 149
  predicting, cause of lack of results in, 38
  problem of concepts, 88, 89, 92, 93
  semantics, 10, 11, 15, 16, 103–105, 238–240
  status, 261–263
  synthesis of, 77, 78, 88–91, 106, 107
  tests of validity of theory, 26
Management theory and research, importance of, 236

Management theory and research, need for realism in, 152–154
  relation to progress in social theory, 154–156
  role of university, 187, 188
  what practicing manager expects, 149, 150–186
Managerial attitudes, realism in, 152
Managerial behavior, 190
  and teaching, 189–190, 197, 199
Managerial competence and performance, 174, 175
Managerial decision making, 190
Managerial facts, 22, 23
Managerial stereotypes, 150–152
Managers, nature of tasks, 141, 142
  required abilities, 192
Morale and productivity, 52
Motivation of executives, 182, 183

Normative decision theory, 68, 69
Normative propositions, 59–61, 68, 69
Normative theory, 99, 100

Operational approach to management, 29–33, 39
Operations research, 9
Organization success, ingredients for, 145–148
Organization theory, 156–160
Organizational behavior (*see* Human behavior school of management)
Organizations, as complex systems, 82–85
  formal and informal, 46–48
  function and equilibrium, 48, 49
  meaning of, 11
  and objectives, 146
  as place for study, 42
  selection of alternatives, 179–181
  as social system, 46–48

Personality in organizations, 34
Power, 114
Probabilities and decisions, 71–73
Problem solving and theory, 176–179
Process school of management, 3
Profit maximization, 23
Propositions, confusion between descriptive and normative, 59–61

Quantitative tools, 81, 82

Representatives, reliance on, in management, 128–133
Research (*see* Management research)
Resource allocation problems, 184

Semantics and management theory, 10, 11, 15, 16, 103–105, 238–240
Sensitivity training, 57
Social system school of management, 7
Span of control, 13, 30, 31, 100

Teaching and business schools, 197–199
Theory, nature of, 37, 48, 242–244
  need for, 244
  normative, 99, 100
  organization, 156–160
  problem solving and, 176–179
  (*See also* Management theory)

Universal manager, 26, 27
"Universalists," 12
University, role of, in management research, 207–216
  in management theory, 187, 188